Frommer's™

England
with your
family

by Ben Hatch &
Dinah Hatch

WILEY

A John Wiley and Sons, Ltd, Publication

Copyright © 2010 John Wiley & Sons Ltd, The Atrium, Southern Gate, Chichester,
West Sussex PO19 8SQ, England
Telephone (+44) 1243 779777
Email (for orders and customer service enquiries): cs-books@wiley.co.uk.
Visit our Home Page on
www.wiley.com

UK Publisher: Sally Smith
Executive Project Editor: Daniel Mersey
Commissioning Editor: Mark Henshall
Development Editor: Sasha Heseltine
Project Editor: Hannah Clement
Cartographer: Tim Lohnes
Photo Research: Jill Emeny

Wiley also publishes its books in a variety of electronic formats. Some content that appears in
print may not be available in electronic books.

British Library Cataloguing in Publication Data
A catalogue record for this book is available from the British Library

ISBN: 978-0-470-72168-1

Typeset by Wiley Indianapolis Composition Services

Printed and bound in China by RR Donnelley

5 4 3 2 1

Contents

About the authors

Ben Hatch started out as a tea boy in the Royal Bank of Scotland. He became a recruitment consultant, sold advertising space then lawnmowers, worked in a video shop, as a postman and on the McDonald chicken sandwich station before finally becoming a journalist on various local papers. He quit reporting to become a novelist in 1997. He has written two works of comedy fiction, *The Lawnmower Celebrity* and *The International Gooseberry* and is now on his third. Ben was tempted into travel writing by his wife Dinah who he lives with in Brighton. Together they authored *Frommer's Scotland With Your Family*.

Dinah Hatch went into travel journalism after deciding that crime reporting for regional papers involved just a few too many evenings talking to dodgy people in dark alleys. Since then she has worked for a wide variety of national newspapers, magazines, trade publications and websites and writes extensively for the travel industry. Dinah co-authored *Frommer's Scotland With Your Family*.

Acknowledgements

My sister Penny Hatch for looking after our kids so well at a crucial moment en route; Marion and Bert Robinson for the fun trip to Lyme Regis; my aunt, Romey Martin, for her roast chicken and biscuits in Sidmouth; Jacey Stasiulevicuis for the bed and meal in York, Simon and Julie Heap for the joke about Captain Cook in Gisborough Hall; Pete Williams and Gemma McCann for laughs in Bristol; Vic and Dan Richardson for Oxford; Simon Hudson and Belinda Gannaway for the vital sheets and pillows intervention; Paul Dickson, Norfolk Tourism PR for his great tips; Alison Ruddick, Colette Walker from the Yorskshire Tourist Board and Pat Edgar for the same. Thanks also to Mark Henshall, Jill Emeny and Sasha Heseltine at Frommers. Finally, a thank you to our two kids, Phoebe and Charlie.

Dedication

This book is dedicated to my wonderful step-mum: Mary Clancy Hatch.

An Additional Note

Please be advised that travel information is subject to change at any time and this is especially true of prices. We therefore suggest that you write or call ahead for confirmation when making your travel plans. The authors, editors and publisher cannot be held responsible for experiences of readers while travelling. Your safety is important to us however, so we encourage you to stay alert and be aware of your surroundings.

Star Ratings, Icons & Abbreviations

Hotels, restaurants and attraction listings in this guide have been ranked for quality, value, service, amenities and special features using a star-rating system. Hotels, restaurants, attractions, shopping and nightlife are rated on a scale of zero stars (recommended) to three (exceptional). In addition to the star rating system, we also use 5 feature icons that point you to the great deals, in-the-know advice and unique experiences. Throughout the book, look for:

FIND   Special finds – those places only insiders know about

MOMENT   Special moments – those experiences that memories are made of

VALUE   Great values – where to get the best deals

OVERRATED   Places or experiences not worth your time or money

GREEN   Attractions employing responsible tourism policies

The following abbreviations are used for credit cards:

AE   American Express
MC   MasterCard
V   Visa

A Note on Prices

In the Family-friendly Accommodation section of this book we have used a price category system.

An Invitation to the Reader

In researching this book, we discovered many wonderful places – hotels, restaurants, shops and more. We're sure you'll find others. Please tell us about them, so we can share the information with your fellow travellers in upcoming editions. If you were disappointed with a recommendation, we'd love to know that too. Please email: frommers@wiley.co.uk or write to:

Frommer's England With Your Family, 1st edition
John Wiley & Sons, Ltd
The Atrium
Southern Gate
Chichester
West Sussex, PO19 8SQ

Photo Credits

Cover Credits

Main Image: © Pete Seaward - Britain on View / Photolibrary
Back Cover: © Pawel Libera / Corbis

Front Matter Credits
Pi: © Pete Seaward - Britain on View / Photolibrary.

Inside Images

All images: © Ben Hatch with the following exceptions:

© Chambers Apartments, Leeds: p 199.
Courtesy of PCL: p 23 (© Monica Wells); p 30 (© Picture Finders).

1 Family Highlights of England

The English are seen by outsiders to be an insular, slightly quaint race of people living in chocolate-box thatched cottages, doffing their hats respectfully to the Queen and going to their drab civil service jobs in bowler hats and pinstripe suits on big red London buses. The impression is that the English are polite, deferential, not terribly bright and perfectly content when drinking tea and eating a good sponge cake.

Is this really accurate though and all there is to the English and our ambition? Hasn't this version of Englishness for those of us who live on this island and know it been consigned to the dustbin? Yes, we do love our tea (I am drinking a cup as I write) but the English are less reserved than they once were and if not as effusive in the company of children as the Italians, they are not openly hostile any more. Restaurants, attractions and places to stay are geared increasingly towards families. Many go out of their way to ensure children are not only seen but also heard and ungrudgingly cleaned up after as well.

England itself has so much to see for families within easy travelling distance. From toddlers and older children to teenagers, parents and seniors our diversity of landscape, regional identity, range of activities and seasonal change offer an astonishing choice. As an island we have a distinctive character you can see in our rich arts, historic and romantic ruins, the beautiful gardens and parks that abound, vibrant towns and pretty, independent villages.

From the craggy mountains of the north to the flat expanses of Midlands and rolling hills of the south you'll see glinting waterfalls, daffodils and blue bells carpet the ground in spring, an autumnal colouring of trees and wooded areas throwing a patchwork of sunlight and shade.

Families in England can wake to fresh, rolling mists, experience distinct landscapes and exceptional, unspoilt countryside with abundant wildlife and take dramatic cliff walks as the waves break and crash below. There are festivals and events year long and seaside and beaches miles wide, there are film and music, markets, architecture and tradition, and more reasons than we'd ever thought to get out there.

We drove 8,000 miles round England researching this book. We went as far north as Berwick and as far south as the Lizard in Cornwall, we went east to the Broads and west to Eardisland. Our conception of England changed over the four months we spent on the road with our two children (Charlie age one and Phoebe age four). The patchwork of memories that constituted this country for us were joined up. The dots connected to give an overall impression of the country we were born in. And actually, guess what, at the risk of a little swagger, we're pretty damn good. We live in a fantastic country to holiday in. We knew, of course, about the great family beaches of Devon and Cornwall before, but not that there were quite so many miles of them. And then there's the little-visited coastline of Northumberland, possibly the most beautifully unspoiled seaside scenery in England. The cities of Liverpool, Leicester, Birmingham and Manchester in particular have had sums lavished on their redevelopment and look as sleek as anything you'd find in continental Europe. In addition to family zoos and theme parks and aquaria, we still do our history well; there are scores of wonderful castles and old country houses to visit, full of children's activities. Perhaps a legacy of our view of ourselves as eccentric, we also have some of the most curious museums in the world – what other country would have a museum boasting the world's largest pencil? Eating out is a different ball game entirely from when I was a child. English food, the laughing stock of Europe, has come on leaps and bounds. Most places have children's menus and it isn't always of the burgers and chicken nuggets variety either, while the accommodation range is enormous. In 120 nights away we never stayed in two places remotely alike. We had a tremendous time researching this book – and hope you'll have as good a time reading it as we did writing it.

ENGLAND'S FAMILY HIGHLIGHTS

Best View The jagged Cornwall coastline from the summit of Tintagel Castle over the cave that Merlin, of King Arthur lore, is said to have lived in (see p 156). Although it could equally be looking at stunning Bamburgh Castle in Northumberland (see p 181) from the beautiful sandy deserted beach below.

Best City In our (biased) opinion it is Brighton where we live, love and can watch the flocks of starlings above the rusting West Pier joining and parting to make giant geometric shapes in the sky against a tangerine-orange sunset across the sea. On top of this, there is the wonderfully over the top Royal Pavilion, the Palace Pier and some of the best restaurants outside London. See p 46.

Brighton seafront

Best Day Trip To Brownsea Island in Dorset to see red squirrels in the woods having borrowed (free) an all-terrain buggy that made us feel like very smug parents (see p 162). Drayton Manor Theme Park (see p 115),

3

with its host of toddler rides, is also up there and might well have won if it wasn't for the fact that occasionally in idle moments my brain reverts to our three hours in Thomas Land and I once more start humming the 'Thomas the Tank Engine' theme tune.

Best Adult Games Try a grown up kind of Dr Who at the Jorvik Viking Centre where you can time travel to the year 975 when York was the Viking town of Jorvik. Learn Norse words and see how much Viking blood you possess. See p 192.

Best Animal Park Drusillas in Alfriston, East Sussex, where we have been to so many times because of the great children's activities. We know most of the animals by their first names and even which fruit peel is whose favourite. See p 49.

Best Aquarium The National Marine Aquarium in Plymouth for its fantastic Discovery Centre, where our daughter checked out a whale skull, completed a fish jigsaw and made an electric eel hat. See p 159.

Best Historic Attraction The Tower of London, where you can stand at the site of the execution of two of Henry VIII's wives, and Blenheim Palace, where you can enter the bedroom Sir Winston Churchill was born in. See p 29.

Craziest Story We Heard That Adolf Hitler used to work as a waiter at the family-friendly Adelphi Hotel in Liverpool (see

p 233). In the Museum of Hartlepool, there is a display about a monkey who was washed ashore in the town during the 19th-century Napoleonic Wars; it was hung for being a French spy. See p 183.

Best Walk Nunnery Wood at the Worcester Countryside Centre for the short circular walk along a buggy-friendly and wheel-chair friendly path under a canopy of trees with animal sculptures along the way. For older children and adults the nine and a half mile ramble through the oak and conifer woodland of Grizdale Forest Park, Cumbria to spot red deer and buzzards. See p 127.

Best Museum The Natural History Museum in London, with its blue whale room, hands-on creepy crawly gallery and dinosaur exhibition. You could spend a week exploring and still not do it justice. See p 28.

Best Castle Norwich Castle, so full of children's entertainments like drawing, sticking, model building and interactivity, that it could only have been more fun if it had been a bouncy one. See p 82.

Best Dressing Up Alnwick Castle in Northumberland, the setting for the quidditch game in the Harry Potter movies with Potter tours and quests for younger and older children. Also, where our daughter dressed as a 'lovely court lady, Daddy – do you like my beautiful dress?' See p 181.

Dressing up at Alnwick Castle

Best Sunset From the Esplanade Hotel overlooking the surfer's paradise of Fistral Beach in Cornwall. See p 168.

Best Wildlife Spotting Take a boat trip to the Blakeney Point seal colony on the sand bar in Norfolk. See p 80.

Best Close-up Animal Encounter Experience dozens of hungry parakeets crawling all over you at Friskney, Lincolnshire, pecking for millet seed, at the walk-through aviary of the National Parrot Sanctuary. Home to more than 1,400 birds, and the largest collection of parrots in the UK.

Most Comical Attraction The Cumberland Pencil Museum in Keswick featuring the world's longest pencil (see p 226), and also, of course, the Museum of Dog Collars at Leeds Castle in Kent. See p 36.

Place Where the Riskiest Emergency Wee Stop Occurred Either the tiger enclosure of Woburn Safari Park (see p 54) or the field marked as part of a Military Zone in Offerburn Northumberland, which was full of ordnance debris. See p 203.

Best for Seniors Top sites for seniors include: Bronte Parsonage Museum (Yorkshire), Castle Howard (York), The World of James Herriot (N Yorkshire), Tank Museum (Dorset), National Marine Museum (Plymouth), SS Great Britain (Bristol), Severn Valley Railway (Kidderminster), Constable Country (Bridge Cottage).

Best for Pre-teens Good interactive bets for the 5 to ten year-olds include Think Tank in Birmingham, The Science Museum and The Natural

Parrots, Friskney

History Museum, London. Rides to keep up pre-teen spirit include Legoland and Drayton Manor Theme Park. See p 115.

Best Island The holy island of Lindisfarne, home to the world-famous priory that was the cradle of English Christianity. See p 186.

Best for Teenagers Two places that cannot fail to impress even the most world weary teen are the Eden Project and Goonhilly@futureworld with their Segway transporters. Failing that one of the country's many roller-coaster rides including the excellent one at Blackpool Pleasure Beach. See p 222.

Best Adventure Splash down in Searle's Wash Monster (Hunstanton), a one-time 1960s' US marines amphibious landing craft. Feel the thrill of paragliders jumping and leaping on your wash and learn about the history of smuggling in the area. See p 85.

Weirdest things to do Visit dank Mother Shipton's Cave in Knaresborough, home of a prophetess who predicted the Great Fire of London, the Plague and the Internet. It is also home to petrifying waters that have turned to stone, among other things, an old woolly hat of Seth's from TV's *Emmerdale*. See p 193.

Best Conservation At Slimbridge Wetland Centre, a nature reserve home to 30,000 birds, you get to go canoeing, go on hour-long guided tours and see wildlife films in a cinema. The observation tower has great views across the Severn to the Forest of Dean. See p 147.

Best Art There's an excellent, eclectic array of art and other intriguing objects at Ashmolean Museum of Art and Archaeology (Oxford). Here you'll find a lantern carried by Guy Fawkes, some posie rings said to have inspired J.R.R Tolkien's One Ring in his novel *Lord of the Rings* and the remains of Europe's last Dodo (see p 47). The Wallace Collection (Manchester) has a beautiful sculpture garden and one of the world's best collections of 18th century French paintings. See p 32.

Best Educational Attraction Hartlepool Maritime Experience, where you can board the oldest warship still afloat, The HMS Trincomalee, and experience a recreated 19th century dockside. See p 183.

Spookiest Attraction The Kelvedon Hatch Secret Nuclear

Mother Shipton's Cave, Knaresborough

Bunker in Essex, where we learned how 57 million of us could die in the event of nuclear war without meeting a single other person in the bunker, making us feel that we may have missed a nuclear war while on the A12 getting there. See p 78.

Best Walking 'Letterbox' walking through beautiful countryside on Dartmoor and walking the chalk-down land path of the white cliffs of Dover to see Peregrine Falcons and ravens. See p 62.

Best Cycling Mountain biking in North Yorkshire's Dalby Forest, with graded routes for difficulty, including the tough red routes with hazards such as jumps, steps and steep inclines. Cycling the moors the Bronte sisters made famous on a circular 13 and a half mile cycle ride offering spectacular views over valleys taking in Thornton Moor and Leeway reservoirs. And riding the Bristol and Bath Railway Path, crossing the River Avon through ancient woodland with views of the Cotswold Hills.

Mostly Unlikely Interactive Activity Handling mineralized mammoth poo at the Dinosaur Farm Museum on the Isle of Wight. See p 41.

Scariest Moment The spooky story of the mysterious disappearance of the Sandringham Company at Gallipoli during World War I (see p 84). The old Victorian prison at Lincoln Castle with its tales from the 'gentlemen' executioner and its grisly hangings from the castle ramparts (see p 69). The slamming of prison doors and ghost stories of former inmates at the Galleries of Justice, Nottingham (see p 120). The haunted suites at Hazlewood Castle where a monk killed himself in the Reformation (see p 201). Lastly, the dark corridors and sense of dread at the Dracula Experience in Whitby (see p 190).

The Funniest thing Overheard

A German man behind me in the queue at an ice-cream stand at Chester Zoo ordering 'von Nobbily-Bobbily'. See p 214.

Best Sporting Goosebumps

The Anfield Tour of Liverpool Football Club where you can pose underneath the shirt of Anfield hero Steven Gerrard, sit in the manager's seat in the stands and stand in the legendary tunnel listening to a tape of the roaring crowd at the height of Liverpool's 1970's dominance. See p 217.

Most Inspiring Poetry

Dove Cottage where Wordsworth spent his time of 'plain living and high thinking'.

BEST FAMILY ACCOMMODATION

Most Child-friendly Hotel

Knoll House, Enid Blyton's favourite place to stay in Dorset; it felt exactly like being at Aunty Fanny's house at the start of a *Famous Five* mystery. See p 165.

Most Tranquil Place to Stay

The remote and beautiful Kielder Leapish Waterside Park in Northumberland, based on the banks of the largest man-made reservoir in Europe. The birds-of-prey centre is fantastic and there are boat rides across the reservoir.

Most Friendly Place to Stay

The Rooftree Guesthouse in Sandown, Isle of Wight, a few minutes' walk from the beach. It

Bracken Bank Lodge, Penrith

Ettington Park, Stratford-upon-Avon

serves Japanese meals on request, has a pet's corner and our daughter was given a free ballet lesson by the owner and former professional dancer Anne Abe.

Most Eccentric Hotelier/ Guesthouse Owner The aristocratic Stuart Burton of Bracken Bank Lodge in Penrith, who can tell you about how his grandfather was responsible for shooting many of the animals whose pelts line the walls of the lodge. His lovely wife also makes a great breakfast and you may find is mysteriously obsessed with the village of Plumpton. We kept a tally of her utterances of it (14).

Kindest Member of Staff The welcome and enduring great service at Ettingham Park where the owner, Damon, also turned a blind eye to the aromatic duck vomit down my shirt when I checked in with food poisoning and then brought pints of cola to my room and talked to me about Norman Cook. See p 129.

Hotel with most Children's Stuff Fritton House Country Park in Norfolk. There's an adventure playground with an enormous play castle, slides, a jumping pillow, pony rides (£2), boat rides, a barn with small buggies and ride-on diggers. See p 87.

Hotel with Strangest Children's Activity Armathwaite Hall Hotel in Keswick, Cumbria, where they have Young Etiquette classes, involving lessons for children on how to use a knife and fork, which glasses to use for what drinks and why it is bad form to shovel peas. See p 231.

BEST FAMILY DINING

Most Child-friendly Restaurant The Disney-esque Outside Inn in Blackpool, with its fibreglass wonderland of lanterned trees, ruined castles, waterfalls and Tudor houses. Regular pirate nights are staged, during which staff dress as buccaneers and children can help themselves from a treasure chest of sweets. See p 240.

Largest Portions Breakfast at the 202 West Parade Guesthouse in Lincoln. See p 90.

Best Ice Cream The Leonardo da Vinci at Morellis in Broadstairs, where the comic actor Tony Hancock went wooing John Le Mesurier's wife. See p 61.

Best Cheese Selection The dessert trolley at Holbeck Ghyll in the Lake District. See p 232.

Best Retro Dining Betty's Cafe Tea Rooms (Harrogate) whose waitresses in old-fashioned black and white serve more than 300 different varieties of cake, chocolate and bread on cake stands.

Freshest Fish My haddock at the Magpie Café in Whitby; it could probably have swum in my brown sauce if I'd made the puddle any deeper. See p 207.

Least Likely Place to Celebrity Spot The Essex Rose Tea House in Dedham, where Sting, Griff Rhys-Jones and Dave Hill from Slade have visited; it's also where Chelsea and England midfielder Frank Lampard pops in for a rock 'n'roll tuna jacket potato with no tomatoes. See p 93.

The popular Magpie Café at Whitby

The Poshest Pier Food At Southwold Pier, Suffolk, you can buy a Roquefort salad. See p 93.

Most Welcome Appearance of a Person in a Bear Costume Brewster bear at the Hampton restaurant in Peterborough after a harrowing row with my wife about directions. My daughter and son hugged him and, emotionally wrought by the evils of the ring road, we felt like hugging him too. See p 94.

Most Historic Place to Eat a Stilton Ploughman's In the high-backed settle seat of the Lord Nelson pub in Norfolk's Burnham Thorpe. It was Nelson's local and he came here between ship commands. See p 92.

2 Planning Your Trip

ENGLAND

Researching this book we visited hundreds of attractions, stayed in dozens of hotels, hostels and bed and breakfasts and ate out so much our daughter came to see everything she came across that was laminated (including one time a flyer at PC World) as a menu ('What's that Daddy – that looks nice'… 'er… that's a bubble jet printer, Phoebe'). We did our best to be comprehensive but England is large and there will be attractions we missed or hadn't room for. We've divided the country up into six area chapters – London and the South-east, Shakespeare and the Heart of England, The Lakes and the North-west, the Northeast, Eastern England and the Southwest. Each chapter contains a brief and often fairly glib overview of the area demeaning, jok-ingly where possible, its inhabitants and their customs. England's great strength is its regional diversity, something to be celebrated and some-times teased although we're aware we're as odd ourselves. After this we'll tell you about the best places to visit, the best food to discover and the best places to stay. We'll probably tell you too much about what our children said and the personal mishaps we had but we've slapped it in anyway (a) because we're bored of reading travel guides ourselves described as knowledgeable and informative, shorthand for bland and unreadable, (b) because it made it more fun to write and hopefully to read. England has so many outdoor activities we'd never considered and landscapes we'd never imagined. You'll need to plan carefully to make the most of each day, but it will be well worth it. Driving around the country researching this book was one of the most memorable and enjoyable experiences I've had as a parent. Have fun on your own travels.

VISITOR INFORMATION

It won't be long before high street travel agents are seen as quaint timepieces like those olden day shops selling Bath Oliver biscuits. That's how good the Internet is as a research tool when investigating a family holi-day. A few useful websites for England include *www.visit england.com* with many two for one offers and downloadable money-off vouchers as well as a special family fun page with ideas for days out while *www. enjoyenglanddirect.com* has similar offers and suggestions. If you are planning more of a tour-based holiday (you lazy couch potato) then *www.britannia.com* is also worth a look as are the fol-lowing: *www.english-heritage.org. uk* and *www.nationaltrust.org.uk*.

This being England, where the weather is the national obses-sion, biggest drawback and also crutch conversation when all else fails, you'll be wanting to have some information on this. See *www.news.bbc.co.uk/weather*. Other useful sites include: *www. takethefamily.com*; *www.child friendly.net*; *www.babygoes2.com*; *www.mumsnet.com*; and *www. visitlondon.com/family*.

Family Festivals

Festivals for families have come on leaps and bounds in England or perhaps it's just that they've returned to the relaxed, welcoming atmosphere of the original festival scene. For families it's a real opportunity to try something new with a bit of planning, some wet wipes and for younger children headphones, toys and blankets. You can make it a day trip or a long weekend and it may be the only place you can go and get some cred with your older children (although don't expect to see them much). Don't discount seniors either, there's lots for all the family; many grandparents returned to the Isle of Wight Festival in 2002 after it restarted to see how the line up compared to Hendrix, Jefferson Airplane and The Who 32 years ago!

At Camp Bestival, Lulworth Castle, Dorset, 30 July – 1 August (**www.campbestival.net**) there's a kid's Garden area with sea views behind the Castle with a Circus Big Top, a Kid's Dressing Up Tent (and Catwalk), a Bouncy Castle, Donkey Rides, a separate Toddler's Area, Nickelodeon's SpongeBob SquarePants, a Penguin Children's Book Tent, the English National Ballet presenting Angelina Ballerina workshops, the Insect Circus & Museum, a Maypole (for little and big kids to dance around) and a Punch & Judy stall. Got you thinking?

Other top family festivals include:

Wychwood, Cheltenham, 4-6 June. **www.wychwoodfestival.com**

Guilfest, Guildford, 16-18 July. **www.guilfest.co.uk**

Latitude, Southwold, 15-18 July. **www.latitudefestival.co.uk**

Ben & Jerry's Sundae on the Common, Clapham Common, July. **www.benjerry.co.uk/sundae**

The Innocent Village Fete, Regent's Park, August. **www.innocentvillagefete.com**

Shambala, Central England, 26-30 August. **www.shambala festival.org**

Solfest, West Cumbria, August. **www.solwayfestival.co.uk**

WOOD Festival, May, Oxfordshire. **www.thisistruck.com**

Womad, 23-25 July, Wiltshire. **www.womad.org**

Sunrise, 3-6 June, Somerset. **www.sunrisecelebration.com**

For more information on festivals and events go to: **www.whatsonwhen.com**.

Getting There & Around

The fact that Britain is an island surrounded by sea complicates driving here somewhat, although the Channel Tunnel provides a waterless route direct from the continent from Folkestone. The journey is about 35 minutes long. The main routes from Scotland are the A1 and the A74(M) and M74. From Wales there are numerous routes into England including via the Midlands the A458 and the A483.

Driving around England is relatively easy provided you are prepared for the inevitable traffic

Teen Spirit

If you are on holiday with your teenage children then one of two things will have had to have happened. 1) you will either have bribed them to come with you with money or gifts or 2) you will have forced them to come with you and they are right now lashed to the back seat in inch thick rope muttering swear words at you. Now you have them with you the first thing you must appreciate is that teenagers need to stay in contact with their friends. More important than food and probably oxygen to the average teenager is mobile phone coverage and an internet connection for them to be able to Facebook their friends about what "a pratt you were today on the log flume ride". Also, don't expect gratitude for the £26 ticket to Windsor castle. There are two places however, we can think of that cannot fail to impress even the most world weary teen – the Eden Project and Goonhilly@futureworld with their Segway transporters. Remember, you were a teenager once, too.

jams, especially on the outskirts of major towns and cities and almost always on the notorious M25. In the countryside and in particular the Lakes, Yorkshire Dales and North York Moors there are narrow roads where it is impossible to overtake and where you are likely to encounter sheep, cows and chickens in the road.

Useful driving websites include **www.theaa.com** and **www.rac.co.uk** which have free route planning tools while **www.multimap.com** provides useful-ish area maps and traffic info. **Sat nav** Having criticised these in the past we now don't know how we managed without one. They are the best money you will ever spend on your car. We love our sat nav, we love Jane the voice of our sat nav. We trust her more than we trust each other and ourselves. If I could ask it what to wear I would.

By Train Travelling to England by train can be achieved via

Eurostar (℡ *08705 186186*, *www.eurostar.com*), which has services from Paris and Brussels via Lille that connect to Ashford in Kent and London St Pancras. The journey from Paris takes around two and a half hours and costs from £120 return, while it is half an hour less from Brussels. As for train travel within the country, unfortunately, despite inventing it, the English have one of the worst transport systems in the world. In fact it's like a child who made a great Lego model, got bored of it and so started to gradually knock it down. The best way to travel by train is to check out your route with **National Rail Enquiries** (℡ *08457 484950*, *www.nationalrail.com*), get a white witch to cast a spell for good fortune and take a long book to read when you get stuck in Swindon because of a signal failure.

By Coach The main hub for coach travellers is London's

Tips for Driving with Young Children

There are two small difficulties associated with driving with children and they are: (1) Getting children into the car and (2) being with them in the car.

Ok, I can you hear you saying, that is everything. And yes, that's right. Children and driving don't go well together. Children, on the whole, hate driving. We do, however, have some tips to help you. These are as follows.

The reason it is hard to get young children into the car is because once in their bucket seats they remember how boring it was the last time they were there and will buck and twist into strange shapes making them impossible to strap in. Even when the twisting and bucking has stopped, right as you are about to connect the buckle they push their tummies out to prevent you fastening them up and slide down the seat onto the floor, necessitating starting the process again. To counteract this, do one of two things. Try to distract your child. As you put them in the seat point at an object through the window and say, 'Hey, look, a doggie', or even 'Hey, look a magic rabbit with gifts for you'. But if your children are veterans of this technique you must be subtle, and this involves bribery. Not to carry sweets in a family car is like walking through a vampire-infested graveyard at midnight without a wooden cross. Provided that you have sweets in your car, what you do is this: as your child bucks say, loud enough for them to hear, but not loud enough for other judgemental parents to hear, 'Please – you can hold the chocolate gem packet'. If this fails return to the house in tears.

To amuse a child in the car is tricky. Many games have been invented for this purpose, including I-Spy and collecting car registration plates but none of them work. I am, of course, talking about – cue scary music – the in-car DVD player. Yes, I know their inquisitive minds demand stimulation every second of the day and that it's not fair to chloroform them for an hour with the talking mouse that is Angelia Ballerina. But what do you do on a plane when you're bored of your John Grisham? Do you play I-Spy? What we are saying is, is it better they cry, fight and draw all over their hands and faces with felt-tip in dirty protests? Anyway, and I can see you backing away from us fearfully now, all we will say is that they can be bought at Argos for under £100.

Victoria coach station on Buckingham Palace Road (☎ 0207 730 3466). The major operator is National Express (☎ 0870 580 8080, www.nationalexpress.com). For shorter journeys (good ones by bus) the main operators are Arriva (☎ 0844 8004411, www.arrivabus.co.uk), and FirstGroup (☎ 01224 650100, www.firstgroup.com) serving more than 60 towns and cities in England while Greenline (☎ 0844 8017261, www.greenline.co.uk) has a number of services from London to the home counties including one (the 757) from London to Luton Airport.

By Air There are lots of airports in England that claim to be in London but which are actually often ages away. London's main airports are Gatwick (☎ *0870 00002468*, *www.baa.co.uk*) and Heathrow (☎ *0870 0000123*, *www. baa.co.uk*). Heathrow, about 25km west of central London, has hundreds of airlines serving it, including main carrier British Airways (*www.britishairways.com*), **Air Canada** (*www.aircanada.com*), **Air New Zealand** (*www.airnew zealand.co.uk*), **Continental** (*www.continental.com*), **Qantas** (*www.qantas.com*), **Singapore Airlines** (*www.singaporeair.com*), **United** (*www.united.com*) and **Virgin Atlantic** (*www.virgin-atlantic.com*). To get to London from Heathrow the cheapest option is via the Piccadilly Line on the London Underground (*www.tfl.gov.uk/tube*). The journey takes about 55 minutes and will costs about £5.50 Alternatively the Heathrow Express (☎ *0845 6001515*, *www.heathrow express.co.uk*) runs from each of the airport's four terminals to London Paddington Station in 15 minutes. It costs around £16.50. Alternatively a taxi costs about £55.

INSIDER TIP ≫

ANIMAL WELFARE

Ask zoos and other animal attractions about their animal welfare policy if you have concerns. The more public pressure to ensure the protection of animals will help put an end to animal cruelty. *www.wspa.org.uk*.

By Foot

Dartmoor, (☎ *01392 832768*). *www.dartmoorletterboxing.org*

The best England has to offer, of course, is found on two feet, exploring the countryside, the flora and fauna, tumbling through forests and over the downs to enjoy nature. One unique way to get outdoors is 'letterboxing' on Dartmoor. This outdoor hobby combines the rigours of orienteering with the nerdiness of stamp collecting and involves walkers searching for weatherproof boxes that are hidden in various places on the National Park. These boxes that might be under rocks, say, or in the roots of a tree contain inky stamps and a visitors' book. You then use the stamp to make a mark in a special book you bring along with you, after this using your own stamp (you must make one – see website) you then make a print in the visitor's books to prove you found it. Although it sounds a little bit like quite a busy morning of mindless bureaucracy at the DVLC it's very popular with thousands of letterboxes now dotted all over the moor. The aim is, of course, to find as many boxes as possible and an excuse to get out there and discover England's excellent National Parks: Dartmoor, Exmoor, New Forest, South Downs, Broads, Peak District, Yorkshire Dales, Lake District, North York Moors and Northumberland.

TIP ▷ **When to Go?** ◁

There is no real best time to travel in England. There are worst times to make a big trip – once every four years, for instance, around the quarter-final stage of the World Cup, when as the England football team makes a courageously predictable exit English men traditionally take to the streets draped in St George crosses to cry in doorways. In terms of the weather it can't be denied that it does rain quite a lot in England. There is no real rainy time – every time is potentially a rainy one although marginally November (6.4cm on average) is the worst month. The temperature ranges from $-1°$ C to $43°$ C ($30°$–$110°$ Fahrenheit), although very rarely drops below $2°$ C ($35°$ F) or goes above $26°$ C ($78°$ F). The cheapest time to come to England is in the off-season from 1st November to around 12th December and then from 2nd January to 14th March. Prices tend to rise between mid-March and early June and peak between 6th June and early September when the school holidays end. Most of us living here hope and pray for a sunny July and August when we book time off. In terms of prettiness – the spring is when the country is at its greenest, it's beautiful too under a bed of winter snow although on balance the summer would probably be the best choice.

Gatwick Airport is about 50km south of London and is served by among many others **American Airlines**, **British Airways**, **Delta Continental**, **Northwest**, **Qantas** and **Virgin Atlantic**. The best bet into central London from here is the **Gatwick Express** (📞 *0870 002468*, *www.gatwickexpress. com*), which takes half an hour into London Victoria Station (roughly £16). Trains run every 15 minutes. The **Thameslink** service (📞 *0845 7484950*, *www. firstcapitalconnect.co.uk*) runs from Gatwick to London Kings Cross with a slightly cheaper fare although the journey is 15 minutes longer. The service runs every 15 minutes.

The other London airports and we are using the term London fairly loosely here are: **Stansted Airport** (📞 *08700*

000303, *www.baa.co.uk*), which is used mainly for European and domestic flights, **London City Airport** (📞 *0207 646 0088*, *www. londoncityairport.com*), which serves European destinations and **Luton Airport** (📞 *0158 405100*, *www.london-luton.com*) which handles mainly charter flights.

The country's other major airports are **Manchester Airport** (📞 *0161 48980000*, *www. manchesterairport.com*), **Birmingham Airport** (📞 *0844 5766000*, *www.bhx.co.uk*) and **Bristol Airport** (📞 *0871 3344344*, *www. bristolairport.co.uk*)

For detailed information on air connections to/from:
Heathrow, see p 17
Gatwick, see p17
Stansted, see p 18
London City, see p 18
Luton, see p 19
Manchester, see p 216

London can be fiercely expensive, so if you plan to use London public transport a lot, Travelcards offer unlimited use of buses; Underground, including Dockands Light Railway and trains (except Heathrow Express). Cards can be for one day, three days, a week, a month, and up to four months for children, also offering a third off riverboat cruises. You can buy an off-peak version to save money for travel after 9.30 weekdays. Remember children under 11 on the tube and DLR travel for free if accompanied by a ticket holder. If you are visiting lots of sights it may be worth investing in a London Pass offering free admission to 55 attractions (*www.londonpass.com*). Also check out deals on: *www.discount-london.com*. For the quickest routes around London see: *www.tfl.gov.uk* and live updates countrywide: *www.nationalrail.co.uk*. Booking family travel online and going midweek or off-peak will save you your pounds, too. For bike, wheelchair and pushchair access see Chapter 3.

Birmingham, see p 104
Bristol, see p 141

INSIDER TIP ⟩⟩

VALUE ACCOMMODATION
Staying on a **university campus** is cheaper than normal self-catering. If you're lodging in a big city over the summer holiday, most big universities have rooms suitable for families. They're generally cleaner and more modern than the average B&B. You'll need to book well ahead, especially in London, Oxford and Cambridge. For more details contact **Venuemasters** (*www.venuemasters.co.uk*).

ACCOMMODATION

Camping

Camping is so much more fun today. Tents, for one thing, don't take a degree in structural engineering to construct, sleeping bags are warmer and campsites aren't as primitive as they were when I had to have my hair washed under a crusty looking standpipe used to clean out the cattle shed. Washing facilities have improved to include showers with clean water and at superior places there are children's play areas with actual real toys and almost always there will be a shop selling basic supplies and the strong wine you'll need to sleep through your son's incredibly loud snoring your wife at first mistook for a badger shuffling around the food box outside the tent. Useful websites include *www. camp-sites.co.uk*, *www.camping andcaravningclub. co.uk*, *www.bigfreeguide.com*, *www.alanrogers.com/camping* all of which provide a list of campsites region by region often with links to the campsite's own websites including sometimes photos to give you a better idea of what to expect.

Self-catering

If you are going away for any length of time self-catering is often a more attractive option than a hotel or B&B in that you have more room to spread out, a home from home to keep children's routines going and you end up more in control of those hotbeds of temper – mealtimes. There are reams of places available although these lists are a good place to start your search *www.cottageguide.co.uk*, *www.easycottages.com*, *www.oas.co.uk*, *www.cottagesdirect.co.uk*, *www.britainexpress.com/cottages* and *www.independentcottages.co.uk*.

B&Bs

Generally speaking these aren't always ideal for young families as chances are you'll be in one room that causes problems if anyone is a light sleeper. Also, unless there is a within-baby-monitor-range lounge to retreat to after the children are in bed you'll be turning in yourselves after the Cbeebies night-time hour at 7pm feeling wide awake still thinking about the Pontypines and the Whatingers. You can obtain a good list of those available from Bed & Breakfast Nationwide (☎ *01255 831235, www.bedandbreakfastnationwide.com*), or *www.bedandbreakfasts-uk.co.uk*, *www.bedandbreakfast-directory.co.uk* and *www.visitus.co.uk*.

Hotels

A more luxurious and expensive option, most hotels offer

Breakfast at 202 West Parade Guesthouse

half-board, full-board, B&B options and often private self-catering alternatives sometimes not in the hotel itself but in a lodge or cottage next door. If you are travelling with a young family interconnecting rooms are a good bet if you have the purse, or failing that be creative and ask for a family room that's maybe in an L-shape so you can put the children's beds somewhere away from the main section of the room you might want to watch TV in. We quite often re-arranged entire hotel rooms to hide our son's cot behind sofas and chairs so my wife could watch *The X-Factor* in relative peace. At the higher end of the scale are the luxury family hotels, often old manor houses set in grounds with spas, children's clubs, crèches, pools and almost every activity you can imagine from canoeing to badminton and including even in one case, an etiquette school for toddlers anxious to learn how to use the correct cutlery at dinner. Useful websites include *www.tripadvisor.com*, which reviews attractions and *www.laterooms.com* with daily updated lists of discounted hotel rooms. Other sites worth a look include *www.hotels-england.co.uk* and *www.heavenlyhotels.co.uk*.

Youth Hostels

With not a woolly jumper in sight (well, not all the time) the Youth Hostel Association (YHA) has done a lot to change its image and offering. These former cold and bleak out-houses are now often comfortable and simple lodgings in often idyllic areas. Perhaps it's a bit of a jump for some families with younger children, but for older children they offer freedom and fun.

Breakfasts now feature posh sausages and FairTrade coffee and there's over 150 locations in England.

Families are an important clientele, and rooms which used to be full of bunks now sleep four or six, and are often en-suite. All for a nightly cost of around £14, less for children. *www.yha.org.uk*.

DINING

Although we, the English, may feel we've moved on, England still has a sorry reputation abroad for serving low-quality meals featuring bizarre desserts like spotted dick and unhealthy main courses made up of largely, either cold meats like spam and corned beef, or hot food like fish and chips, whereas in actual fact no-one eats like this any more. Thanks to the advent of the celebrity chef and the popularity of foodie TV shows, restaurant-goers expect a whole lot more than a prawn cocktail and a steak and crinkle chips when they sit down for £15 a head. Thanks to the smoking ban, pubs too are now a good bet for a healthy meal these days. The pickled egg and bags of cheese–and-onion crisps of yesteryear eaten amongst the fog of a 100 cigarettes have given way to the ubiquitous brie and cranberry panini, the saucer of black olives and the tzatziki dip. This explosion in the choice of places to eat has forced pubs that were already serving food to raise their games and the result is the gastro-pub, pubs really in name only specializing in freshly prepared, locally sourced food.

As a child I can recall eating out as a family maybe once before the age of 12. It was a Harvester and I had the Ploughman's Lunch with a Stilton so hard from the fridge I would have needed an angle grinder to cut it into slithers to place in my stale roll. There was nothing geared towards children then, and for amusement you were expected, between courses, to stare at the rustic farming memorabilia nailed to the walls. ('Ooh look, another hoe.') Nowadays all good restaurants with an eye on the family market have children's menus, highchairs and usually crayons and colouring-in books. They also now tend to open earlier than 7pm to allow younger families the chance to dine together before the witching hour of bath and bed.

Family Dining Tips

❶ In big cities, especially London, the pre-theatre (5pm–7pm) menu is often 10–20% cheaper than the later menu.

❷ Some hotels offer free children's meals if you're (a) staying there and (b) eating *en famille*. Ask about this when you book, and on check-in be cheeky and ask for an upgraded room.

❸ Ring ahead, say you'll be bringing children and book a restaurant table away from the main action, so if they kick up you won't feel so self-conscious when you bellow: 'I said BE QUIET'.

❹ A good way to avoid the baby-in-the-lap dinner is to bring along the car seat. Also most restaurants have highchairs, so always ask for one on arrival.

❺ Ask for crayons and colouring books to keep the children occupied. Lots of restaurants have these, although you'd better make sure the crayon goes on the colouring book and not the expensive linen tablecloth.

Older Travellers

We've added an age icon throughout this book to show parents which attractions may be better for different aged children, however we know families take all shapes and sizes (older children, single parents, extended families, grandparents, disabled travellers) and so have kept this in mind when making our choices.

From our experience of visiting attractions with seniors two obvious things are vital: one to be near somewhere you can rest and get something to eat and drink, and the other to avoid a walk up the steps to the top of the spire at Durham Cathedral if one of your parents have just had a new hip fitted (although they'll still go faster than you). A few banker attractions you cannot go wrong at include SS Great Britain (Bristol), Severn Valley Railway (Kidderminster), Constable Country (Bridge Cottage).

And before you get smug as multi-generational juggling parents, remember they brought you up, have lived longer than you, know more than you and *are* wondering why their grandchildren are pushing Alphabet Spaghetti up their noses.

LONDON & THE SOUTHEAST

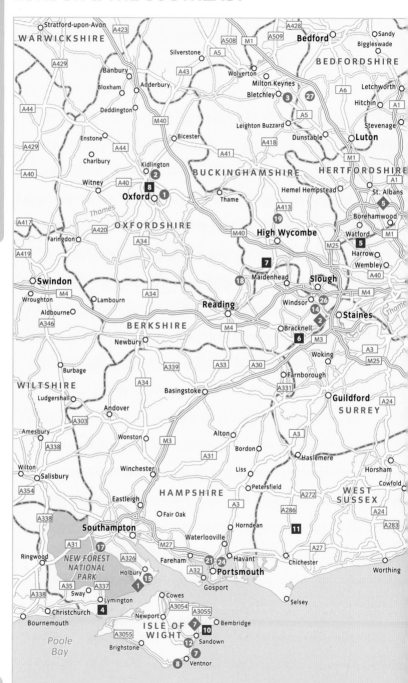

Attractions ●

Ashmolean Museum of
  Art & Archaeology **1**
Blenheim Palace **2**
Bletchley Park **3**
British Airways London Eye **4**
Canterbury Cathedral **5**
The Canterbury Tales **6**
Dinosaur Farm Museum **7**
Dinosaur Isle **8**
Drusillas Wild Animal Park **9**
Historic Dockyard **10**
The Hop Farm **11**
Isle of Wight Zoo
  & Tiger Sanctuary **12**
Leeds Castle **13**

Legoland **14**
National Motor Museum **15**
Natural History Museum **16**
New Forest Museum **17**
The River & Rowing Museum **18**
The Roald Dahl Museum
  & Story Centre **19**
Royal Engineers Museum **20**
Royal Navy Historic Dockyards **21**
The Royal Pavilion **22**
Science Museum **23**
Spinnaker Tower **24**
Tower of London **25**
Windsor Castle **26**
Woburn Safari Park **27**

Accommodation ■

Ashdown Park Hotel & Country Club **1**
Browns **2**
Eastwell Manor **3**
Elmers Court Hotel **4**
The Grove **5**
Macdonald Berystede Hotel & Spa **6**
Macdonald Compleat Angler **7**
The Old Bank Hotel **8**
The Pavilion **9**
Rooftree Guesthouse **10**
Woodstock House Hotel **11**

Dining ◆

The Captain's Cabin at Buckler's Hard **1**
Carluccios **2**
Don Vincenzo **3**
Hummus Bros **4**
Inn on the Park **5**
Morellis **6**
The Spyglass Inn **7**
Tootsies **8**
The Wallace **9**

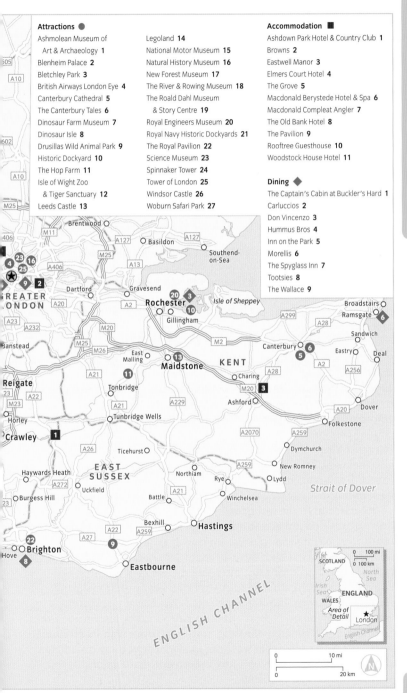

This vast area encompasses a chunk of the country stretching from the New Forest around the south coast to Chatham in Kent, up through London, fanning out to the Home Counties and out as far as Oxford to the west. The wealthiest area of England, the Southeast isn't really a region in the sense that the Northeast or Southwest are, but is simply a collection of counties with their own distinct characters that happen to be within striking distance of the capital. London is the heartbeat of the region and, as you'd expect of Europe's largest city, has plenty for families including two of the best museums in the world – the Natural History Museum and the Science Museum – as well as hundreds of places to eat and stay. In fact, London has so much to offer we feel a little light-headed trying to convey its scale as we write this. I am afraid we cannot hope to do it justice in this guidebook and so while happy to point out a weekend's worth of attractions, if you're planning a longer stay, we suggest you pick up a copy of the excellent Frommer's *London with Kids*, which will tell you more than you'll ever need to know.

Nicknamed the Garden of England for its preponderance of orchards and hop farms, Kent is the furthest Southeast county in England and is home to historic Canterbury and the oldest cathedral in England, and also the former royal naval dockyards of Chatham. Further along the coast, the boho town of Brighton in East Sussex has more restaurants per head of population than anywhere else in the country, and is a great spot for a family meal or a jaunt to the best small zoo in England, Drusillas Wild Animal Park. Moving west again, Hampshire boasts some of the country's last remaining unenclosed pastureland. Known as the New Forest, it is strangely controlled by the Court of Verderers, a legal body whose laws are enforced and overseen by Agisters, who, we suspect, may actually employ goblins. The best things to do here besides driving around staring at the ponies, wondering if it is safe to pet them (it isn't) and give them sugar lumps (it isn't), include visiting the National Motor Museum at Beaulieu and Buckler's Hard and cycling the trails of the New Forest.

Separated from the mainland by the Solent, the Isle of Wight is the best place to find dinosaur fossils in Europe and perhaps the most insular area of England (tourists are known as 'grockles' and cars 'grockle cans'). That said, there are many family-oriented places for grockles to visit in their cans, including the Isle of Wight Zoo and two dinosaur-based attractions. A ferry ride away on the mainland, the town of Portsmouth is home to the Royal Naval Dockyards, where you can board Nelson's flagship *HMS Victory*. Elsewhere in the Southeast you'll find the university town of Oxford with its dreaming spires, the palace Churchill was born in, and a drive away from here along the M40, two of the country's most visited attractions – Windsor Castle and Legoland.

CHILDREN'S TOP 10 HIGHLIGHTS

❶ Test your ability to stand on one leg against a flamingo's at Drusillas Wild Animal Park. See p 49.

❷ Check out the mini-Madame Tussauds exhibition at the Hop Farm in Maidstone where my wife and I greatly enjoyed/were alarmed by a geriatric-looking wax model of Marilyn Monroe seemingly breaking wind over a recreated New York subway vent. See p 39.

❸ Stare at the Beefeaters with 'Father Christmas Beards' and try a family tail at the spooky Tower of London. See p 29.

❹ Experience an earthquake and be tracked by a T-Rex at the Natural History Museum in London. See p 28.

❺ View the capital city from the top of the world's highest observation wheel. See p 28.

❻ Visit Lord Nelson's flagship, *HMS Victory*, on a day out at the Royal Navy Dockyards in Portsmouth. See p 44.

❼ Hold mineralized mammoth poo at the Dinosaur Farm Museum on the Isle of Wight. See p 42.

❽ See children make rainbows and feel the breath of a dinosaur on the back of their necks at the Science Museum in London. See p 29.

❾ Enjoy a Winnie the Pooh teatime of honey sandwiches and Kanga cupcakes close to Ashdown Forest, inspiration for A.A. Milne's 100 Acre Wood at Ashdown Park Hotel and Country Club. See p 54.

❿ Have your children rub shoulders with celebrity sprogs in the Anouska nursery at Hertfordshire's Grove Hotel. See p 57.

LONDON

Here's a brief outline of a suggested weekend bearing in mind the main rules when sightseeing with children in London: keep it simple, don't try to do too much and spend the least amount of time you can on the underground shouting 'stay away from the rails'. In terms of getting around, the least painful method is the London underground although that is fraught, especially if you have young children in a buggy, as lifts are scarce and members of helpful staff even rarer. To minimize the stress pick up a tube map that marks the 50 or so stations with no steps or with lifts to platforms. To further complicate matters you're not allowed unfolded buggies on the trains themselves between 7.30am–9.30am and 4pm–7pm, although this is rarely enforced. Tube stations are marked with a red circle and blue crossbar bearing the word 'Underground'. The colour-coded map designating the various lines is fairly straightforward. Basically you can transfer as many times as you want as long as you stay on the underground and have a ticket valid for the zones in which you have travelled. Some stations have ticket-dispensing machines while in others you'll have to queue to buy them. The flat fare for one trip within Zone 1 or between Zone 1 and any other zone is £4 and £2 for children over 10 (photocards needed). Hold on to your tickets – you need them on exit or you risk a fine. Tube hours are 5.15am–11.45pm.

The Top Four Family Attractions

British Airways London Eye

★ ★ ★   ALL AGES

Millennium Jubilee Gardens, SE1, ☏ 0870 9908883, www.ba-londoneye.co.uk. Nearest tube: Westminster or Waterloo.

The best way to get an overview of the capital is from the top of the world's tallest observation wheel (135m), commanding 360-degree 40km views. From your glass pod (seating 25) you can see all of the London bridges and Buckingham Palace. To get the most of the experience it's a good idea, for an extra £2, to hire a guide who'll talk you through the history of the city, point out landmarks and try and interest your children in activities other than banging on the glass and shouting, 'I'm the king of the castle and you're the dirty rascal'. Booking online saves 10% and queuing (this is now the country's busiest tourist attraction).

Open Oct–May 10am–8pm, June and Sept 10am–9pm, July–Aug 10am–9.30pm. Adm £17, children (5–15) £8.50, conc £14. Amenities baby-changing. Credit Cards all cards accepted.

Natural History Museum ★ ★ ★   ALL AGES

Cromwell Road, SW7, ☏ 0207 945011, www.nhm.ac.uk. Nearest tube: South Kensington.

I can still remember dropping my chocolate Penguin biscuit in shock at the sheer size of the three-double-decker-long Blue Whale exhibit when I visited this museum as a child (or as our daughter said here with considerably more savoir faire, 'Yes, daddy I know it's big but when are we going to have the chocolate yoghurts. You said after the fish'. The highlight for our son was the Dinosaur Gallery with its super-sensing T-Rex that followed his movements around the room with its scary head ('That dinosaur looking at me'). Investigate is a hands-on science lab for 6–15 year olds, and at The Power Within you get to experience an earthquake. There are Discovery Guides (80p) to inspire children (4–16) in their explorations of volcanoes, dinosaur teeth and the source of the earth's energy, while for under sevens the Explore Backpacks (free, £25 deposit) come with explorer hats, binoculars and drawing materials and are worth picking up and keeping your eye on. Ours was dumped in the Darwin Centre because 'I want to look at Archie the giant squid'.

Open daily 10am–5.50pm. **Adm** free (except temporary exhibitions). **Amenities** café. **Credit Cards** all accepted.

Science Museum ★ ★ ★ ALL AGES

Exhibition Road, SW7, ☎ 0870 8704868, www.sciencemuseum. org.uk. Nearest tube: South Kensington.

Here our daughter made a rainbow, our son felt a dinosaur's breath on the back of his neck, and I managed to demean my wife's ancestors.

A dauntingly huge museum on five floors, it's a good idea to head straight for the third floor Launch Pad gallery where there are more than 50 hands-on exhibits. As well as making a rainbow at the Light Table, children can see through a thermal-imaging camera how licking their lips cools them down while orange-shirted guides are on hand to explain the various forces of nature. The Imax cinema (adults £8, conc £6.25) shows 3D films on its double-decker-bus-sized screens including, when we visited, one about hunting for dinosaur remains in New Mexico. Elsewhere we learnt how the technologies used in Formula One racing had (a) helped the *Beagle 2* space mission to Mars and (b) developed a type of rubber footwear that prevented pet-shop workers slipping over in Doncaster. In Who Am I? you can trace the roots of your surname enabling you to remind your wife that while relatives of yours were geniuses (John Couch-Adams) who discovered

the planet Neptune, most of hers were, according to parish records, flogged in Buntingford.

Open daily 10am–6pm. **Adm** free (except some exhibitions, rides and the IMAX cinema). **Amenities** café, baby-changing. **Credit Cards** all accepted.

Tower of London ★ ★ ALL AGES

Tower Hill, EC3, ☎ 0870 7567070, www.hrp.org.uk.

Here visitors can walk across Tower Green, the famous site of the executions of two of Henry VIII's wives – Anne Boleyn and Catherine Howard – see the Crown Jewels and feed ham to the ravens (our son). Built in the 11th century by William the Conqueror, this is one of the best medieval castles in the world, you'll find instruments of torture, graffiti on a prison wall left by the distraught husband of tragic queen Lady Jane Grey, and learn what it was like to be held in the Bloody Tower. There are family trails, although if you're short of time skip round on an hour-long guided yeoman tour. The famous beefeaters, all Tudor-outfitted ex-British servicemen, with 'Father Christmas beards, Daddy' will tell you about how Colonel Blood tried to steal the Crown Jewels in 1671 and his accomplice Robert Perot was caught with a golden orb down his pants. They'll pose for pictures and advise that ham sandwiches are not the ideal meal for one of the six resident ravens, each of which has their wings clipped, because as the

Tower of London

legend goes if the ravens fly away (or choke to death on ham fat) the tower will fall.

Open Mar–Oct Tues–Sat 9.30am–5.30pm, Sun–Mon 10am–5.30pm, Nov–Feb Tues–Sat 9am–4.30pm, Sun–Mon 10am–4pm. **Adm** adults £17, children under 16 £9.50, conc £14.50. **Amenities** café, baby-changing. **Credit Cards** all accepted.

FAMILY-FRIENDLY ACCOMMODATION

VERY EXPENSIVE

Browns ★★

35 Albermarle Street, W1S, ☏ 020 7493 6020, www.brownshotel.com.

Children are given an age-specific gift on arrival at this 19th-century hotel where Rudyard Kipling wrote our children's favourite Disney film *The Jungle Book*. Bathrooms come with children's bathrobes, rubber ducks, slippers and even a thermometer to test the bath-water temperature while as part of the 'Family Affair' offer, children booking a deluxe room on certain days of the week net their parents another deluxe room free. Probably more fun than all of the above, however, is the interconnecting door between the two deluxe rooms, situated Narnia-style at the back of a wardrobe. Under threes eat and drink for free and 3–12 year olds pay half-price on the hotel menu.

Rates from £310 for a double room, deluxe rooms £480. **Amenities** baby-sitting, restaurant, spa, gym, massage, dry cleaning. **In Room** DVD player, hairdryer. **Credit Cards** all accepted.

MODERATE

The Pavilion

34-36 Sussex Gardens, W2, ☏ 0207 2620905, www.pavilionhoteluk.com.

Family-Friendly Accommodation

Let's be clear, London accommodation can be expensive, even extortionate, so for families it's worth considering what your main needs will be in the capital. For younger families this could be proximity to key attractions, the ability to manage your own routine, lots of children's amenities and child-friendly staff. With older children you may have more flexibility and even get (but don't hold your breath) some parent cred with a glam stay (see Pavilion above). For most of us though, budget and openness – even, dare we say, warmth – to families will be the key factors. London has got better in recent years for family travellers and below is a few of our best bets over a range of budgets and style: self-catering, hotels, B&Bs and apartments.

Family-friendly: One Aldwych (**☎ 0207 73001000, www.onealdwych. com**); **Neighbourhood options:** Europa House (**☎ 0207 7245924, www.europahouseapartments.co.uk**); La Gaffe (**☎ 0207 4358965, www.lagaffe.co.uk**); **Views:** Four Seasons Canary Wharf (**☎ 0207 5101999, www.fourseasons.com**); Wyndham Grand (**☎ 0207 8233000, www.wyndhamgrandlondon.co.uk**); **Hip:** Zetter Restaurant & Rooms (**☎ 0207 3244444, www.thezetter.com**); **Price no object:** Berkeley (**☎ 0207 2356000, www.the-berkeley.co.uk**); Athenaeum Apartments (**☎ 0207 4993464, www.athenaeumhotel.com**); **Price main object:** Crescent (**☎ 0207 3871515, www.crescenthotelof london.com**); **Teens:** Myhotel Chelsea (**☎ 0207 2257500, www.my hotels.com**); **Pool:** Hilton London Metropole (**☎ 0207 4024141, www. hiltonlondonmet.com**); Crown Moran (**☎ 0208 4524175, www.crown moranhotel.co.uk**); **Chains:** Citadene (**☎ 0800 3763898, www. citadenes.com**); Premier Travel Inn (**☎ 0870 2428000, www.premier travelinn.com**); Travelodge (**☎ 0870 1911600 www.travelodge.co.uk**); **YHA:** (suitable for children under three) St Pancras Hostel (**www.yha. org.uk**); **Residence halls:** High Holburn Residence (**☎ 0207 1075737, www.lse.ac.uk/collections/vacations**); Rosebury Hall (**☎ 0207 1075875, www.lse.ac.uk/collections/vacations**) **Value:** Cherry Court Hotel (**☎ 0207 8282840, www.cherrycourthotel.co.uk**); Rushmore Hotel (**☎ 0207 3703839, www.rushmore-hotel.co.uk**); Oxford Hotel (**☎ 0207 4026860, www.oxfordhotellondon.co.uk**).

A lively B&B set up by a former model and often used in boho photo shoots (Leonardo di Caprio has been spotted here), this place has quirkily themed rooms slightly older children will enjoy, including the Honky Tonk Afro room (inspired by Starsky and Hutch). Rooms are fairly small but all en suite and there's one family room for two adults and two children.

Rates family room (inc. continental breakfast) £130. *Amenities* laundry

London's Variety Show

London's parks, theatre and museums provide children of all ages with an amazing variety in the capital from innovative outdoor pursuits to award-winning workshops. Outdoor spaces range from the eight royal parks (*www.royalparks.gov.uk*) to North London's quirky Clissold Park with its deer and aviary. Theatre lovers are spoilt with long running West End shows such as *The Lion King* and *Billy Elliot* to children's theatre companies such as Little Angel Theatre (*www.littleangel theatre.com*). Attractions such as Shakespeare's Globe (*www. shakespeares-globe.org*) meanwhile hold children's workshops, while the British Museum (*www.britishmuseum.org*) has themed sleepovers for older kids and Kew Gardens hosts midnight rambles (*www.kew.org*).

service, dry cleaning. **In Room** TV. **Credit Cards** all except DC.

FAMILY-FRIENDLY DINING

MODERATE

Hummus Bros

88 Wardour Street, W1, ☏ 0207 7341311, www.hbros.co.uk

We must admit we thought this was a pretty crazy idea – a restaurant dedicated solely to the chickpea – although our children loved it. Basically anything you can think to add to hummus (boiled egg, fava beans, etc.) is available here. Adult alternatives include: tabouleh, greek salad, falafel and Moroccan meatballs. There's also refreshing smoothies, fresh mint and ginger lemonade and baklava for dessert. Perfect for a quick snack; over a glass of hot spiced apple juice with cinnamon you can try and think of broadening the concept.

'What about the Mayonnaise Sisters'.

'No. The Horse Radish Cousins. It's more upmarket yet folksy at the same time'.

Open Mon–Wed 11am–10pm, Thurs–Fri 11am–11pm, Sat 12pm–11pm, Sun 12pm–10pm. **Main Course** £3.40–£8. **Amenities** highchairs, smaller portions at reduced prices for children. **Credit Cards** all cards accepted.

The Wallace ★

The Wallace Collection, Manchester Square, W1, ☏ 0207 5639505, www. wallacecollection.org

To maximize sightseeing time, it's a good idea to eat out at the restaurant of an attraction you're visiting. Based in the beautiful glass-roofed Sculpture Garden of the Wallace Collection, this place offers more than the usual baked potato and soup choices (try the ox tongue or the steak tartare with truffles) at reasonable prices. The Wallace Collection has one of the world's best collections

Family-Friendly Dining

British food and the welcome British families get in many restaurants in London has come on leaps and bounds. Rather than just tolerated, families are now seen as a significant part of the food scene and there's some really excellent choices, which can make rather than break a frazzled parents' day. Here's a few of our best bets for eating in the capital. **Best family-friendly:** Giraffe (various: *www.giraffe.net*); **Best children's menu:** Carluccio's Caffe (various: *www.carluccios.com*); **Best neighbourhood hangout:** Bush Garden Cafe (59 Goldhawk Road, W12, ☏ 0207 6362228); **Best outdoor eating:** Frizzante City Farm (☏ 0207 7392266, *www.hackneycityfarm.co.uk*); **Best park café:** Inn at the Park (☏ 0207 4519999, *www.innthepark.com*); **Best museum café:** Camden Arts Centre (☏ 0207 4725516 *www.camdenartscentre.org*); **Best view:** Peter Jones: top floor (☏ 0207 7303434, *www.peterjones.co.uk*); **Best breakfast:** Boiled Egg & Soldiers (63 Northcote Road, SW11, ☏ 0207 2234894); **Best brunch:** Smiths of Smithfield (☏ 0207 2517950, *www.smithsofsmithfield.co.uk*); **Best fish & chips:** Fish Central (☏ 0207 2534950, *www.fishcentral.co.uk*); **Best pizza:** Italian Graffiti (☏ 0207 2534970, *www.italiangraffiti.co.uk*); **Best burgers:** Gourmet Burger Kitchen (various: *www.gbkinfo.com*); **Best sausages:** S&M Café (various: *www.sandmcafe.co.uk*); **Best vegetarian:** The Place Below (☏ 0207 3290789, *www.theplacebelow.co.uk*); **Best fast food:** Masala Zone (various: *www.masalazone.com*); **Best Asian food:** Blue Elephant (☏ 0207 3856595, *www.blueelephant.com*); **Best ice cream:** Marine Ices (☏ 0207 4829003, *www.marineices.co.uk*); **Best girls' day out:** Yauatcha (☏ 0207 4948888, *www.yauatcha.com*); **Best boys' day out:** Café Kick (☏ 0207 8378077, *www.cafekick.co.uk*).

of 18th-century French paintings and more importantly suits of armour for your children to try on/fall over in. There are children's trails and a free Little Draw drop-in art workshop on the first Sunday of every month where our son drew his first self-portrait/scribble and said, 'That me'.

Open Sun–Thurs 10am–3pm, Fri–Sat 10am–3pm and 5pm–9.30pm. Main Course £12–18. Amenities highchairs, children's menus. Credit Cards all accepted.

CANTERBURY & AROUND

From our research of this city one fact leaps out – pretty much every hundred years or so somebody tries to destroy Canterbury. As a Belgic settlement the Romans sacked it, as a Roman settlement the Saxons destroyed it, as a Saxon settlement the Danes wrecked it, as a Danish settlement the Normans messed it up, and finally, Hitler attempted to make large holes in the town when he identified targets in England from the Baedeker travel guide books (we are not making this up) according to their historic importance and dropped bombs on them. Canterbury, despite being destroyed many times, has managed to preserve the most famous cathedral in England. Elsewhere in Kent there are many places that haven't been destroyed and others perhaps that should have been. Not that we are saying Chatham, home to the famous Historic Dockyards, is one of these. OK, we are. Maidstone, meanwhile, boasts Leeds Castle and the wonderful child-friendly Hop Farm.

Essentials

Getting There

By Train From London Waterloo there are services every 30 minutes from South West Trains (☎ 08456 000650, *www. southwesttrains.co.uk*). The journey takes roughly one hour 30 minutes. From Brighton to Canterbury the same company has trains every 30 minutes to Canterbury. The journey takes up to two hours and 45 minutes.

By Bus National Express (☎ 0870 5808080, *www.nationalexpress. co.uk*) has services running throughout the day from London Victoria coach station. The journey takes roughly two hours. From Brighton to Canterbury the same company has coaches

throughout the day. The journey takes roughly five hours.

By Car From London to Canterbury take the A2 to Rochester, then the M2 to Canterbury. From Brighton take the M23 to the M25 exit, and then it's the M26 to Maidstone, then the M2 on to Canterbury.

Visitor Information

The **Dover Tourist Information Centre** (☎ *01304 205108*) is based at Townhall Street, Dover. The **Broadstairs Visitor Information Centre** (☎ *08702 646111*) is based at the Dickens House Museum, 2 Victoria Parade, Broadstairs. The **Canterbury Tourist Information Centre** (☎ *01227 378100*) is at 12-13 Sun Street, The Buttermarket, Canterbury. The **Maidstone Tourist Information Centre** (☎ *01622 602169* or *01622 602048*) is at Town Hall, Middle Row, High Street, Maidstone. The **Margate Visitor Information Centre** (☎ *08702 646111*) is at 12-13 The Parade, Margate. The **Rochester Tourist Information Centre** (☎ *01634 843666* or *01634 338105*) is at 95 High Street, Rochester.

What to See & Do

Canterbury Cathedral ALL AGES

11 The Precincts, Canterbury, Kent, ☎ *01227 762862, www.canterbury-cathedral.org*

Canterbury Cathedral is famous for being the Mother Church of the Church of England, seat of

Canterbury Cathedral

the Primate of All England and scene of the murder of Archbishop Thomas Becket. The oldest cathedral in England has been a place of worship since 602, and of pilgrimage since Thomas Becket's slaying in 1170 by four knights, who overheard Henry II declaring, rhetorically, he later claimed, 'Who will rid me of this turbulent priest?'. The knights thought, 'actually we will', and rode to Canterbury to cut part of his head off. Kids can try out the 'Childrens Trail' or you can tell them the story of Archbishop Parker (see box). The cathedral, half Gothic and half Romanesque in style, has helpful staff in Blake 7's-style purple sashes to answer any questions and pretend not to see your son trying to pull a poppy wreath to Major E

Mannock V.C. D.S.O off the wall.

Open daily summer 9am–5.30pm, winter 9am–5pm. **Adm** adults £7.50, children and conc £6.50. **Amenities** refreshment kiosk, baby-changing. **Credit cards** all except AX.

> **INSIDER TIP**
>
> A good hiding place for small children: the baptismal font in the Holy Innocent's Chapel of the western crypt.

Historic Dockyard ★★★
ALL AGES

Chatham, Kent, ☏ *01634 823800,* ***www.chdt.org.uk***

Where Britain's navy was built, manned and repaired for the last 400 years, children get the chance to board two ships – the 19th-century *HMS Gannet* and 20th-century *HMS Cavalier.*

Nosy Parker

Parker, Archbishop of Canterbury under the reign of Elizabeth I (1559–1575), was obsessed with finding independent evidence for the origins of a Christian church in England independent of that in Rome. So assiduous was Parker in this quest it gained him the epithet 'Nosy Parker'. The result of his work was catchily named *De Antiquitate Britannicae Ecclesiae et Privilegiis Ecclesiae Cantuarensis cum Archiepiscopis eiusdem*, said to be the first privately printed book in England. It was presented to Queen Elizabeth I, who we suspect said, 'thank you – that's just what I wanted for Christmas', and shoved it in her knicker drawer, never reading a single word.

Both ships have audio-guided tours, and there are pirate story-telling sessions below deck in the summer holidays on *HMS Gannet*. There is also a 1960s' submarine here, the *HMS Ocelot*, where we were pleased to hear 'divers were forced to wear man-sized nappies to exit from because the water pressure would squeeze urine from them like a crushed orange'. Of the two galleries, Wooden Walls follows the life of William Crockwell, an apprentice shipwright in 1758, and the less interesting second is

Historic dockyard at Chatham

about rope making. In the Kent Police Museum based here you'll discover the world's largest working padlock and the pickled scalp of a manager from the Blue Moon Chinese Restaurant in Chatham. If you can, come on a pirate-themed day, where if you have a receding hairline like me, expect to be told by an in-character actor (and then taunted by your wife) 'His thoughts is so lewd 'is follicles is falling is out'.

Open *daily 14th Feb—28th Mar 8am–4pm, 29th Mar—24th Oct 10am–6pm, 25th Oct–1st Nov 10am–4pm, weekends in Nov 10am–4pm.* **Adm** *adults £14, children (5–15) £9.50, conc £11.50, families (two adults, two children) £39.50.* **Amenities** *café, baby-changing, parking.* **Credit Cards** *all except DC.*

Leeds Castle ★ ★ ★ ALL AGES

Maidstone, Kent, ☏ *01622 765400,* **www.leeds-castle.com**

This 900-year-old castle based on two small islands in a lake formed by the River Len (yes, that's a real river) and once the home of Catherine of Aragon, was where our baby son Charlie slid under the table that saw the

FUN FACT ▶ Pirate Rules

An equal share in the spoils, compensation if you lost an arm, no gambling, and, oddly, a very strict bedtime of 8.30pm or else you were made to walk the Naughty Plank.

signing of the precursor to the Camp David agreement and refused to come out until he was given – no, not his half of Jerusalem but something harder to obtain – an unbroken breadstick from my wife's hand-bag. While it isn't very family friendly inside the castle (buggies are banned – you're given a baby sling nobody knew how to work) and staff are jumpy when orange juice is spilt close to former owner Lady Baillie's precious 1926 ebony floor – the beautiful grounds full of swans and wandering peacocks more than make up for this. There are falconry displays at 1.30pm and 3.30pm featuring buzzards, eagles, hawks and

vultures. Elsewhere there is the Knight's Realm playground, a maze and also the only museum in the country, we believe and hope, dedicated to dog collars. Children (6–12) can also become keeper for the day and get to feed swans, stand around looking knowledgeable during aviary talks and assist bravely/look terrified during birds of prey demonstrations involving swooping eagles. Meanwhile at the Castle Craft Café in the Wykeham Martin Centre, children can paint their own T-shirts (£12.95) and make fired pots (£3–£6).

Open *daily 1st Apr–30th Sept 10am–6pm (grounds) and 10.30am–5.30pm (castle), 1st Oct–31st Mar 10am–5pm*

Leeds Castle, Maidstone

(grounds) and 10.30am–4.30pm (castle). **Adm** adults £16.50, children (4–15) £9.50, conc £13.50. **Amenities** car park, café, baby-changing. **Credit Cards** all except AX.

Royal Engineers Museum ALL AGES

Prince Arthur Road, Chatham, Kent, ☎ *01634 822839, www.remuseum. org.uk*

Warmongering youngsters can wander excitedly through corridors of military memorabilia here, which include an actual Ninja RAF Hawker Harrier, while more sensitive souls like our daughter ('I don't like war, Daddy, it's too noisy') can talk to a stuffed, dead dog called Snob. The museum telling the story of the **Corps of Royal Engineers** has Zulu shields captured at Rorke's Drift, the map Wellington used at Waterloo, and some bombs. There is an education room open in the school holidays (usually from 10am) where children are taught to make shields and medals. There's also a children's quiz, helpful small stands for children to see higher up exhibits and displays teaching them how to use a compass, see through night vision goggles and (a stepping stone in every toddler's progress) sink an enemy ship with mines.

Open Tues–Fri 9am–5pm, Sat–Sun 11.30am–5pm. **Adm** adults £6.99, conc £4.66, families (two adults, two children) £18.64. **Amenities** car park, baby-changing, picnic area. **Credit Cards** all except AX.

The Canterbury Tales AGES 5 AND UP

St Margaret's Street, Canterbury, Kent, ☎ *01227 479 227, www. canterburytales.org.uk*

The medieval models at this recreation of Geoffrey Chaucer's *Canterbury Tales* (see box) so frightened our daughter we were forced to flee midway through the visit via an emergency exit. Visitors walk unguided through mocked-up rooms (including the realistic smell of urine unless that was our baby son's nappy) telling each of the pilgrim's tales and although dark, it's suitable for all children except those unaccountably frightened of models of people with hairy faces ('I just don't like them, Dad'). It's a funny and fascinating trip back to 14th century England where you can join 'Geoff' Chaucer and his band of merry characters on their magical pilgrimmage from London to the Shrine of St.Thomas Becket in Canterbury Cathedral. The historic building of St. Margaret's Church brings the experience to life as you

FUN FACT **It's a Dog's Life**

Snob was found with the body of a dead Russian soldier after the Battle of Alma in the Crimean War by the 11th Company Royal Sappers and Miners. Brought back to Chatham, the dog was named Snob because it preferred the officer's mess to the guardroom. It was later awarded a medal of honour and, when it died, was stuffed.

The Canterbury Tales, written by Geoffrey Chaucer in the 14th century, is a collection of stories by pilgrims from the London borough of Southwark told on their way to visit the shrine of St Thomas a Becket at Canterbury Cathedral.

hurtle back 500 years. There are separate audio guides for adults and children.

Open *Jan–Feb 10am–4.30pm, Mar–Jun 10am–5pm, Jul–Aug 9.30am–5pm, Sept–Oct 10am–5pm, Nov–Dec 10am–4.30pm.* ***Adm*** *adults £7.75, children (5–15) £5.75, conc £6.75.* ***Amenities*** *toilets.* ***Credit Cards*** *all except AX and DC.*

The Hop Farm ★★★ ALL AGES

Maidstone Road, Paddock Wood, Tonbridge, Kent, 📞 *01622 872068,* ***www.thehopfarm.co.uk***

Here our daughter got to shout 'howdy pardner' at the Rootin' Tootin' cowboy show and our son stroked an escaped rabbit called Bramble. Home to the world's largest collection of oast houses, there are also Shire horses and a host of other indoor and outdoor activities including go-karts (5–9 only), and the pet's corner where Bramble the rabbit escaped from his hutch and ran amok (OK, sat twitching its nose in a corner). Other highlights at this 400-acre site include the Jumping Pillows, which our son bounced practically into the ionosphere when a cube from Chatham flopped onto the canvas shouting, 'Jeronimo'. And we cannot go without mentioning the Legends in Wax – a sort of mini-Madame Tussauds, where my wife and I greatly enjoyed/were alarmed by a geriatric-looking wax model of Marilyn Monroe seemingly breaking wind over a recreated New York subway vent. The Hop Story exhibition is full of clips of old men saying: 'is hard work on an 'op farm but I love it'. There's also, oddly, a tank museum here.

Open *10am–5pm (last admission 4pm).* ***Adm*** *adults and children (3-15) £13, under threes free, families (two adults, two children) £45. Booking online saves £2 per ticket.* ***Amenities*** *café, parking, baby-changing, gift-shop.* ***Credit Cards*** *all except AX.*

The Canterbury Tales

Cycling in the New Forest

There's more than 100 miles of traffic free cycle routes and flat(ish) terrain in the New Forest (*www.thenewforest.co.uk*). It is one of the best and safest areas in England to go cycling with a family. All tracks are signposted, trails are well maintained and easy pedalling can be enjoyed all year round. The Forest has been in good use for a while – William the Conqueror established it in 1079 as a Royal Hunting Ground and even today, 'commoners' still retain their ancient rights – and animals roam freely across open heathland. In April 2005, the forest was given National Park status. There's camping, B&Bs, country house hotels and cottages to stay in and gardens, museums, leisure and wildlife parks to explore. Most cycle hire places will be able to supply families with maps and routes, map holders, helmets, gloves, rain covers, locks, trailers, visibility jackets and energy food etc.

www.newforestcyclehire.co.uk
www.countrylanes.co.uk
www.cyclex.co.uk/product/new_forest_bike_hire/index.html

THE NEW FOREST, THE ISLE OF WIGHT & AROUND

Created as a royal hunting forest by William Conqueror in 1080, the New Forest isn't any longer actually a forest, but a tract of scrubby land on which commoners have retained the right to graze ponies. Along the coast there's a motor museum and Buckler's Hard, the 18th-century village where Lord Nelson's navy was built up. A ferry ride across the Solent from Portsmouth or Lymington lies the country's smallest county, the Isle of Wight, with its zoo, dinosaur-based attractions. Back on the mainland, Portsmouth has two great attractions – the Royal Naval Dockyards and Spinnaker Tower.

Essentials

Getting There

By Air The closest airport is at Southampton (📞 0870 0400009, *www.southamptonairport.com*), which handles internal flights from and to Belfast, Edinburgh, Glasgow, Isle of Man, Isles of Scilly, Leeds Bradford, Manchester and Newcastle and international flights to among other places France, Germany and Austria.

By Train From London Waterloo to Portsmouth Harbour South West Trains (📞 08456 000650, *www.southwesttrains.co.uk*) has services every 30 minutes. The journey takes one hour and 40 minutes. From Bristol to Portsmouth Harbour there is one train per hour provided by the same company. From Brighton to Portsmouth Harbour there are South West trains running every 30 minutes. The journey takes up to one hour and 30 minutes.

By Bus National Express services (☏ 0870 5808080, *www.nation alexpress.co.uk*) leave London Victoria coach station throughout the day for Portsmouth. The journey takes about two and a half hours. From Bristol to Portsmouth Harbour the same company has daily services that take up to six hours, the same journey time the daily service takes from Brighton to Portsmouth Harbour.

By Car Take the A3 from Portsmouth to London. From Bristol it's the M4 to Newbury, the A303 to Winchester, then the M27 to Portsmouth. From Brighton the A27 will take you to Portsmouth.

By Ferry There are two main crossing points from the mainland to the Isle of Wight – from Lymington to Yarmouth and from Portsmouth to Fishbourne. The crossings take roughly half an hour. For more information contact **Wight Link Ferries** (☏ 0871 3764342, *www.wightlink ferries.co.uk*).

Visitor Information

The **Portsmouth Visitor Information Service** (☏ 02392 826722) is based at Clarence Esplanade, Southsea, Hampshire. **The Lymington Visitor Centre** (☏ 01590 689000) is at St Barbe Museum, New Street). The **Portsmouth Tourist Information Centre**

(☏ 023 92826722), is based at The Hard, Portsmouth. Cowes Tourist Information Centre (☏ 01983 813818) is at 9 The Arcade, Fountain Quay, Cowes, Isle of Wight. The Ryde Tourist Information Centre (☏ 01983 813818) is at 81-83 Union Street, Ryde, Isle of Wight. The Sandown Tourist Information Centre (☏ 01983 813818) is at 8 High Street, Sandown, Isle of Wight. Shanklin Tourist Information Centre (☏ 01983 813818) is at 67 High Street, Shanklin, Isle of Wight. Yarmouth Tourist Information Centre (☏ 01983 813818) is at The Quay, Yarmouth, Isle of Wight.

What to See & Do

Dinosaur Farm Museum ALL AGES

Military Road, Brighstone, Isle of Wight, ☏ *01983 740844, www. dinosaur-farm.co.uk*

Our daughter held in her hands some mineralized mammoth

The Needles, Isle of Wight

excrement during a talk at this museum, briefly uniting our children's two main interests in all the world – dinosaurs (him) and poo (her). There is a fossil pit to explore, where our daughter found a real 20-million-year-old shark tooth, dinosaur rubbings and jigsaws for children, while for adults experts explain the Isle of Wight's history as a treasure trove of fossil remains and also how you get to have a dinosaur named after you. Encouraged by this, you can then place your family (you must visit the museum to do this, there are no phone bookings) on a beach fossil comb where everyone is guaranteed to find a fossil (and children do surprisingly well) and not so long ago a brachiosaurus turned up. Fossil trips run between July and August every day and sometimes twice a day. The rest of the time it's twice a week.

Open daily Apr–Oct 10am–5pm. **Adm** adults £3, children under 16 and conc £2.50, under fours free, families (two adults, two children) £9.50. **Amenities** baby-changing, parking. **Credit Cards** cash and cheques only.

Dinosaur Farm Museum, Isle of Wight

Dinosaur Isle ★ ALL AGES

Cuilver Parade, Sandown, Isle of Wight, ☎ *01983 404344, www. dinosaurisle.com*

Children get to design a stegosaurus, complete jigsaws, smell the breath of a herbivore, and, in a great activity room (with magazines for parents to read), they can paint, read about and play with/throw at each other, cuddly dinosaurs. The museum, displaying over 1,000 fossils, tells the story of the island back through time to the Cretaceous period and houses the famous

FUN FACT ≫ **Giant Steps** ≪

A new species of dinosaur is discovered on average every three years on the Isle of Wight. This is because 120 million years ago the island was joined to England, which was itself joined to Europe. Dinosaurs would walk from Cornwall across the Isle of Wight and on to Belgium and France. The area was then located at the same latitude as North Africa today. The most common dinosaur found on the island is liguanodon, a plant-eater the size of a bus that travelled in herds.

and also least dinosaur-sounding dinosaur found on the island – the Barnes High Sauropod. You can book fossil walks (adults £3.90, children £2.30) to Yaverland, Shanklin and Compton Bay (they go four times a week and last one and a half hours) and drive away speculating on what a Barnes High Sauropod might look like – pinstriped, we suggest, with a pocket watch, an unflappable old English charm, possible homosexual leanings and a hangover from an ugly incident at a minor public school involving a dominating older male Allosaurus.

Open *Apr–Sept 10am–6pm, Oct 10am–5pm, Nov–Mar 10am–4pm.* **Adm** *adults £5, children (3–15) £3, under threes free, conc £4.* **Amenities** *car parking on street outside (charged Apr–Oct £3.40 for up to four hours, £2.50 of which can be reclaimed on admission).* **Credit Cards** *all except AX and DC.*

Isle of Wight Zoo and Tiger Sanctuary ☆ ALL AGES VALUE

Yaverland Road, Sandown, Isle of Wight, ☏ 01983 403883, www. isleofwightzoo.com

So inured to the almost daily presence of wild animals in her life, after visiting our 14th zoo in England, our normally nervous daughter stood fearlessly in front of a Siberian tiger pacing its cage and said to me tiredly, 'make him roar, Daddy'. This zoo, which we think the most reasonably priced in Britain, has the largest collection of tigers in the UK, along with plenty of other big cats including jaguars, leopards and, in an inventive enclosure, two lions we saw licking their paws on top of an upturned zebra-striped jeep; the inference being that the rangers inside had been eaten. There are also monkeys, lemurs and snakes here among other creatures, as well as informative keeper talks, where we learnt about a tiger's Flehman response. This enables them, through drawing air across the Jacobsen's organ in the roof of their mouths, to physically taste a scent, something we are convinced our son does when I secretly open cheese-and-onion crisps in the driver's seat.

Open *14th Feb–31st Mar 10am–4pm, 1st Apr–30th Sept 10am–6pm, 1st–31st Oct 10am–4pm, Nov weekends only 10am–4pm.* **Adm** *adults £5.95, children (5–16) and conc £4.95, under fives free, families (two adults, two children) £19.75.* **Amenities** *parking, baby-changing, children's playground.* **Credit Cards** *all except AX and DC.*

National Motor Museum
☆ ALL AGES

Beaulieu, Brockenhurst, Hampshire, ☏ 01590 612345, www.beaulieu. co.uk

The museum has more than 250 cars on display, ranging from Del Boy's yellow Reliant from *Only Fools and Horses* to several world land-speed record-breakers. When we visited, there was also a James Bond Experience featuring exhibits including Oddjob's razor-rimmed bowler hat from *Goldfinger* and the skidoo from *Die Another Day*. My daughter's favourites were a pod ride through a display telling the story of the motor car, the old Routemaster London bus she climbed aboard, and dressing up in Victorian clothes to drive a 1904 Pope Tribune. There are go-kart rides and driving games while Beaulieu House itself and the cloisters of the abbey next door are also worth a snoop. The gardens certainly live up to the name (Beaulieu means 'beautiful place') and have been in the Montagu family for generations. They include the fragrant Victorian Flower Garden, the informal Wilderness Garden, the Ornamental Kitchen Garden and Mill Pond Walk.

Open daily Oct–22nd May 10am–5pm, 23rd May–Sept 10am–6pm. **Adm** adults £15.75, children (5–12) £8.50, under fives free, conc £14.75. **Amenities** café, highchairs, children's menu, parking, baby-changing. **Credit Cards** all except AX and DC.

New Forest Museum ALL AGES

The New Forest Centre, The Main Car Park, Lyndhurst, Hampshire, 0238 0283444, www.newforest museum.org.uk

Here you'll learn about Harry Busher Mills, famous in his day for catching adders, where the grave of Alice from *Alice in Wonderland* is, and something boring we will not trouble you with called pollarding. The highlight for our daughter was selling Chaumes cheese from a pretend child farmer's market stall. There are also books, jigsaws, feel-in-the box stations, colouring-in, quizzes and dressing up for children.

Open daily 10am–5pm. **Adm** adults £3, under 16s free, conc £2.50. **Amenities** disabled toilet, lift for buggy pushers. **Credit Cards** all except AX and DC.

Royal Navy Historic Dockyards ★★ ALL AGES

Victory Gate, HM Naval Base, Portsmouth, Hampshire, 023 92839766, www.historicdockyard.co.uk

Here you can visit the Mary Rose Museum and take tours aboard a number of warships including the *HMS Warrior*, built in 1860, which was Queen Victoria's pride and joy because it was the fastest ship in her navy. The highlight of a visit, however, is the 50-minute visit to *HMS Victory,* Nelson's flagship and the oldest still-commissioned warship in the world. On the tour (booked through the visitor centre) you see Nelson's original writing table and a replica of an officer's cot, which doubled as a coffin, while learning – among other things – that sailors cleaned (not dirtied, cleaned) their clothes in urine. There is also a soft-play centre and harbour tours are available, although we found the lacklustre highly statistics-focused commentary reminded us more of reading the back of a Top Trump playing card, 'And the battleship to our right has 56 guns and weighs x-number of tons, which is x-number of tonnes lighter than the next battleship to my left, which has 45 guns', and so on until you fall asleep.

FUN FACT ⟫ A Loose Canon ⟪

How things started: A loose cannon – firing a 24-pounder cannon ball involved a 60mph recoil which was very dangerous if you were standing behind it, in that they weighed over two tons. Three square meals a day – sailors were given fiddles when they boarded ship. These were square trays on which their meals were placed. If you tried to get more food than your fair share, you were 'fiddling'.

Open *Apr–Oct 10am–6pm, Nov–Mar 10am–5.40pm.* *Adm* *for a single attraction adults £12.50, children (5–16) £8.50, conc £10.50, families £33. Annual admission adults £18, children £13.50, conc £16, families £50.50.* *Amenities* *café, baby-changing.* *Credit Cards* *all except AX.*

Spinnaker Tower ALL AGES

Gunwharf Quays, Portsmouth, Hampshire, ☎ 023 92857520, www. spinnakertower.co.uk

There are wonderful 40km panoramic views across Portsmouth's Historic Dockyard and the Solent from the top of this 170m tower opened in 2005, which you can marvel at while staring over your daughter's head while she is saying, 'Dad, if we fell from here we would bang our heads so hard, wouldn't we? We would have to go to the docy's wouldn't we? And we'd need a big, big plaster . . .' The audio guides (£3) tell you the history of the city and its naval associations, while on viewing deck 2 there was a plastic owl (to scare off pigeons) that our baby son quite liked. There is a children's activity sheet and a glass floor at 100m up – the highest in the world – that you can spend 20 minutes plucking up the courage to walk across. The Spinnaker Tower is the centre-piece of the renaissance of Portsmouth Harbour Project and is taller than the London Eye, Blackpool Tower and Big Ben, although it only takes 30 seconds to whisk you to the top in the internal high-speed lift. It's an eye-catching sight, especially at night, as it's illuminated in different colours. The tower was designed by local architects to resemble a billowing sail and built by National Lottery cash; it has been abseiled down by among others, Children in Need mascot, Pudsey Bear.

Spinnaker Tower, Portsmouth

Open 1st Feb–31st July 10am–6pm.
Adm adults £7, children (3–15) £5.50,
under threes free, conc £6.20. **Amenities** café. **Credit Cards** all except
AX and DC.

OXFORD, WINDSOR & AROUND

Many historical events have happened in Oxford. It was where
Charles I set up court during the
English Civil War in 1642 and
was also where Roger Bannister
broke the four-minute mile in
1954. The city is, however, most
famous for its university and the
ornate colleges that lend Oxford
its nickname, the 'city of dreaming spires'. However, while
walking tours of the colleges are
informative (I sneaked away
from my family and had a great
time on one) they're not child-
friendly. If you have young children not that keen on standing
around listening to someone discussing how many people the
Sheldonian Hall holds on gradu-
ation day, the Ashmolean
Museum is your best bet. And if
you visit other attractions in
Oxfordshire Blenheim Palace is
hard to beat, as is the little-
known River and Rowing
Museum in Henley-on-Thames.
About a half-hour's drive away
Windsor has Legoland and the
royal residence at Windsor Castle. In neighbouring Buckinghamshire, The Roald Dahl
museum has plenty to offer, and
across the Chilterns, Woburn
Safari Park and Bletchley Park
make great days out.

Essentials

Getting There

By Train Services from First
Great Western 📞 08457 000125,
www.firstgreatwestern.co.uk leave
London Paddington roughly
every 15 minutes for Oxford.
The journey takes about one
hour. From Birmingham direct
trains from the same company
run every 29 minutes. The journey takes one hour 10 minutes,
and from Bristol running every
30 minutes, the journey is about
two hours.

By Bus Services from National
Express 📞 0870 5808080, **www.
nationalexpress.co.uk** leave London Victoria coach station
around every 15 minutes. The
journey takes between one and
two hours. The same company
has daily coaches to Oxford
from Birmingham International
airport and from Bristol as well.

By Car From London to Oxford
take the M4 and then the M40.
From Birmingham it's the A452
towards Oxford and then the
M40. From Bristol simply take
the M4.

Visitor Information

**Aylesbury Tourist Information
Centre** 📞 01296 330 559 is at
The Kings Head, Kings Head
Passage off Market Square,
Aylesbury. **The Royal Windsor
Information Centre** (📞 01753
743900 or 01753 743909) is at The
Old Booking Hall, Central Sta-
tion, Windsor. The **Henley-on-
Thames Visitor Information**

Centre (📞 *01491 578034* or *01491 412703*) is at King's Arms Barn, Kings Road, Henley-on-Thames. The **Oxford Information Centre** (📞 *01865 252200*) is at 15/16 Broad Street, Oxford. The **St Albans Tourist Information Centre** (📞 *01727 864511*) is at Town Hall, Market Place, St Albans.

What to See & Do

Ashmolean Museum of Art and Archaeology ALL AGES

Beaumont Street, Oxford, 📞 *01865 278000, www.ashmolean.org*

At the time of writing closed for a £60 million facelift, the world's first university museum, established in the 17th century to house the collection of art and archaeological finds of Elia Asmole, has among its prize exhibits a lantern carried by gunpowder plotter Guy Fawkes, a collection of Posie (finger) rings said to have inspired J.R.R. Tolkein's One Ring in his novel *Lords of the Rings* and the remains of Europe's last dodo. There is an activity trolley for children enabling them to play object-detective and for you to ask them fun questions like: 'Phoebe, what do you definitely know about zips?' Children are given sheets requesting they find and then describe various paintings, and also questions on how various works have made them feel. Hungry in the case of our children, who subsequently caused such a commotion queuing to be served in the basement café, I was forced to steal armfuls

of the free bread next to the soup terrine to keep them within the borders of sanity. The architect Rick Mather has created a new building that has doubled the Ashmolean's gallery space. Its six floors – one underground – boast 39 new galleries, including four for temporary exhibitions, together with an education centre, offices and Oxford's first rooftop restaurant. It's an impressive revamp for Britain's oldest public museum but a deserving one for a space that contains art from the Dutch masters to Picasso and fragments from Minoan excavations.

Open *Tues–Sat 10am–5pm, Sun 12pm–5pm.* **Adm** *free.* **Amenities** *café, baby-changing.* **Credit Cards** *all accepted. Reopens 2009.*

Blenheim Palace ★ ★ ★ ALL AGES

Woodstock. Oxfordshire, 📞 *08700 602080, www.blenheimpalace.com*

Constructed as a hunting lodge and where Queen Elizabeth I was jailed for a year prior to her succession to the throne in 1555, this Baroque palace was given to John Churchill, the first Duke of Marlborough, in recognition of military triumphs against the French in the 18th century. It was also famously where Winston Churchill grew up and I must confess it gave me goose pimples to stand in the bedroom where he was born on 30th November 1874. While staring at the kiss curls chopped from his five-year-old head, I felt palpably close to an event in history that changed the world. Or as my wife said as we left the

A family event at Blenheim Palace

room, 'Oh God, please don't do his voice the whole way around. You sound more like the Churchill Insurance dog'. There are quizzes for children, frequent Family Days, including when we visited, a falconry show and a great jousting demonstration where our daughter got to hold up a severed head (made from polystyrene) in a large arena and shout 'We fight for the king'. Other highlights include a butterfly farm and a play park, while the rolling grounds are ideal for contemplating the fragility of history: 'We were just one dimension – time – away from being here at Churchill's birth. Think of what's happened between then and now. His birth and the achievements since led to the nows we're in and the nows of now . . .' My wife: 'Let's drive to Cheltenham for an early check in. You've been in the sun too long. You're talking gibberish'.

Open *palace and gardens daily 10.30am–5.30pm, park daily* 9am–4.45pm. **Adm** *palace, park and gardens peak time adults £17.40 children £10, conc £14, families £46; off-peak time adult £14.50, children £7.80, conc £11.50, families £38. Park and gardens peak time adults £10, children £5, conc £7.50, families £25; off-peak time adults £7.70, children £2.70, conc £5.40, families £18.50.* **Amenities** *café, parking, baby-changing.* **Credit Cards** *all except Solo and DC.*

Bletchley Park ALL AGES

The Mansion, Bletchley Park, Milton Keynes, ☎ 01908 640404, www. bletchleypark.org.uk

Codenamed Station X, this, the country's main decryption centre during World War II is now a museum dedicated to the efforts of the mathematicians who worked here. Winston Churchill said of them: 'they were the goose that laid the golden egg but never cackled'. He was speaking – maybe after a few drinks – about the famous German enigma code that was cracked here; he believed it did more than any one other single thing to help the Allies win the war. Ian Fleming, author of the James Bond books, worked here as one of the code-breakers during the war. He also wrote *Chitty Chitty Bang Bang*, which we let our daughter watch on the drive over 'to give the attraction a context'. A good idea you might think. No. She misunderstood the context and expected to see the actual flying car at this attraction. Maybe she thought she would receive a head-pat from Truly Scrumptious as well; we cannot tell because after her disappointment she simply sulked. A harrier jump jet outside Hut 9 was scorned. 'That's a plane not a car, Dad'. The Toy and Household Memorabilia collection featuring wartime dolls didn't wash either. The main exhibition is in Block B and tells the Bletchley story while there is also an old 1940s' cinema, and a room containing the largest collection of Winston Churchill memorabilia in the world. Older children will enjoy the 'spooks' like tales of spies, strategic deception and misleading the enemy with impenetrable communications, while adults can enjoy a walk by the lake where there's wildlife and for youngsters a playground. There's an unfathomable mathematical talk on how the Colossus computer helped break the German code, the opportunity to ferret in the grounds for a silver hoard that maths genius and enigma code-breaker Alan Turning hid here during the war (we are not

sure why) and a café to practise your Churchill speeches in. 'You may ask what is my aim. I can answer in one word. Sausage rolls. Sausage rolls at whatever cost…'

Open 1st Nov–31st Mar 10.30am–4pm, 1st Apr–31st Oct 9.30am–5pm (weekends 10.30am–5pm). *Adm* adults £10, children (12–16) £6, under 12s free, conc £8, families (two adults, two children) £22.50. *Amenities* café, parking (£3). *Credit Cards* all except AX.

Drusillas Wild Animal Park

★ ★ ★ **AGES 11 AND UNDER**

Alfriston, East Sussex, ☏ 01323 874100, www.drusillas.co.uk

If I visited this zoo any more often my wife reckons they'd give me a green T-shirt and a bucket of fish and get me to feed the penguins. This is the best small zoo in Britain. To start with children are given a spotter book. Around the zoo there are various stamps and children stamp their spotter books when they see each of the main animals. Our children love the bureaucracy of this. Getting the book out, identifying the animals, aligning the stamp, checking the ink on the stamp, pressing down unnecessarily hard and then admiring the red ink tick. There are also interactive exhibits – buttons to press to hear animal noises, information flaps, boxes that roar when you lift their lids. There is a tunnel to crawl through to look at the meerkats, and a periscope enabling you to see from the height of a giraffe. A 'zooolympics'

Celeb Spotting in Brighton

Brighton became fashionable during the time of the Prince Regent (later King George IV) in the 18th century when the upper classes turned against the health-giving affects of natural spring waters and decided sea air was the new thing. The city has been fashionable ever since. Attractions where you can expect to bump into celebrities include the former retreat of the Prince Regent, the Royal Pavilion (Richard Attenborough once and Julie Burchill, we think) the seafront children's playpark next to the remains of the West Pier (where I have personally spotted Samantha Janus, Patsy Palmer and once Marcus Brigstock talking to his agent in a sandpit) while further out, Drusillas Wild Animal Park (Patsy Palmer again) is a great day out. Also worth visiting if you're in the area at the right time is the Christmas pantomime at the Theatre Royal. Sightings of the bithneth man Chris Eubank are not recorded as he can be seen every day driving around Brighton in his huge black lorry nipping out to buy milk.

theme runs through the park whereby you can compete against the animals and, say, beat a flamingo standing on one leg. They have play areas, both indoor and outdoor. There's gold panning, giant slides, a Thomas the Tank engine train circling the park every 10 minutes and in summer a paddling area. And I haven't even mentioned our daughter's favourite thing – pressing the button that makes an elephant fart noise so she can say, 'Daddy, was that you doing a poo poo in your pants?'

Open daily 10am–5pm. **Adm** peak times adults and children over 2 £13.80, under twos free, conc £13.30; off-peak times adults and children over 2 £10.80, under twos free, conc £10.30. **Amenities** baby-changing, café, microwaves to heat up baby food and bottles. **Credit Cards** all except AX.

Legoland ALL AGES

Winkfield Road, Windsor, Berkshire, ☎ *0871 2222001, www.legoland. co.uk*

Before we set off a friend said to me, 'It's a bun fight. I pity you'. We came on a hot summer day and made two fatal mistakes. The first was to arrange to meet

Go-karting at Legoland, Windsor

friends. Do not attempt to meet friends here. You'd be safer meeting on the slipway of a major motorway wearing a blindfold. The other mistake was not to pre-book tickets. It meant after we had queued to get into the theme park, and queued to park and queued to buy our tickets and queued to run our tickets through the barriers, we then had to queue to get onto each ride. We queued so much at Legoland my wife's legs began to seize up – she lost the ability to stride. Her knee-bending capacity was impaired. That said, a good place to start is Miniland, where we visited the Miniature World of Lego, created from over 40 million bricks and Duploland, where our children played in water-splash fountains until our son's nappy weighed so much he could no longer stand up. Other highlights include watching Bob the Builder in 4D, the Kingdom of the Pharaohs (mainly for older children) and the Land of the Vikings. Throughout the park rides range from white knuckle to gentle toddler carousels. A tip from us: the Ferris wheel queue moves faster than most and we managed a go-kart ride, to operate a child's JCB and see a puppet show, before we finally met up with our friends, who we believe are possibly still queuing for the Jungle Coaster. We left, my wife telling me sourly, 'I noticed all the bricks were stuck together. That's not really in the spirit of Lego, is it?'

Open *daily 18th Jul–31st Aug 10am–7pm, other peak times daily 10am–6pm and Mar–Oct daily 10am–5pm.* **Adm** *adults £36, children (3–15) and conc £27, under threes free.* **Amenities** *cafés, baby-changing, parking.* **Credit Cards** *all cards accepted.*

> **INSIDER TIP**
> Booking online for Legoland saves 10% on entrance prices.

The Roald Dahl Museum and Story Centre ★ AGES 11 AND UNDER

81-83 High Street, Great Missenden, Buckinghamshire, 📞 *01494 892192,* **www.roalddahlmuseum.org**

Children can dress up, stage puppet shows, paint, stick and make animated movies at this museum dedicated to the famous children's author of *Charlie and the Chocolate Factory.* The highlight is the Story Centre, where children are encouraged to think up their own tales, and are asked what

---

FUN FACT **Roald Dahl (1916–1990)**

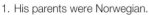

1. His parents were Norwegian.
2. *Charlie and the Chocolate Factory* was inspired by an incident at Repton boarding school, where boys were employed by Cadbury to taste-grade prototype chocolate bars.
3. Dahl missed home so much at boarding school in Weston-super-Mare he always slept with his bed pointing to his parents' house.

props they would have on their own writing desks to inspire them. On his, Dahl always kept a model of a hurricane plane in recognition of the one he flew in World War II, a paperknife of his father's and his thighbone, which was removed by a surgeon who later remarked it was the biggest one he had ever seen. Our daughter would keep on her writing desk her cuddly rabbit and my wife rather unimaginatively said 'spare pens'. Also here is the top hat Johnny Depp wore playing his inferior version of Willy Wonka (Gene Wilder every day of the week).

Open daily Tues–Fri 10am–5pm, Sat–Sun 11am–5pm. **Adm** adults £6, children (5–18) and conc £4, families (two adults and up to three children) £19. **Amenities** café. **Credit cards** all except AX.

The River and Rowing Museum ☆ ALL AGES

Mill Meadows, Henley-on-Thames, Oxfordshire, 📞 01491 415600, www. rrm.co.uk

Children get to walk through recreated scenes from Kenneth Grahame's children's novel, *The Wind in the Willows*, at this museum on the Thames that contains a host of interactive exhibits based around rowing. Downstairs there are drawing tables, jigsaws, the chance to dress up like an Olympic rower (oddly enough a German one) and to test your ability not to fall out of a rowing boat when standing in it. Upstairs you can learn about the history of the Thames and its association with poetry, the novel and also popular music while your children attempt to upturn a Canadian canoe. In the rowing gallery there's lots about Steve Redgrave, the Henley regatta and the Olympics along with a rowing game where you try to synchronize your stroke with three others, a cox urging you on.

Open daily May–Aug 10am–5.30pm, Sept–Apr 10am–5pm. **Adm** adults £7, children and conc £5, under fours free. **Amenities** café, parking, baby-changing. **Credit Cards** all except AX.

Royal Pavilion

4/5 Pavilion Buildings, Brighton, 📞 03000 290900, www.royalpavilion. org.uk

Kenneth Grahame

The Wind in the Willows was published in 1908 and inspired by the unhappy life of Kenneth Grahame (1859–1932). His mother died of scarlet fever when he was five and because his father was an alcoholic, his grandmother brought him up. He dreamed of going to university but never made it and ended up working as a secretary in the Bank of England. The book is about escape from the real world. Grahame's son Alistair committed suicide when he was 20 and Toad was based on his excesses. He wrote one other book, *The Reluctant Dragon*, which was turned into a Disney film.

Windsor Castle

Living locally our trip here was hotly anticipated by our daughter, who'd learned a little about Prince George already ("And he was fat because he ate his dinner all the time"). Prince George, the model for Hugh Laurie's insanely dim-witted, upper-class twit character in Blackadder, lived and lavishly entertained in the pavilion as regent and later as King George IV. The pavilion itself is almost as eccentric as the man. Built by John Nash in the 19th century as a version of an Indian Moghul's palace it is uniquely ornate, and so inappropriately exotic in its setting off the roundabout to Brighton pier, it looks like a bad movie set when seen for the first time. The most interesting rooms our children crawled under the security ropes of were the fantastically-equipped Great Kitchen, which the Prince would proudly show to his guests, and the Banqueting Hall with its dragon-supported central chandelier. There are adult and children's audio tours.

Open daily Oct-Mar 10am-5.15pm, and Apr-Sep 9.30am-5.45pm. **Adm** adult £8.80, children (5-15) £5.10, conc £6.90, family ticket (2 adults, 2 children). Brighton and Hove residents are entitled to half-price admission and up to four children can enter free per adult. **Amenities** shop. **Credit Cards** All except AE.

Windsor Castle ALL AGES

Windsor, Berkshire, 📞 *0207 7067304,* **www.windsor.gov.uk**

Being a major royal fan (she drinks her morning cuppa from a 1977 Jubilee mug), my wife insisted that we visit this, the oldest and largest occupied castle in the world, and the official residence of Her Majesty, The

Queen. The castle, with a history spanning almost 1,000 years, is fully buggy accessible and its highlight for our daughter (along with the paper crown she was given by a security guard) was seeing perhaps the largest and most expensive doll's house in the world, made for Queen Mary with – we kid you not – its own electricity and running water. After a whiz round the palace, where you can see the doll's house in the grand vestibule along with a suit of armour worn by Charles I as a child, it's worth visiting St George's Chapel where Henry VIII is buried. There are special events throughout the year such as 'Henry VIII: A 500th Anniversary' for all ages and each Christmas family activities take place in December. These include special activity trails where children can learn about planning for a ball and past celebrations at the castle, design their own costume for a Christmas Ball and make a Christmas tree decoration to take home.

Open daily 1st Mar–31st Oct 9.45am–5.15pm, 1st Nov–28th Feb 9.45am–4.15pm. **Adm** adults £15.50, children £9, conc £14, families (two adults, up to three children) £41. **Amenities** café. **Credit Cards** all accepted.

Woburn Safari Park ★ ALL AGES

Woburn, Near Milton Keynes, 📞 *01525 290407, www.woburn.co.uk*

We had a fun day here that was only slightly blighted by our daughter's sudden and violent protestation that I need 'a wee, I'm desperate. Quick!' in a traffic jam in the lion enclosure. After an incident like this, you can relax through the rest of the safari park, which includes other highlights such as the car-aerial-ripping monkeys, various talks and animal feeds (check ahead for times) as well children's boats and the Mammoth Playpark. For older children there's the excellent Go Ape! where you can slide down zip wires, climb the trees, cross rope bridges, crawl through tunnels and walk the

Rhino, Woburn Safari Park

planks. The high wire forest adventure course of rope bridges and tarzan swings takes around 2.5 – 3 hours and you're fitted with a climbing harness and given full instructions beforehand. The abbey itself is worth a look and is home to a collection of paintings by amongst other masters, Canaletto and Gainsborough, as well as the famous Blue Drawing Room, where the English tradition of tea was said to have been invented in 1840 by Duchess Anna Maria, who found the gap between luncheon and dinner just too long.

Open *weekends only Nov–Mar 11am–3pm, 7th Mar–1 Nov 10am–5pm.* ***Adm*** *winter adults £10.50, children (3–15) £8.50, conc £9; spring and early summer adults £17, children £12, conc £14; high summer adults £18.50, children £13.50, conc £15.50.* ***Amenities*** *café, parking, baby-changing.* ***Credit Cards*** *all except AX.*

FAMILY-FRIENDLY ACCOMMODATION

EXPENSIVE

Ashdown Park Hotel and Country Club ★ ★

Wych cross, Near Forest Row, East Sussex, ☎ *01342 824988, www. ashdownpark.com*

Close to Ashdown Forest, the inspiration for A.A. Milne's 100 Acre Wood, this luxury hotel offers a special Winnie the Pooh tea for children dining without parents that includes honey sandwiches, Kanga cupcakes and Owl's popcorn. Other children'

Ashdown Park Hotel and Country Club

perks in the Tigger Escape package include activity packs on check-in, free milk and cookies at bedtime, entry to Ashdown Llama Park, which backs on to the hotel and a children's map to local Winnie the Pooh attractions. For older children there are outdoor games, a putting green and swimming lessons. The hotel, set in 186 acres, is 8km from the spot that A.A. Milne based the Pooh Sticks bridge scene. The Tigger package also includes a meal for two at the Anderida Restaurant (two AA rosettes), which has a children's menu, or a babysitting service can be laid on. There is 6,400 acres of ancient woodland, much of it criss-crossed by footpaths and bridleways surrounded by immaculate lawns, secret gardens, lakes and woodland trails ideal for youngsters and older children to explore. For adults there's an indoor pool, sauna, spa, tennis court, indoor golf nets, putting green, croquet lawn, jogging trails and an 18-hole, par 3, golf course.

Rates the best way for families to stay is on a special family break that includes dinner, bed and breakfast for two adults, and bed and breakfast for children at £260 per night. For this you get a bedroom and a separate sitting room for the children to sleep in. *Amenities* swimming pool, golf nets, baby-listening, baby-sitting, travel cots, sauna, steam room, tennis courts, snooker table, table tennis. *In Room* TV, phone, en suite bathroom, tea and coffee making. *Credit Cards* all accepted.

Eastwell Manor

Eastwell Park, Broughton Lees, Ashford, Kent, ☎ *0800 089 3929, www.prideofbritainhotels.com*

This historic country house was where Richard Plantagenet was discovered hiding after his father Richard III was killed in the Battle of Bosworth in 1485. Eastwell Manor is surrounded by a 3,000 acre Estate with many designated walks and footpaths to experience – great for children to muck around on and discover. The Manor, in a quiet spot, has origins dating back to the Norman conquest with carved panelled rooms, massive baronial stone fireplaces and many four-poster beds. The Pavilion Spa has all the things a gym addict or spa hedonist could desire for a weekend away including indoor and outdoor pools, plus there's a 9-hole golf course.

Rates Mews Cottage £600 for a two-to three-night stay, £850 for a week. Family suites (with bunk-bed room for children) £350–£440. Large family room £295. *Amenities* outdoor

heated swimming pool, DVDs to rent, spa pool, sauna, steam room, Jacuzzi, gym, wifi, tennis court, croquet and petanque, car parking, beauty treatments, baby-sitting, baby-listening. *In Room* phone, TV (no Cbeebies), DVD player, hob, microwave, fridge, hairdryer, ice box, free Madeira sherry decanter – red and white, kettle, free mineral water. *Credit Cards* all accepted.

Elmers Court Hotel

South Baddesley Road, Lymington, Hampshire, ☎ *01590 676011, www.macdonaldhotels.co.uk*

Set in a manor house dating from 1820 and surrounded by 23 acres of private grounds, staff hand out activity packs for children on check-in at this hotel, a few minutes' walk from Lymington's old town centre and closer still to the ferry for the Isle of Wight. On the edge of the New Forest you can go for long jaunts through the beautiful countryside, pony trek or learn how to sail on the Solent. Also within reach are Paultons Family Park, wild animals at Marwell Zoo and Bournemouth Aquarium. As our son was ill we couldn't go for dinner at the family-friendly Sails Bar & Brasserie, but remembering how when our daughter was born we couldn't afford to go out any more, we repeated the trick of Friday nights in by pushing a small table to the window and surrounding it with pot plants to make us feel we were at a restaurant.

Rates classic family (with bunk-bed room for children) £147–£245 per night. *Amenities* pool, spa, tennis courts, restaurant, parking. **In Room** TV, phone, tea and coffee making. **Credit Cards** all except DC and JCB.

The Grove ★★

Chandler's Cross, Hertfordshire, 📞 *01923 807807, www.thegrove. co.uk*

Once a wartime HQ of great strategic importance called 'Project X' (six old air raid shelters still here are now home to one of Europe's largest colonies of Pipistrelle bats), The Grove is set in 300 acres of beautiful parkland and canal ideal for walking, running or cycling. Inside are spacious family rooms, 200 pieces art and the Sequoia Spa looking out onto walled garden and woods.

There is a nursery here – Anouska's (three months to 10 year olds, £6 per hour) – where your children have the chance to scratch the face of a celebrity sprog (Charlie had a pop at Take That's Mark Owen's boy here), and a mini beach complete with sand, a volleyball court and beach huts. There is an adventure playground, baby-sitting and activities ranging from remote-controlled car racing to Frisbee flinging. Children are given activity packs and there's a wonderful restaurant where I consumed pan-fired foie gras so soft you could stuff a small teddy with it. In fact the food was so good my wife and stepmum Mary became so befuddled with wine and rich food that they ate a plate of sugar lumps believing (until we spoke with

the chef) that they were very sweet chocolate delicacies.

Rates superior family suite (two bedrooms) £490 per night B&B. **Amenities** pool, tennis courts, Xboxes, PlayStations. **In Room** TV, DVD player, phone. **Credit Cards** all accepted.

McDonald Berystede Hotel and Spa

Sunninghill, Ascot, Berkshire, 📞 *0844 8799104, www.macdonaldhotels. co.uk*

Children receive their own check-in card, activity pack and bubble bath at this sprawling hotel close to family attractions such as Thorpe Park, Chessington, Go Ape! in Swinley Forest and perhaps for older children, paintballing in leafy Maidenhead. It offers family rooms and interconnecting rooms, wheelchair accessible rooms, special children's menus, a summer children's activity programme and staff leave small Lego toys on children's pillows on check-in and can arrange cheaper tickets for entry to Legoland.

The Grove Hotel, Chandler's Cross

Dinner is a strange affair with extremely expensive wine (£20 for the cheapest bottle) served from a confusingly laminated-style menu that looked like the takeaway ones taped to the counters of flamegrilled chicken outlets. Friendly hotel staff will also refrain from calling the police when they see you throw your bags from the family suite window into the car park below to save the walk.

Rates £129 per room per night B&B, £194 for two inter-connecting rooms. **Amenities** pool, spa, thermal suite, parking. **In Room** phone, TV, tea and coffee making. **Credit Cards** all except DC.

Macdonald Compleat Angler

Marlow, Buckinghamshire, 📞 *0844 8799128, www.macdonaldhotels. co.uk*

The hotel, named after the title of Izaak Walton's famous fishing book written in and around Marlow in 1653, has long been the haunt of the rich and famous. Naomi Campbell, Princess Diana, Clint Eastwood, Omar Sharif, F. Scott Fitzgerald, J.M. Barrie and the Queen have all dined here. We were given a room away from the main hotel usually reserved for the disabled, which meant our children attempted to pull all the red emergency chords. One other bugbear: there was no Cbeebies in the room although that wasn't anything 20 minutes of Channel 4 Racing couldn't put right. ('Those horses have people on their backs, Dad!') The setting, on the banks of the swollen Thames in the shadow of the Tierney suspension bridge, is spectacular with gardens for children to run about and for wives to spot celebrities.

Rates £138 per room per night. **Amenities** room service, restaurant, boat hire. **In Room** phone, TV, tea and coffee making, cots, fold-out beds. **Credit Cards** all accepted.

The Old Bank Hotel

92-94 High Street, Oxford 📞 *01865 799599, www.oldbank-hotel.co.uk*

A sophisticated hotel surrounded by Oxford's ancient academic institutions with 42 bedrooms in a Georgian stone building. Nearby you can visit Modern Art Oxford for international contemporary art, go punting with a picnic or take a hotel bicycle for a ride. Inside bedrooms have marble bathrooms, there's art collected by the owner over the last 35 years, jazz on Sunday afternoons and a good restaurant with highchairs, children's menus and colouring sheets. Staff and guests are also gracious (and waive dry cleaning) as evidenced when emulating the famous scene from *Trainspotting* and frustrated Charlie would not eat, my wife whipped the napkin from his neck and pebble-dashed three breakfasting professors behind us with scrambled egg. The property is ideal for local attractions as it's bang in the centre, so you can explore the Botanic Garden, Radcliffe Camera, Bodleian Library, the famous Magdalen Bridge and the River Cherwell.

Woodstock House Hotel

If you have the time and older children (or sleeping children) you can also take advantage of a complimentary tailor-made walking tour with a local art expert. It was also here my wife confided that she wished she'd gone to Oxford at which point I reminded her: 'Your favourite programme is *Britain's Got Talent*.'

Rates *family room £185–£210 per night, family suite £325–£350 per night.* **Amenities** *small car park, wifi.* **In Room** *TV, phone.* **Credit Cards** *all except DC.*

Woodstock House Hotel

Charlton, Near Chichester, West Sussex, ☎ *01243 811666,* ***www. woodstockhousehotel.co.uk***

A smartly run hotel in the South Downs with a family annexe serving food at the weekends and light meals in the week, and where we spent the last night of our four-month trip around England. The annexe has two bedrooms up a flight of stairs you can leave your buggy at the foot of. Staff are friendly, they have highchairs for children to eat at/throw their breakfast cereal to the floor from, while the Rose Room patio is an ideal place to relax with a glass of wine, watching the sun disappear after a long walk on the Downs competing with your wife about who would make the greater sea lord (me who did a talk on Nelson for his O-level oral and has always understood that great mistress the sea, or her who can't step in a puddle without getting sea sick).

Rates *annexe £80–£148 per night B&B.* **Amenities** *parking.* **In Room** *TV, tea and coffee making.* **Credit Cards** *all accepted.*

Rooftree Guesthouse ★

26 The Broadway, Sandown, Isle of Wight, ☎ *01983 403175, www.roof tree-guesthouse.co.uk*

Our daughter was given a ballet lesson here by the friendly host and former professional dancer Anne Abe, who looks like – and very bizarrely – also once worked with Bonnie Langford. There is a trampoline, lots of children's toys, a pet's corner with guinea pigs, chipmunks and rabbits, and our children were given hot milk and biscuits before bed. The hotel, a few minutes' walk from the beach, has baby-listening devices and serves Japanese meals on request.

Rates family room £29–£33 per person per night. Children up to £25 per night. Under twos free. Amenities travel cots, car parking, large lounge. In Room TV, tea and coffee making. Credit Cards all accepted.

FAMILY-FRIENDLY DINING

Carluccios ★

Windsor Royal Station, Windsor, Berkshire, ☎ *01753 852019, www. carluccios.com*

This chain delivers consistently good, simple food for families of all ages with friendly staff and a child friendly atmosphere – ours have been exploring in the kitchen before. It was while eating here with the in-laws that Bert, my wife's father, trumped my kidney stone story in Leeds

(see p 199) by discussing, to the alarm of several tables around us, the goitre once discovered in his saliva glands that was 'the size of a Malteser'. Unfazed, even when my father-in-law went into great detail about 'the pus actually hitting the ceiling' when it burst, our children woofed their pasta and between courses were content to colour in pictures on the children's menus, while chat around them escalated alarmingly to even more competitive and alienating heights. A very speedy good-food stop.

Open Mon–Fri 8am–11pm, Sat 9am– 11pm, Sun 9am–10.30pm. Main Course £6.95–£13. Amenities baby-changing, children's menu. Credit Cards all except DC.

Don Vincenzo

108-110 High Street, Rochester, Kent, ☎ *01634 408373*

A friendly Italian known locally as Don V's with pictures of Robert De Niro in the *Godfather* on the wall and a lurking sense of the Sicilian way of doing things as evidenced in the following exchange: 'I have a friend, he run restaurant in Italy. He buy 60 copies of guidebook he get in guidebook. Is like this?' And when I said no, Frommer's don't operate like this, 'Maybe something to think about'. The ingredients are fresh, the meat organic and the menu is excellent. Smaller portions are served at half price for children and the paper tablecloths mean spillages cause no anxiety and can be drawn upon. Baby changing is a no-nonsense bench affair outside the restaurant.

Open Mon–Fri 12pm–3pm and 6pm–10.30pm, Sat 12pm–4pm and 6pm–10.30pm, Sun and bank holidays 12pm–8.30pm. **Main Course** £6–£14.50. **Amenities** highchairs, on-street parking. **Credit Cards** all except DC.

The Spyglass Inn

Esplanade, Ventnor, Isle of Wight, 📞 *01983 855338, www.thespyglass. com*

Overlooking the English Channel and next to a great beach for the children to play on, this inn with seafaring memorabilia on the walls serves wonderful locally caught lobster and crab. Full of families when we visited, they have children's meals like fish fingers and cottage pie and menus for your dinosaur-obsessed son to open and arrange into a small pen containing sachets of mustard and ketchup because as you daughter will point out for me 'Dad he thinks they are really baby stegosauruses having a picnic'.

Open Mon–Sat 12pm–9.30pm, Sun 12pm–9pm. **Main Course** £8.50. **Amenities** highchairs. **Credit Cards** all except DC.

INEXPENSIVE

Inn on the Park

Off St Michael's Street, Verulamium Park, St Albans, Hertfordshire, 📞 *01727 838246, www.inn-on-the-park.com*

Set between the Verulamium Museum (great children quizzes and trails) and St Albans Cathedral in a 100-acre park next to a play-park, this café has messy children's days in a next-door room on some Friday mornings (£3.50 a session). In the summer the nearby splash-pool opens and a stroll away our children enjoyed feeding ducks and swans the remains of the hand-cut sandwiches we bought for lunch.

Open daily 9.30am–4pm winter and 9.30am–5pm summer. **Main Course** sandwiches £5. **Amenities** highchairs, baby-changing, children's lunchboxes. **Credit cards** all except AX and DC.

Morellis

14 Victoria Parade, Broadstairs, Kent, 📞 *01843 862500, www.morellis.com*

Opened in 1932, this upmarket café (they have a branch in Harrods) is where the comic actor, Tony Hancock, used to visit while wooing John Le Mesurier's wife. We can understand why. They sell more than 60 varieties of ice cream, including the very special Leonardo Da Vinci, useful to bribe your children with to eat their tomato and cheese paninis. Like one of those old men who pretend to be grumpy around children but when you're out of the room are as soft as putty, the restaurant has signs up about children not running about which, if our children's behaviour was anything to go by, they turn a blind eye to. The café, overlooking Viking Bay and a stone's throw from the Dickens House Museum (toby jugs, crimping irons, tea cosies), has slot machines for your children to beg you for money to play on and a juke box necessitating them dancing energetically on the fairly slippery floor before banging their heads against table legs prior to be being lugged down to the beach below for a calm down.

Open daily winter 8am–5pm, summer 8am–10pm. *Main Course* paninis £3.50. *Amenities* highchairs. *Credit Cards* cash and cheques only.

The Captain's Cabin at Buckler's Hard

Beaulieu, Brockenhurst, Hampshire 📞 *01590 616293, www.bucklershard. co.uk*

Three ships that fought at Trafalgar with Lord Nelson were built at this now idyllic riverside spot often used by film-makers looking for somewhere that conveys the Thames as it was in the 16th century. There is a museum next to the café that has a lock of Nelson's hair, a bonnet he wore as a nipper and several recreated shipyard scenes from the 18th century although you do not have to pay for the attraction to eat here. The café sells light lunches such as soup, rolls and sandwiches.

Open daily winter 10am–4pm, summer 10am–5pm. *Main Course* sandwiches £3.25. *Amenities* baby-changing, highchairs. *Credit Cards* all except AX and DC.

Walk the White Cliffs of Dover

White Cliffs of Dover Visitor Centre, Langdon Cliffs, Upper Road, Dover CT16 1HJ, 📞 *01304 202756, www.nationaltrust.org.uk*

With stunning 20 mile views to France along a chalk down-land path rich in rare butterflies and Exmoor ponies, even our effort-shy children enjoyed this walk, one of the most popular in the country for its staggeringly beautiful scenery and easy access. The walk, that ends in the beautiful St Margaret's bay, starts from the visitor centre, a former Victorian prison, and is basically a three-mile slice of the Saxon Shoreway path that stretches from Gravesend to Hastings. Along the way you might catch sight of peregrine falcons and ravens nesting in the 250-foot high cliff-tops, and if you're here between May and August you'll see the endangered Silver Spotted Skipper and Small Blue Butterflies specific to this area. Around 14 Exmoor ponies graze the slopes identified as a Site Special Scientific Interest. For younger kids borrow one of the 15 tracker packs available at the visitor centre. They contain magnifying glasses, binoculars, compasses, a map and checklist of wildlife to look out for. We stopped for our picnic 2 miles into the walk at the Foreland Lighthouse decommissioned in 1987. Meanwhile, St Margaret's Bay is great for rock-pooling and the visitor Centre has displays about conservation in the area and also about the former prison here that provided the forced slaves that helped build the port of Dover.

Open (visitor centre) daily in the summer 10am-5pm; winter daily 11am-4pm. *Amenities* café, gift-shop, parking (£3 for the day).

4 Eastern England

EASTERN ENGLAND

Attractions ●

Blakeney Point Seals **1**
Burghley House **2**
Constable Country **3**
Cressing Temple **4**
Dinosaur Adventure Park **5**
Grantham Museum **6**
Imperial War Museum **7**
Kelvedon Hatch Secret
   Nuclear Bunker **8**
Lincoln Castle **9**
Merrivale Model Village **10**
National Parrot Sanctuary **11**
The National Stud **12**
Norwich Castle **13**
Orford River Trip **14**
Oxburgh Hall **15**
Pleasure Beach Great Yarmouth **16**
Rutland Belle **17**
Sandringham Estate **18**
Searle's Wash Monster **19**
Time & Tide Museum of
   Great Yarmouth Life **20**

Accommodation ■

202 West Parade Guesthouse **1**
Beech House **2**
Black Lion Hotel **3**
The Cambridge Belfry **4**
Congham Hall **5**
Elm Farm Cottages **6**
Fritton House Country Park **7**
Kesgrave Hall **8**
The Old Brewery **9**
Sprowston Manor Marriott **10**
Titchwell Manor Hotel **11**

Dining ◆

Ask **1**
Boardwalk Restaurant **2**
Essex Rose Tea House **3**
The Farmers Arms Inn **4**
The Hampton **5**
Ickworth Hotel **6**
The Lemon Tree **7**
The Lord Nelson **8**
The Wheatsheaf Inn **9**

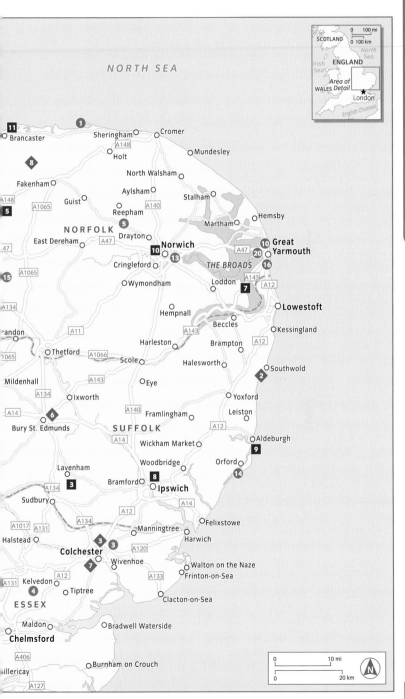

NORTH SEA

SCOTLAND

ENGLAND

WALES

Area of
Detail

London

North Sea

Irish Sea

English Channel

0   100 mi
0   100 km

11 O Brancaster

1

Sheringham O ── O Cromer

A148

O Holt

O Mundesley

8

North Walsham O

Fakenham O

Aylsham O

Stalham O

A148

A1065   Guist O

Reepham O

A140

O Hemsby

5

NORFOLK

Drayton O

5

Martham O

47   East Dereham O

A47

10 Norwich O

O

13

Great **10**
Yarmouth

A47

20 O

15   A1065

Cringleford O

THE BROADS

16

A134

Wymondham O

Loddon O

A143

7 A12

Hempnall O

O Lowestoft

andon O

A11

Beccles O

A143

O Kessingland

1065 O Thetford

A1066

Harleston O

Brampton O

A12

Mildenhall

Scole O

Halesworth O

A134

A143

2 O Southwold

A14 O **6**

O Ixworth

O Eye

Bury St. Edmunds

A140

Framlingham O

O Yoxford

Leiston O

SUFFOLK

A12

Lavenham O

A14

Wickham Market O

O Aldeburgh

3

Bramford O

8

Woodbridge O

Orford O

9

Sudbury O

O Ipswich

14

A12

A134

A14

A1017   A131

A134

Manningtree O

O Felixstowe

Halstead O

Harwich O

3 O **3**

Colchester

A120

Walton on the Naze

7

Wivenhoe O

A133

Frinton-on-Sea

A131   Kelvedon O

A12

O Tiptree

Clacton-on-Sea

4

ESSEX

O Maldon

O Bradwell Waterside

Chelmsford

A406

O Burnham on Crouch

illericay

A127

0   10 mi
0   20 km

N

Norfolk is cut off from the rest of England by the sea on three sides and on the fourth side by the lack of a motorway. Its relative isolation and image as a backward county is not new and stems from the fact that from the Middle Ages through to the 1800s it was easier to cross the sea to the continent than reach the Midlands or London by road from Norfolk. Its reputation became synonymous with the phrase 'Normal for Norfolk', a term doctors routinely abbreviated to NFN in a patient's notes to mean 'intellectually challenged'. In fact Norfolk has many intellectual claims to fame. The first book ever written by a woman, *Revelation of a Divine Love*, was written in Norfolk, albeit a woman with a man's name, Julian of Norwich (1342–1416). The county town of Norwich meanwhile famously has a school of painters named after it, and a university that has produced Booker Prize-winning alumni. The county's ungrammatical motto – Do Different –while hardly bolstering its brainy credentials, does sum up Norfolk. They do things differently here. And by differently we mainly mean they do things much more slowly.

Not that this is the case in neighbouring Cambridgeshire, parts of which have been nicknamed Silicon Fen for their preponderance of high-tech science parks. Many of these companies have, of course, spun out of Cambridge University, whose world-famous ornate, bike-lined colleges churn out prime ministers and Nobel Prize winners year after year almost as fast as Norfolk does apples, and goes a long way to defining the vibrancy of the city. Nearby Newmarket, meanwhile, is the only town in England where there are more horses than people, a fact reflected so deeply in its culture that pelican crossings have raised buttons for riders to press while on horseback. The barracks town of Colchester in Essex further south is the country's oldest and East England is also home to the beautiful Constable country around East Bergolt, as well as the stunning Suffolk coast where you'll find England's most middle-class pier in Southwold and the quintessentially old English seaside village of Aldeburgh. Lincolnshire has its own distinct character. Again, set apart from the rest of the country, locals here will confusingly greet you with the words 'now then' instead of 'hello', are 'mardy' instead of 'cross' and 'frit' rather than frightened when they think you've checked out without paying for your broadband supplement. Lincoln, the main city in the county, has a world-famous cathedral and castle, and Stamford, a town so scrumptiously pretty, clean and well-kept that you half want to wrap the streets in greaseproof paper, sprinkle them with sugar and see what they'd taste like topped with almond shavings. The *Rutland Belle* is fun and also worth a day out is Rutland Water, which, along with our bathroom floor following a game of 'I be the pirate, Daddy,' is one of the largest man-made reservoirs in Europe. The county is also home to the hilarious National Parrot Sanctuary, where ill informed Londoners would argue the birds have a more understandable vocabulary than the locals.

CHILDREN'S TOP 10 ATTRACTIONS

❶ Hunt for a crazy T-Rex on the loose at Dinosaur Adventure Park in Norfolk. See p 81.

❷ Cruise a couple of metres from a colony of 100 basking grey and harbour seals at Blakeney Point. See p 81.

❸ Have dozens of colourful parakeets crawl over you at the National Parrot Sanctuary. See p 70.

❹ See if you have the hand–eye coordination to be a pilot at the Imperial War Museum in Duxford. See p 73.

❺ Wander around the eerie secret nuclear bunker in Kelvedon Hatch. See p 78.

❻ Draw your own coat of arms at Norwich Castle. See p 82.

❼ Hang out with stars like Sting at the Essex Rose Tearooms. See p 93.

❽ Visit the Queen's official country residence at Sandringham House. See p 84.

❾ Treat your children to all the activities at the Fritton House Country Park. See p 87.

❿ Ride the Hunstanton Wash Monster. See p 85.

LINCOLN & AROUND

The city of Lincoln is famous for producing the colour Lincoln green, as sported by legendary outlaw Robin Hood, and for being home to Lincoln Cathedral that would have been, up until the early 1960s, the tallest building in the country if bits hadn't fallen off it. Lincoln is also renowned for its castle, scene of what in its day was the equivalent of the Big Chill music festival, when n'er-do-wells were hung from its ramparts and huge crowds gathered to drink ale, munch venison and comment on the speed of strangulation like they might do a Ray Manzarek keyboard solo today. The broader county of Lincolnshire has some lovely unspoilt towns, one of which isn't Skegness (the Fens' answer to Blackpool Pleasure Beach) and two of which include the birthplace of Sir Isaac Newton, Grantham, and Stamford, the town we have to thank/curse/burn to the ground for the proliferation of BBC costume dramas on TV.

Essentials

Getting There

By Train From London (Kings Cross) there are services to Lincoln every hour. The journey takes approximately two hours and has one change normally at Newark Northgate. For information call East Midlands Trains (☎ 08457 125678, *www.eastmidlandstrains.co.uk*). From Birmingham (New Street) the same operator has services every hour to Lincoln. The journey takes about two hours 30 minutes with one change at

Nottingham. From Leeds to Lincoln there is an indirect service from National Express East Coast Trains (08457 225 333, *www.nationalexpresseastcoast.com*). They leave every hour with the journey lasting between one hour 30 minutes and two hours.

By Bus From London, National Express (08705 808080, *www.nationalexpress.com*) has services from Victoria coach station running daily with the journey lasting four hours and 20 minutes. From Birmingham the company has a single daily direct service taking just over three hours, while from Leeds there is a single daily service with one change in Leicester, the journey lasting six hours and 20 minutes.

By Car From London to Lincoln take the A1 north and then the A46 to Lincoln signposted from the A1. From Birmingham take the M6 or M42 to pick up the M1 headed north then the A57 to Lincoln at junction 31.

From Leeds take the A63 to the A1(M) headed south then the A57 to Lincoln at junction 31.

Visitor Information

The Stamford Tourist Information Centre (01780 755611) is based at St Mary's Street, Stamford and is open Mon–Sat 9.30am–5pm and Sun 10.30am–3.30pm. The Grantham Tourism Information Centre (01476 406166) at Guildhall Centre, St Peter's Hill is open Mon–Fri 9.30am–4.30pm and Sat 9am–1pm. The Rutland Tourist Information Centre (01780 686800) at Sykes Lane, Empingham is open seven days a week 10am–4pm. The Lincoln Tourist Information Centre (01522 873213, *www.visitlincolnshire.com*) based at Castlehill (between the cathedral and the castle) is open Mon–Thurs 9.30am–5pm, Fri 9.30am–4.30pm and Sat 11am–4pm.

What to See & Do

Burghley House ALL AGES

Stamford, Lincolnshire, 01780 752451, www.burghley.co.uk

The famous home of the ancient Cecil family was used during the filming of *The Da Vinci Code* and *Pride and Prejudice* and has hosted among other distinguished guests Prime Minster Benjamin Disraeli and Queen Victoria. The tour of the house, where children are encouraged to identify animals in various portraits was, however, a slight disappointment. Our children were unmoved by a projected audiovisual show featuring the present owner of the house, Lady Victoria, and continued to loudly sing 'the bear necessities of life will come to you' all through it. Buggy access was also poor – we could only get to the kitchen and great hall on the ground floor. The Orangery restaurant got a thumbs down too, selling such overpriced ice cream we were morally forced to swipe free croutons from the soup stand to give to our children as an alternative (and quite literal) credit-crunch snack. The grounds, designed by Capability Brown, are more fun. There is a ha ha to roll/fall down while chasing a plastic football, while the contemporary statue garden is full of eccentric water features specially designed to soak everyone within a 1.5km radius of them.

Open 28th Mar–29th Oct Sat–Thurs 11am–5pm. The gardens are open the same times as well as Fri. Adm house and gardens adults £11.30, children (5–15) £5.60, conc £9.90, families (two adults, two children) £29. Gardens only adults £6.50, children £3.15, conc £5.40 and families £17. Amenities café, parking. Credit Cards all accepted.

Grantham Museum ALL AGES

St Peter's Hill, Grantham, Lincolnshire, ☎ 01476 568783, www.lincolnshire.gov.uk

An intelligent local history museum wisely concentrating on its town's two chief claims to fame – that it was home to both Sir Isaac Newton and Lady Thatcher. You can see some of Thatcher's old dresses, and the museum has a few good low-level interactive exhibits on Newtonian experiments for your children, enabling you and your wife the time and luxury of rewriting Newton's laws on motion as applied to a toddler, these being as follows:

Newton's first law of (toddler) motion: if a toddler is standing still to make it move you must apply a packet of chocolate buttons. Once the toddler is moving it will continue to move at the same speed and in a straight line unless another force acts upon it. This force is known as 'seeing a sibling with more chocolate buttons'.

Newton's second law of (toddler) motion: a moving toddler moves even faster when a packet of mini-eggs acts upon it. The toddler accelerates in the direction of the mini-eggs, the amount of acceleration depending on the exact number of eggs and their perceived chocolateness.

Newton's third law of (toddler) motion: if a toddler is pushed or pulled it will push and pull to an equal extent in the opposite direction until somebody is in tears and all the mini-eggs are scattered on the floor of the museum and the curator is staring at you questioningly and it is time to leave for Rutland.

Open Mon–Sat 10am–4pm. Adm free. Amenities gift-shop. Credit Cards all except AE.

Lincoln Castle ALL AGES

Castle Hill, Lincoln, ☎ 01522 511068, www.lincolnshire.gov.uk

Whilst the guided tours (not good for buggies), heavily focused on grisly hangings from the castle ramparts, are interesting for older children, toddlers, more used to the jolly parp of the Pinky Ponk horn, might find it too distressing. Wedding parties from services in the cathedral next door often spill into the grassy grounds for their group photos and it's a great place for children to run around while your wife lounges about on

Lincoln Castle

an elbow saying dismissive things about the bridesmaids' dresses ('You should never, never, wear salmon pink'). There is an old Victorian prison here, where you'll learn about William Marwood, the gentlemen executioner (he pioneered the quicker and less distressing long-drop hanging method), while the highlight is glimpsing one of the four remaining original copies of the Magna Carta. Signed in 1215 by King John at Runnymede and outlining a list of rights granted to the barons of the day, it's stored to protect its fragility in a very dark room that our baby son refused to enter because 'a dinosaur a-coming, Daddy'. Lincoln Castle's history and the site on which it stands, spans the centuries from 60 AD to the present day. In 1068, two years after the Battle of Hastings, William the Conqueror began building Lincoln Castle on a site occupied since Roman times. Many original features still remain and a walk around the walls provide you with excellent views of the Cathedral, the City of Lincoln and the surrounding countryside.

Open *daily 10am–4pm Oct–Mar, 10am–5pm Apr and Sept, 10am–6pm May–Aug.* **Adm** *adults £4, children and conc £2.65.* **Amenities** *café.* **Credit Cards** *all except AX.*

National Parrot Sanctuary

⭐ ALL AGES

Dickonhill Road, Friskney, Lincoln-shire, 📞 *0871 3841130, www. parrotsanctuary.co.uk*

Home to more than 1,400 birds, and the largest collection of parrots in the UK, the highlight is a walk-through aviary where, when we visited, up to 190 parakeets crawled on our shoulders, over our fingers and nibbled our sunglasses looking for millet seed. The experience is so intense it can frighten some (my wife panicked: 'I don't like it Ben – they're out of control!') while in others (the rest of our family, and everyone else we saw) it can't help but provoke a ticklish form of hysterics. Look out for the African Grey, Bill, who, very much like a woman, who served us a battered sausage in Ingoldmells, will talk politely about your plans for the day, and then when your back is turned, mutter the word 't***t'. Our children relished the pathos of the harrowing rehoming stories printed underneath bird cages that involved everything from alcoholism (we assumed the owner's) to abandonment

National Parrot Sanctuary

('what a poor VERY cute parrot, Daddy'). They also enjoyed the Small Animal Experience (best time for the rabbits is late afternoon after they've run about all day and need to recuperate on a warm lap). If you get a chance, have a chat with inspirational owner Steve Nicholls, who'll tell you about Derren Brown's parrots (he failed to control their minds and they are now here).

Open daily 10am–5pm. **Adm** adults £5.95, children (3–15) £4.50, under threes free, conc £4.95, families (two adults, two children) £18.50. **Amenities** café, parking. **Credit Cards** all except AE.

Rutland Belle ALL AGES

Whitwell Harbour, 📞 *01572 787630,* **www.rutnet.co.uk**

The cruise has onboard commentary that's not particularly engaging for children or even adults, focusing on brown trout and the water-retentive properties of clay so that in the end it was more interesting overhearing a pensioner on the top deck loudly bragging about her third appearance on *The Antiques Roadshow*. In the end we commandeered the prow of the ship with a sliding door we could pull shut so our son couldn't fall

Rutland Water

The best thing to do here on a sunny day is lounge around the North Shore with an ice cream from the Funky Fox Café looking out at the sailing boats close to local sculptor Alexander's ('my statues communicate the unspoken elements of everyday life') 30-feet bronze Great Tower, in front of which our son tried to eat pellets of duck poo.

overboard between the large gaps in the railings. Rutland Water itself is a 3,100 acre reservoir, built in the 1970s to supply water to the East Midlands. It offers activities for all ages with sports such as windsurfing, rock-climbing, canoeing, dinghy hire, cycling and fishing. You can also visit the Egleton and Lyndon nature reserves, or just take in the scene by the water around the 25 mile shoreline.

The boat sails on the hour daily in the afternoons 4th Apr–25th Oct. **Adm** *adults £7, children (3-15) £4.50, families (two adults, two children) £20. A limited number of under threes can sail free.*

Open *Sun–Thurs 9am–10pm, Fri–Sat 9am–11pm.* **Adm** *free. Wristbands covering all eligible rides peak season for under 12s £12 (off peak £6), for over 12s £17 (off-peak £12).* **Amenities** *restaurants, parking (£1–£4 depending on the season).* **Credit Cards** *all accepted.*

CAMBRIDGE & AROUND

The city is famous primarily for its university whose world-renowned colleges have produced more than 80 Nobel Prize-winners, 10 prime ministers, Charles Darwin (see box), and more importantly darts commentator, Sid Waddell. The city is easy to walk across (but take care to dodge students flying down the centre of the street on bicycles), and based on the attractive River Cam, where students carelessly punt along, faces in books, while across the county you'll find the huge and impressive Imperial War Museum at Duxford and the town of Newmarket of racing fame, where horses we are reliably informed outnumber people, and we believe actually run the town themselves using a tri-party first-past-the-post democracy criticized for its exclusion of full voting rights to donkeys.

Essentials

Getting There

By Train There are First Capital Connect (☎ *0845 0264700*, *www.firstcapitalconnect.co.uk*) services every 10 minutes or so from London direct to Cambridge. The journey takes about 45 minutes. To get to Cambridge from Birmingham New Street take a Virgin Trains (☎ *0845 0000800*, *www.virgintrains.co.uk*) service to London Euston, the underground to London Kings Cross and then the First Capital Connect service mentioned earlier. The journey is a sapping three hours.

By Bus From London Victoria coach station there are hourly (and sometimes half-hourly) National Express (☎ *08705 808080*, *www.nationalexpress.com*) services to Cambridge. The journey takes two hours and 10 minutes. From Birmingham's Digbeth coach station the same company has two hourly services to Cambridge. The journey takes between three and a half to five hours depending on the wait at Milton Keynes.

Skegness

Skegness was home to the first-ever Butlins holiday camp in 1947 and is strangely still often voted the best place to retire to, because of its laid-back atmosphere, tanning studios and the fact if you are male and over 15 you must go out in a baseball cap or be labelled gay. Its sandy beach has £2 donkey rides, and proudly, if slightly offputtingly, publicizes next to the car park the fecal *streptococci* content of its waters with a sad- or happy-faced public sign. While there are plenty of places to buy fish and chips, the seascape view is strangely modern, the middle distance obliterated by an oil-type platform and an ugly windmilling line of rusting turbines. The chief attraction Fantasy Island (☎ *01754 615860*, *www.fantasyisland.co.uk*) is a short drive away on Sea Lane, Ingoldmells. Though not an island and some would say not that fantastical, there are more than 29 rides ranging from whitish-knuckle roller-coasters to the ones our four-year-old daughter went on in the Main Pyramid including the Magical Sea Aquarium, the Jungle Adventure Ride, the Balloons and, of course, the Jellikins roller-coaster. The highpoint is the toddler show on the Scallywags stage, where amongst other notable performances we saw Pinky and Perky dancing to Reet Petite, and the Jellikins singing robustly about their jelly-megatastical day. The largest outdoor market in Europe is also at Fantasy Island, as are hoards of football-shirted dads striding amongst the mock Polynesian huts flanked by palm trees impatient to get to Wood's Wine Bar because the live football is about to start.

By Car From London to Cambridge take the M25, M11 and then the A1309 and A1134 into the city. The journey takes around one hour and 35 minutes. The journey from Birmingham to Cambridge will take two hours. Take the M6, the A14 and then the M11 followed by a similar route in from London as explained above.

Visitor Information

Cambridge Tourist Information Centre (☎ 0871 226 8006) is at The Old Library, Wheeler Street, Cambridge, and the Newmarket Tourist Information Centre (☎ 01638 667200) is at Palace House, Palace Street, Newmarket.

Imperial War Museum
★ ALL AGES

Duxford, Cambridgeshire, ☎ *01223 835000, www.duxford.iwm.org.uk*

There are several hangers worth visiting here including the American Air Museum built into the side of a hill and looking so like the home of the Teletubbies our baby son wanted to know where La La was. The huge aerodrome is dominated by a B52 bomber, while dozens of other planes are fixed strikingly to the ceiling like

Punting

The best way to visit the many famous Cambridge colleges is on a chauffeured punt with the largest operator Scudamores (☎ 01223 359750, www.scupdamores.com). They depart from Mill Lane or Magdalene Bridge, and combine insights into university life with Cambridge history and, of course, detailed information about Harry Potter film location spots. The success of the tours that depart roughly every 20 minutes and last 45 minutes will be largely influenced by your ability to return to the jetty with all family members alive (i.e. not for under threes), and by the quality of your guide, ours it has to be said being on the more basic side of informative ('That's the Wren library built by a man named Sir Christopher Wren... And this is Queen's College. A man called Stephen Fry studied here. He's on the telly'.) That said, during occasional lulls when our one year old settled/was held down/was force-fed toffee, watching all the life of Cambridge go by – students revising, fisherman casting for pike, louts in Michael Ballack Chelsea football shirts smacking either other round the head with oars – the cruise was fun and almost relaxing. One word of advice: don't sit in the seat in front of the punter (the freshing seat) – you'll get splashed. Actually two words of advice. If you can book online – you'll save yourself a few pounds.

Adm adults £14, under 12s £7, conc £12. **Amenities** umbrella.

pinned butterflies. The land warfare hanger focuses interestingly on the story of the D-Day landings, although more fun for children is the Air Space Museum. It includes a Concorde you can climb aboard, a Polaris missile and, upstairs, many hands-on gizmos demonstrating lift, thrust and drag, all of which I was ironically forced to employ to remove our one year old from the Morse code area later. The site is so huge you take a land train to get around.

Open daily 10am–4pm (winter), 10am–6pm (summer). **Adm** adults £16, under 16s free, conc £12.80. **Amenities** parking, café. **Credit Cards** all except AX.

The National Stud ALL AGES

Newmarket, Suffolk, ☎ 01638 663464, www.nationalstud.co.uk

The tour starts at the coffee shop where children can feed grass to mini Shetlands. After this you get on a bus and are driven to various paddocks to see silky race horses licking mineral blocks, a retired Grand National winner, the headstones of dead horses who won major races and the empty barn where the 'covering' takes place. At the stud itself the highlight for our children was feeding and patting the animals, but be warned it's busy here and every pushy teenage equestrian lover for themselves.

Bury St. Edmunds

Once an ancient Anglo-Saxon kingdom dominated by the Danes, many old villages and market towns abound in East Anglia. Bury St. Edmunds is one good example of this and is still "a handsome little town, of thriving and cleanly appearance," as Charles Dickens described it in Pickwick Papers. It was founded around the powerful Benedictine Abbey in 1020 and derives its name from St. Edmund, king of the East Angles in the mid-9th century. In the Abbey Church, the barons of England united and forced King John to sign the Magna Carta in 1214. Several good parks for families are located just outside town. West Stow Park has man-made attractions but if it's unspoilt nature you seek, Nowton Park will give you relatively easy, quite romantic walks and the most evocative scenery the Suffolk landscape has to offer. The West Stow Anglo-Saxon Village is part of West Stow Country Park and is a reconsructed village holding reenactments on the site of an excavated ancient Anglo-Saxon village (☎ *01284 728718*).

South-east from Newmarket, Lavenham, once a great wool centre and a classic Suffolk village, beautifully preserved today, is well worth a visit. It features a number of half-timbered Tudor houses washed in the characteristic Suffolk pink. The town's wool-trading profits are apparent in its guildhall, on the triangular main "square." Inside, exhibits on Lavenham's textile industry show how yarn was spun, then "dyed in the wool" with woad (the pant used by ancient Picts to dye themselves blue), following on to the weaving process. Another display shows how half-timbered houses were constructed.

Open *1st Feb–30th Sept and Oct half-term.* **Adm** *adults £6.50, children over six and conc £5, under sixes free, families £20.* **Amenities** *parking, café.* **Credit Cards** *all accepted.*

COLCHESTER & AROUND

Stretching back to pre-Roman times, Colchester, England's oldest town and now the centre of a huge army barracks, has an even prouder claim to fame – it provided the setting not only for the children's nursery rhyme *Humpty Dumpty* but also for *Old King Cole* and *Twinkle Twinkle Little Star* (see box). The town is also close to Constable country, the beautiful Suffolk coast, and with family outings nearby in Kelvedon Hatch and Cressing Temple, is currently working on its difficult fourth nursery rhyme featuring, it is rumoured, a cat, a fiddle and some tooled up members of the 16th Air Assault Brigade.

FUN FACT ⟫ **Charles Darwin** ⟪

He once ate an owl.

He wanted to be a doctor but hated the sight of blood.

He almost didn't sail on the *HMS Beagle* to the Galapagos Islands the basis of his famous *Origin of the Species* thesis, because the captain of the ship Robert Fitzroy disliked the shape of his nose.

Oddly the man who gave rise to genetics married his first cousin.

Essentials

Getting There

By Train Take a National Express East Anglia (☏ 0845 600 7245, *www.nationalexpresseastanglia. com*) train from London (Liverpool Street) to Colchester. They go every 10 minutes. The journey takes 50 minutes. From Norwich to Colchester the journey is an hour on the same Liverpool Street–Norwich line. Rail travel from Cambridge is via Ely or Ipswich and the journey takes one hour 45 minutes. Contact: Rail Company.

By Bus From London two National Express (☏ 0870 5808080, *www.nationalexpress. co.uk*) coaches leave each day to Colchester. The journey takes around three hours. From Manchester to Colchester there are services but they have a lengthy wait at Birmingham and can be up to nine hours.

By Car There is good access to Colchester from all parts of the country via the A12, the M25 and the A14.

Visitor Information

The Visit Colchester Information Centre (☏ 01206 282920) can be found at 1 Queen Street, Colchester. It is open 6th Apr–30th Sept Mon, Tue, Thurs, Fri, Sat 9.30am–6pm; Wed 10am–6pm and Sun July, August 11am–4pm. From 1st Oct it is open Mon–Fri 10am–5pm. The Flatford Tourist Information Centre (☏ 01206 299460) is based at Flatford Lane, East Bergholt, Suffolk. The Ipswich Tourist Information Centre (☏ 01473 258070) is at St Stephen's Church, St Stephen's Lane, Ipswich, Suffolk. The Southwold Tourist Information Centre (☏ 01502 724729) can be found at 69 High Street, Southwold, Suffolk. And the Sudbury Tourist Information Centre (☏ 01787 881320) is at the Town Hall, Sudbury, Suffolk.

Constable Country AGES 5 AND UP

Bridge Cottage, ☏ 01206 298260.

The area around East Bergholt has become known as Constable country because John Constable (1776–1837) painted six of his major works around here including The Hay Wain, The Lock and Flatford Mill. Accessed via a car park (£2) and a short walk accessible with a buggy, the small hamlet is an idyllic place consisting of Bridge Cottage housing several of Constable's paintings and a wooden bridge over the river Sour. Here you can hire rowing boats (£3 adults, £1.50 children) while a field on the other side of the bridge is a great spot for a picnic and a stare at cows bathing in the water when the weather gets too hot. If you have children that will stand them, the guided National Trust Constable walks, which leave from behind Bridge Cottage, last approx 45 minutes, cost £2.50 and are fascinating. You can stand exactly where Constable positioned himself to sketch some of our nation's best-loved works of art. Some of these viewpoints are largely unchanged in 150 years, and until our daughter stung herself on a nettle necessitating the 15-minute application of a dock leaf, and our son tried to eat a cowpat after refusing his yoghurt, it was a rewarding experience appreciating the essence of the English countryside that Constable was striving for.

Open *1.30pm–5.30pm peak times and Sat–Sun 11am–3.30pm off peak.*

Cressing Temple ALL AGES

Witham Road, Cressing, Braintree, 📞 *01376 584903, www.cressing temple.org.uk*

Once owned by the Order of Knights Templar (see box) of *The Da Vinci Code* fame, this isn't actually a temple (the knights just liked calling everything a temple apparently) but two huge 13th-century barns and grounds where jousting, falconry shows, car rallies and other family events are regularly staged. In August there are special digs for children in a mocked up archaeological pit and living-history Tudor days, although when we were here it was Divining Day. This saw 14 adults and children moving forward in a zombie-like line holding twisted coat hangers in front of their outstretched hands trying to detect various underground drains. Our four-year-old daughter quickly lost interest and I did too, after I was told that I had lost man's innate sensitivity to the natural rhythms of the world by Barry Hillman, the

---

FUN FACT ➤ **Colchester & Nursery Rhymes** ◄

While Liverpool has Merseybeat and Manchester has 90s' rave, Colchester is home to the nursery rhyme. The legendary Old King Cole of nursery rhyme fame was from Colchester and *Twinkle Twinkle Little Star* was written by Jane Taylor in the town's Dutch Quarter in 1806. Meanwhile Humpty Dumpty wasn't an egg-shaped man with poor balance, but a large cannon used by the Royalists during the English Civil War (1642–49) in the Siege of Colchester. To protect the city walls, Humpty Dumpty was mounted in the belfry (Humpty Dumpty sat on a wall) of St Mary's Church but the wall beneath the cannon was blown apart by the besieging parliamentarians (Humpty Dumpty had a great fall), which couldn't be moved or reassembled (All the Kings Horse and All the Kings Men couldn't put Humpty together again). Thus the castle fell.

instructor, when I failed to detect a ditch. Also there are ducks to chase and flowers for children to illegally pull up from the Tudor-walled garden.

Open 1st Mar–31st Oct 10am–5pm Mon–Fri and Sun. **Adm** adults £4, children and conc £3, families £9.50. **Amenities** tea-rooms, parking. **Credit Cards** all except AX.

Kelvedon Hatch Secret Nuclear Bunker ★ ALL AGES

Crown Buildings, Kelvedon Hall Lane, Kelvedon Hatch, ☎ *01277 364883,* **www.secretnuclearbunker.co.uk**

In a nuclear war it is likely 57 million of us would die. Temperatures would plummet to minus 20 degrees and when the hospital supplies ran out, people would be shot by police to put them out of their misery. The harvest would fail for three years while in the fourth year you'd have to dig through four inches of contaminated soil to plant anything. Marauding gangs would form, put cling film over the shelter air vent and steal our food. Although on the upside, parking would improve. These were some of the stark facts we learnt visiting this 100-feet-deep shelter designed in the 1960s to house 600 military and civil personnel and possibly even the prime minister in the event of a Soviet strike. The tour of the bunker is self-guided via a handset you pick up from a staff-less entrance that adds to the eerie feel you are alone in a post-apocalyptic world – or it would, if you hadn't two toddlers in Mr Tumble T-shirts singing 'Wind the bobbin in' somewhere below your knee. There are several films (some unsuitable for toddlers), military uniforms to try on, and children are given a more upbeat headset featuring a breezy character called Moley. There is a café at the end where you pay your admission and can contemplate grassed-over motorways, law and order disintegrating, and panic that you don't

---

FUN FACT ⟫ Knights Templar ⟨

The Knights Templar, a Europe-wide band, were warrior monks whose job was to protect pilgrims on their way to Jerusalem. They took vows of chastity, obedience to the Pope and poverty but somehow became very rich. They were so rich, and Philip IV of France was so in hock to them, he banded together with Pope Clement V and the Order was rounded up in October 1312 on Friday 13th (hence its association with bad luck) and suppressed. Meanwhile in England they were targeted by Edward II, their lands ceded to the Order of the Hospitallers of John the Baptist of Jerusalem, whose job was to look after the health of pilgrims on their way to the Holy Land. They in turn had this land handed over to the Order of the Filled Baked Potato whose job was to provide snacks to pilgrims on their way to Holy Land, who were suppressed for serving too much chilli and their lands were given to the Order of the Barclaycard . . . you get the idea.

know how to grow vegetables, raise horses or chickens. A seemingly ownerless goat with a bell round its neck wanders around outside scrounging bananas adding to the randomness. Or, as my wife commented, when I passed my observations on to her in the car, 'But they sold some lovely cookies in there. Did you have one?'

Open 1st Mar–31st Oct Mon–Fri 10am–4pm (weekends until 5pm), Nov–end of Feb Thurs–Sun 10am–4pm. Adm adults £6.50, children (5–16) £4.50, families (two adults, two children) £16. Amenities café, parking. Credit Cards cash and cheques only.

Orford River Trip ALL AGES

Orford Quay, Orford, Suffolk, 📞 01394 450169, www.orfordrivertrips.co.uk

Special activity cruises on the 25-feet launch *Regardless* enable children to lift and bait lobster pots and learn about velvet and hermit crabs. Regular cruises (every hour or so but ring ahead)

Kelvedon Hatch Secret Nuclear Bunker

complete a 11km trip to the lighthouse at Orford spit passing the RSPB sanctuary of Havergate Island. Along the way expect to see egrets, shank, cormorants and oystercatchers, and learn how the area was used to test nuclear detonators, and, in World War II, earthquake bombs in preparation for D-Day. You'll see the prison Jeffrey Archer did time in and might have to tell your children, if they are anything like ours, to stop picking valuable things out of your wife's handbag (mobile phone, car keys) to dangle over the side of the boat as ransom for 'One more Chocolate Gem, puhlease'. On your way back, Orford Quay is a great spot for crabbing.

Trips run at 5.30pm every day during the summer school holidays and at 4.30pm every Saturday during term time. Adm adults £7, children (under 16) £5. Amenities parking is 400m away in a pay-and-display car park (£2 for four hours).

NORFOLK

Bishy, bishy, barney-bee
When will your weddin' be?
If it be 'amara day,
Tairk your wings an' floi away.
Sometimes it isn't always easy to understand what a person from Norfolk is saying. If this happens, don't panic. If you panic he will panic and start digging for peat. Over the centuries locals here have created more than 200km of navigable waterways (what we call the Norfolk Broads) by accident through

panicking and digging for peat. Norfolk, home to the villages of Little Snoring, Great Snoring and Really Annoying Snoring That Sounds Like A Whistle, is often seen as a sleepy backwater, although there is much more to the county. For a belt and braces good time Great Yarmouth is hard to beat, while for more sophistication Norwich or the North Norfolk villages – including Burnham Thorpe, the home of Lord Nelson – are worth a visit. The Queen's official country residence, the Sandringham estate is here, and Hunstanton (Sunny Hunny) has a Wash Monster. We had fun in Norfolk. Just don't panic them, OK.

Essentials

Getting There

By Train National Express East Anglia (℡ 0845 6007245, www. nationalexpresseastanglia.com) run half-hourly services between London Liverpool Street and Norwich. The average journey time is 1 hour 50 minutes. A direct service also links Cambridge to Norwich, with an approximate journey time of 1 hour 10 minutes. For more information contact National Rail.

By Bus National Express (℡ 08717 818181, www.nationalexpress.com) operate daily services from London to Norwich. The journey takes approx three to three and a half hours.

By Car Major trunk roads from London and Cambridge to the

Norwich area are the M11, A11, A12, A140 and A14. The journey takes approx two to two and a half hours from London.

Visitor Information

Norwich Tourist Information Centre (℡ 01603 213999, www. visitnorwich.co.uk) is based in The Forum and opens Apr–Oct Mon–Sat 9.30am–6pm (with limited Sun opening), and Nov–Mar Mon–Sat 9.30am–5.30pm (closed Sun). The Burnham Deepdale Tourist Information Centre (℡ 01485 210256) is at Burnham Deepdale, Norfolk. The Great Yarmouth Tourist Information Centre (℡ 01493 846346) is at 25 Marine Parade, Great Yarmouth, Norfolk. The Hunstanton Tourist Information Centre (℡ 01485 532610) is at the Town Hall, The Green, Hunstanton, Norfolk. The North Norfolk Information Centre (Cromer) (℡ 0871 200 3071) is at Louden Road, Cromer, Norfolk. The Norwich Tourist Information Centre (℡ 01603 213999) is at The Forum, Millennium Plain, Norwich, Norfolk and the Wells-next-the-Sea Tourist Information Centre (℡ 0871 200 3071) is at Staithe Street, Wells-next-the-Sea, Norfolk.

Blakeney Point Seals
★★ ALL AGES
The best way to see the seals is on a boat trip with Beans Boats (℡ 01263 740505, www.beansboat trips.co.uk). Because of the tides there were only two trips a day

when we visited, at 9.15am and 5.15pm (but check ahead). You must pick up your ticket from Mr Bean's cottage in Mortson (yes, really, Mr Bean) and then drive down to the quayside car park to take the dinghy. About 100 grey and harbour seals live on the sand bars here. We got to within a few feet of them and it is a fantastic sight. Dozens of them, including pups, like a beach-load of drunks blottoed on the sand, sunbathing, occasionally waving their flippers to the accompaniment of the screeching sandwich terns overhead. The only thing missing was a morning cup of tea, although this was rectified back at the car park when the refreshment kiosk opened. The best time to come is early summer when the pups hatch. On your journey away you might want to check out some of the road signs. We are not sure whether it was just us, but did we really spot the following one after the other on the A419 – Stiff Key and Cock Thorpe – to name but a couple.

Adm *adults £8, under fours £4.*

Dinosaur Adventure Park

★ **ALL AGES**

Weston Park, Lenwade, Norfolk,
📞 *01603 876310, www.dinosaur adventure.co.uk*

An inventive trail through a copse of fibre-glass dinosaurs and abandoned jeeps includes wooden ranger stations with pretend field radios where excited young visitors can swap information about the whereabouts of the deadly T-Rex they're supposedly tracking. My wife took her chelonia phobia a stage further here and found herself scared of something we think was called europloceptallustutus, a dinosaur that looked a bit like a tortoise. Other attractions include a small petting zoo with rabbit-handling sessions while at Xtinction, there is a pit of sand where children can dig for dinosaur bones.

Open *daily Oct–Apr 10am–4pm; daily 13 July-6 Sept 10am-6pm and daily 7 Sept-23 Oct 10am-5p.* **Adm** *adults £7.50–£9.95 (depending on season), under threes free.* **Amenities** *parking, café, baby-changing.* **Credit Cards** *all except AX .*

Norwich

Norwich still holds to its claim as the capital of East Anglia. Despite its partial industrialisation, it's a charming and historic city. In addition to its cathedral, it has more than 30 medieval churches built of flint. It's also the most important shopping centre in east Anglia and has a lot to offer in the way of entertainment and interesting hotels, many of them in its narrow streets and alleyways. A big open-air market is busy every weekday, with fruit, flowers, vegetables, and other goods sold from stalls with coloured canvas roofs.

Merrivale Model Village ALL AGES

Marine Parade, Great Yarmouth,
📞 *01493 842097, www.great
yarmouthmodelvillage.co.uk*

This idyllic model village with a
pint-sized cricket pitch, a charming railway line and some quite
trendy antique and boutique
shops, is somewhere my wife and
I, if we were 5cm high and semi-
retired, would quite like to live.
There are buttons for children to
press to activate models of dancing people, a penny arcade and a
tearoom (real size) where you can
discuss what life would be like if
you really were 5cm high. 'You'd
have to talk into an amplification
system for a start. And I'd sleep
in a biscuit tin. It would smell
lovely when you woke up.' It's all
set in an acre of floral landscaped
gardens on the sea front with a
picnic area.

Open *28th Mar–1st Nov 10am–5pm.*
Adm *adults £5.50, children £3.95,
under threes free, conc £4.95.* **Amenities** *café.* **Credit Cards** *all except AX.*

Norwich Castle ★ ALL AGES

Castle Meadow, Norwich, 📞 *01603
493625, www.museums.norfolk.
gov.uk*

The only castle that could be
more child-friendly than this
would have to be a bouncy one.
Exhibits are cleverly pitched at
exactly the right level, there's
lots of interactivity, jigsaws,
brass rubbings, a soft-play area
and dressing-up opportunities as
well as a Happy Heraldry activity table our daughter happily
drew her own coat of arms on
for half an hour. Elsewhere children can make Egyptian

bracelets while in the Boudica
room there's a mocked-up char-
iot you can stand up on. Other
highlights include a stuffed polar
bear on its hind legs, a gallery of
René Magritte paintings and
outside the meadow is a great
place for a picnic.

Open *Mon–Fri 10am–4pm, Sat
10am–5pm, Sun 1pm–5pm.* **Adm**
*adults £6, children (4–16) £4.40, conc
£5.10.* **Amenities** *café, baby-changing.* **Credit Cards** *all except AX.*

> **INSIDER TIP**
> The museum operates pop-in-
> for-£1 an hour before closure
> and between 12pm and 1pm
> weekdays in school terms.

Oxburgh Hall ALL AGES

Oxborough, Norfolk, 📞 *01366
328258, www.nationaltrust.org.uk*

A moated 15th-century hall with
some rare (yet still not that interesting) embroideries by Mary
Queen of Scots, probably only
worth a visit with children if
there is a living history day. We
happened to call during a Civil
War re-enactment, which was
great fun apart from almost getting our eardrums burst standing
too close to cannon fire and a
minor foot injury I sustained
'charging my pike' in a have-a-go
at being a Roundhead session.
Under various tents whilst sew-
ing, cooking and chatting, living
history actors remained so in
character they refused to abandon
their olden day accents even
when I tried to ask them questions for research into this entry.

   'Does the hall have baby-
changing?'

Civil War re-enactment at Oxburgh Hall

'T'is goodly boiled this potage'. 'Right, OK, what about high-chairs in the café?'

'I have one eye on the ham and yet another on the potage and I cock an ear to the call to arms'.

'I'll check the website then, shall I?'

Open *28th Feb–8th Mar Sat–Sun 11am–5pm, 14th Mar–29th Jul Mon–Wed, Sat–Sun 11am–5pm, 1st Aug–31st Aug daily 11am–5pm, 1st Sept–1st Nov Mon–Wed, Sat–Sun 11am–5pm. The gardens sometimes shut slightly earlier out of season.* *Adm* *adults £6.75, children £3.45, families £19.95. Garden and estate only peak times adults £3.45, children £2. Garden and gatehouse off-peak times adults £5.50, children £2.80, families £13.80.* *Amenities* *café, parking.* *Credit Cards* *all except AX.*

Pleasure Beach Great Yarmouth ALL AGES

South Beach Parade, Great Yarmouth, Norfolk, ☎ 01493 844685, www.pleasure-beach.co.uk

What normally happens at these places is you enter them to be instantly dazzled by hundreds of rides, with loud jingles and flashing lights that are revolving, zig-zagging and flying up and down at high speed. Indeed for younger children there's the Mullan and Pirate Ship, while for older children there's the spinning 'Disko', 22-metre 'Sky Drop', Log Flume and the giant arm of 'Evolution'. With a toddler though it's different and this whole park seemed designed to thwart us. Our four-year-old daughter couldn't go on the carousel with her ice cream. The Fun House banned open-toed sandals, and she didn't meet the height requirement (1m) to go on the Caterpillar Roller-coaster. With only one hour left before our ticket ran out at St Nicholas car park, we panicked. We began barging through crowds like a desperate parent who's lost a toddler shouting out, all self-consciousness vanished, 'Has anyone seen the Snail Ride?' Then, on the point of capitulation we found a clutch of child-friendly rides halfway in. It was like the movie *Brewster's Millions* except with silver tokens. Spend. Spend. Spend. The Formula One ride, the Gallopers, the revolving tea-cups, the Snail Ride. Back to the Formula One ride, the Gallopers again, the snails. Round and round until our pockets were weightless. If you need some respite head for the Beach gardens a short walk from the Pleasure Beach.

Open all year. Adm free. Tokens £1 each. Rides from one to three tokens. Wristbands: maxi for fours and over off peak £16, peak £18; mini for threes and under off peak £10, peak £12.

Sandringham Estate ALL AGES

Sandringham, 📞 01553 612908, www.sandringhamestate.co.uk

The main fun about visiting a royal palace is the hope that a member of the royal family is in, catches sight of you through a mullioned window, and then invites you inside for a cup of tea. There were promising rumours circulating in the visitor centre that Prince Philip had been spotted on a horse and cart in the grounds the day before. Not only that, there had also been pictures of Prince Charles in the papers recently at the Sandringham flower show. However, what we forgot was that when royals are in attendance at their homes, visits are curtailed so that we had to make do with the grounds and

the museum containing some of the toys Prince Charles played with as a boy. (While we as children made do with bent out of shape Action Men he had a perfect, working to-scale replica of the Aston Martin Volante.) There is a collection of shiny full-size royal cars including a racing buggy the Queen Mum rode in when she reached 100. Another interesting room tells the story of the mysterious disappearance of the Sandringham Company (last seen entering a cigar-shaped cloud of smoke) at Gallipoli during World War I. You can discuss this in the café afterwards along with your own mysterious story of disappearance – that of the second packet of Quavers you definitely bought for the family picnic at the Titchwell post office and which you left your wife in charge of.

Open house – every Sat between 11th Apr–24th July and daily 2nd Aug–1st Nov. Museum and gardens daily from 1st Apr. Adm house, museum and gardens adults £10, children (5–15) £5, conc £8, families (two adults, up to three children) £25. Museum and gardens adults £6.50,

Sandringham Estate

children (5–15) £3.50, conc £5.50, families £16.50. **Amenities** restaurant, parking. **Credit Cards** all accepted.

Searle's Wash Monster ★
ALL AGES

Central Promenade, Hunstanton, 📞 *0783 1321799, www.seatours. co.uk*

You can splash down into the Wash from a one-time 1960s' US marines amphibious landing craft here and learn about, amongst other things, smuggling, and Hunstanton history (P.G. Wodehouse liked it here, and the Germans bombed it with Zeppelins). The thrill of being buzzed by paragliders weaving and leaping in and out of our wash was only slightly diluted by the fact I was holding a polystyrene cup for my wife, who suffers seasickness, to be sick into ('You never told me it was a flat-bottomed boat, Ben'). There are five tours on *Willie*, as the boat with shark jaws painted on the sides is nicknamed, ranging from a quick jaunt round the coast to a trip out to Seal Island. *Willie* has proved so popular that many children insist on coming out in their pyjamas to his nighttime 'paddock' to wish him goodnight or, like ours, bully their parents into buying the jaunty/irritating-after-two-plays (never mind the 45 we were forced to endure), Captain Willie single at the promenade kiosk.

Running times: check ahead. **Adm** *adults £12, children £6.* **Amenities** *binoculars.* **Credit Cards** *all accepted.*

Time and Tide Museum of Great Yarmouth Life **ALL AGES**

Blackfriars Road, Great Yarmouth, 📞 *01493 743930, www.museums. norfolk.gov.uk*

Although surprisingly interesting about the process of curing herring – once Great Yarmouth's biggest industry – for our children, more drawn to general freakery, the museum's highlight was standing beside a cut-out figure of local man Robert Hales (1820–1863), nicknamed the Norfolk Giant (2.3m) and the one-time tallest man in the world ('He ate all his broccoli, didn't he, dad?'). The museum, once a smokehouse and still smelling strongly of kippers, is well geared up for children, who can stencil and catch pretend fish on a hook and line. They can also ride in a wooden boat, find ammonites in mock dig-pits and complete jigsaws. There is a lift for buggy pushers.

Open 1st Apr–1st Nov Mon–Sun 10am–5pm, 2nd Nov–31st Mar Mon–Fri 10am–4pm, Sat and Sun 12pm–4pm. **Adm** *adults £5.20, children (4–16) £3.80, under 4s free, conc £4.40.* **Amenities** *baby-changing.* **Credit Cards** *all except AX.*

FAMILY-FRIENDLY ACCOMMODATION

EXPENSIVE

Beech House

Main Street, Clipsham, Rutland, 📞 *01780 410355, www.the olivebranchpub.com*

They have a stylish family room in the annexe here with two bedrooms and a wet room where at bath-time our children slid and clattered around in like Torvill and Dean having a drunken fist fight. A nice touch was the little flasks of milk in a communal fridge in the public area and there was a large cupboard our four-year-old daughter spent two hours sat on the top shelf of with her suitcase of pens drawing rabbit pictures. The only drawback was there was nowhere high enough to put anything breakable or valuable, so for our entire stay, our pockets bulged with cameras, keys, mini-computers and phones. The breakfast in the barn of the Michelin-starred Olive Tree pub was the highlight, our son Charlie gleefully consuming two whole full English breakfasts before flopping bloated into a vase of flowers. Our daughter loved the space-dust they put in the muesli. The evening meals are even better.

Rates *£160–£220 B&B per night.*
Amenities *children's menu, highchairs, parking, colouring- in books, crayons.*

Beech House at the Olive Branch Pub, Clipsham

In Room TV, (extra one in main bedroom,) tea and coffee making. **Credit Cards** all except AX and DC.

Congham Hall

St Andrews Lane, Grimston, Kings Lynn, 📞 *01485 600250, www.conghamhallhotel.co.uk*

This lovely old Georgian manor house has great grounds next to a field of horses set back from the road perfect for children to play their first ever game of croquet

Tides on North Norfolk Beaches

If you're planning to spend time on the beaches of Norfolk it's important to know the tides. The beaches at Snettisham and Heacham on the Wash will be mainly mud at low tide, while from Hunstanton all the way to Wells-next-the-Sea you'll get huge swathes of sand and practically require binoculars to see the waves. At high tide the beaches reduce dramatically from Hunstanton to Wells and there are hazardous currents, while in Weybourne, Sheringham and Cromer at high tide the sand disappears altogether leaving only pebbles. To check out local tides find listings at **www.new.edp24.co.uk** or **www.lynnnews.co.uk**.

on (they pulled up the hoops and threw them in the car park). It was not the most welcoming of hotels, however – we got a warmer reception from Marley the cat than most members of staff. Built in 1780, outside there's a working kitchen garden with over 700 varieties of herbs, while inside, there are log fires to warm yourself up after exploring the local high grassy sand dunes, nature reserves and Areas of Outstanding Natural Beauty.

Rates *Sandringham family suite £305–£340 B&B per night.* ***Amenities*** *parking, restaurant, tennis courts, nearby walks.* ***In Room*** *TV.* ***Credit Cards*** *all accepted.*

Fritton House Country Park ★★

Church Lane, Fritton, Norfolk, 📞 *01493 484008, www.frittonhouse.co.uk*

We realized our children had been away from toys too long on our research trip round England when I caught my son piling bottles of HIPP organic baby food on top of one another to make a tower, and our daughter wrapping up a condiment set in a napkin at dinner, and calling it, 'My lovely new Baby Annabel'. We couldn't have stayed at this intimate country house hotel at a better time. Next to Fritton Lake, it was jammed with all-year-round children's activities including an adventure playground with an enormous play castle, slides and a jumping pillow. There were also pony rides (£2), boat rides (free) and a barn with small buggies and ride-on diggers. The best bet for

families is the attic suite with two bedrooms and a large bathroom, which became the scene of a major triumph for me over my wife. Dismissive of my mosquito fears when we went to bed with the windows open, she awoke at 3am terrified by the loudest buzzing sound she had ever heard ('Ben, can you hear that?'). It turned out to be the bathroom's fluorescent light on the blink.

Rates *family suite £260 B&B per night.* ***Amenities*** *nine-hole golf course, yoga and fitness workshops.* ***In Room*** *TV, DVD player, bottled water, toiletries.* ***Credit Cards*** *all except AX.*

Kesgrave Hall ★

Hall Road, Kesgrave, Ipswich, Suffolk, 📞 *01473 333741, www. milsomhotels.com*

In this convivial country-house hotel in interconnecting rooms with zebra-striped sofas, floor-to-ceiling windows and a roll-top bath, I had a seriously bad night in seriously nice surroundings (kidney stones – enough said). This funky hotel has beautiful grounds for children to roll around in, and fills up in the evenings with families who come here specifically for the relaxed dining atmosphere that was also apparent at breakfast with great service and a special kids menu. Nearby is the historic riverside town of Woodbridge and Rendlesham Forest with picnic areas, cycle ways and waymarked walks.

Rates *interconnecting doubles Mon–Sat £285 per night (including a continental-style breakfast). A family of two adults and two children Mon–Sat*

The Norfolk Broads

One of the most important wetlands of Europe, the Norfolk "Broads" are part of the Broads National Park (www.broads-authority.gov.uk), lying both in Norfolk and Suffolk. Long thought to be natural lakes, they are actually man-made, resulting from peat being excavated for use as fuel. Flooded by a rising water table in the 13th century, these newly formed waterways were named "Broads". The area covers 124 miles of navigable waterways and are home to some of the rarest plants and creatures in Britain. These waterways are fun to explore by boat or canoe but some visitors prefer to ride bikes along the trails. If you want to take your own boat Barnes Brinkcraft in Wroxham is a reliable outfitter (📞 *01603 782625*) or if you want an organised tour contact Broads Tours (**www.broads.co.uk**).

£235 Sun £195. **Amenities** *parking, restaurant.* **In Room** *TV, phone, walk-in shower, wifi.* **Credit Cards** *all accepted.*

The Old Brewery ★★

16 Victoria Road, Aldeburgh, Suffolk,
📞 *01728 638962, www.bestof suffolk.co.uk*

A short walk to the seafront at Aldeburgh (home to Benjamin Britten (1913-76), the festival he founded here in 1948 and his close collaborator on it, W. H. Auden) and a five-minute drive to the beautiful boating lake overlooked by the famous House in the Clouds at Thorpeness, this five-bed house is perfect for a mini-break with friends or your extended family. We stayed here with two other couples and their children (12 of us in all) and it never felt crowded. There is a toy room that had board games for our youngsters to spread the counters and dice from all over the house, a driveway with a sturdy garage door is perfect for a game of 21-and-up,

and there is a lovely dining room for you to sit down at in the evening after a few drinks and go over once again who actually did best following the mass swoop on the Thorpeness boot fair that morning. (Not me – rusty pedal bin: £1.50). Southwold pier isn't too far away, Snape Maltings down the road is worth a snoop and you can hire rowing boats at the Meare boating lake in Thorpeness (£12 for half an hour).

Rates £800–£1700 per week. Three nights start from £600–£900. *Amenities* oven, dishwasher, microwave, parking. **Credit Cards** MC and V.

MODERATE

Black Lion Hotel ★

The Green, Long Melford, Suffolk,
📞 *01787 312356, www.blacklion hotel.net*

On the way to this hotel, after getting lost thanks to Jane, the voice of our brand new Tom Tom, I made the mistake of losing my temper at the wheel and shouting: 'It was bad enough having one person who can't direct. Now we've got two'. This small countryside hotel has a toy box for children and three rocking horses our daughter rode on for almost the whole hour it took for me to make up with my wife. Famous guests have included Jamie Oliver, Delia Smith and Michael Aspel. The best bet for families is the Chianti Suite (one double room and another bedroom with bunk beds). There is a children's menu for evening meals, highchairs and the food is locally sourced.

Rates Chianti family suite with separate bunked room from £168 (every child under 10 £36 on top of this). *Amenities* free wifi, travel cots. *In Room* TV with video recorder and selection of tapes. *Credit cards* all accepted.

Elm Farm Cottages

Elm Farm, Hubberts Bridge, Boston, Lincolnshire, ☏ 01205 290840, www.elmfarmcottages.co.uk

About 3km outside the town of Boston, attached to a farm producing Marks & Spencer's potatoes, there are eight self-catering cottages here set next to a wild flower meadow for children to play in. We slept in Ash Cottage – a converted cart hovel – that had two bedrooms, a kitchen–living room area and an outdoor picnic table. Half-price entry to the nearby National Parrot Sanctuary came with the stay.

Rates £340–£500 per week. *Amenities* microwave, fridge freezer, TV and DVD player, highchairs, oven. *Credit Cards* all except AX.

Black Lion Hotel, Long Melford

Sprowston Manor Marriott

Wroxham Road, Norwich, ☏ 01603 410871, www.marriottsprowstonmanor.co.uk

You cannot stay in a hotel in Norwich without at least once imitating spoof chat-show host Alan Partridge. Perhaps then it was as a punishment for shouting en masse as a family in the echoey swimming pool 'ahhhhhhhha' that we were given the hottest hotel room I have ever slept in. Partly our fault that we didn't see (the telltale there's been trouble in here before) three fans in the hotel wardrobe. Minus the heat, the rooms were what you'd expect of a business-oriented hotel. The staff, great with the children, were some of the most helpful we came across. Nearby family attractions include Bewilderwood (a curious treehouse adventure), Wroxham Barns (farmyard Experience), Pleasurewood Hills and Dinosaur Adventure Park, plus Norfolk Ski Club, horse riding and sailing/kayaking.

Rates £138 B&B. *Amenities* spa, pool, fitness centre, golf course, parking. *In*

Room phone, TV, tea and coffee making. *Credit Cards* all except Solo.

The Cambridge Belfry

Cambourne, Cambridgeshire, ☏ 01954 714600, www.qhotels.co.uk

Our children fed swans close to a small lake outside the breakfast room at this friendly hotel where the manager not only got our Bebetel baby alarm to work but showed no outward sign of annoyance when, for the fifth time in as many hours, we erased the magnetic strip of our room key and called him to let us in. At dinner children are given colouring-in books and pens and ours were served a very clever dessert consisting of fruit (making us happy) in chocolate (making them happy).

Rates £90–£120 per room B&B (the second room for children if you have two interconnecting is half price). *Amenities* swimming pool, spa, steam room and sauna, parking. *In Room* TV, phone, an hour's free wifi, tea and coffee making, free toiletries. *Credit Cards* all accepted.

Titchwell Manor Hotel ★★

Titchwell, Near Brancaster, Kings Lynn, ☏ 01485 10221, www.titchwellmanor.com

If Apple, or Google, ran a hotel it would be like this one. Some hotels get it absolutely right. The right amount of attention, the right level of warmth, efficiency, professional distance. The right surroundings, the right staff and the right attitude to you and your children. The hotel, close to Brancaster beach, has a fine restaurant (highchairs, children's

menu) that serves fantastic food quickly enough to stave off children's tantrums. Baby monitors are provided and the rooms are comfy and homely.

Rates family room (double and two single beds) from £170. Suite from £240. *Amenities* wifi in the bar, walled garden. *In Room* TV, phone, cot. *Credit Cards* all accepted.

INEXPENSIVE

202 West Parade Guesthouse ★

202 West Parade, Lincoln, ☏ 07767 497189, www.202guesthouse.co.uk

I was in a fragile state of health when we checked in here and I couldn't have been better looked after if I'd been paraded into breakfast in a sedan chair to be gently fanned with ostrich feathers. There is a family suite with a twin and a single room, although this was already booked out, so staff kindly rejigged the entire guesthouse to enable our children to sleep in the TV lounge while we slept uninterrupted (apart from my long stories about my hospital stay the night before) upstairs in a double room. The guesthouse was so full we ate our full English breakfast the next morning outside in the garden, my daughter ferrying various twigs and clumps of mud to me that 'are for your kidney stones, OK, dad'. Nearby in the city, there's The Cheese Society, a great place to lunch and The Dog & Bone, CAMRA pub of the year 2009, with a secluded pub garden and unusually no televisions, pool tables, jukeboxes or gaming machines.

Rates £60 per night B&B. **Amenities** garden for children to play in. **In Room** tea and coffee making, wifi, TV. **Credit cards** cash and cheques only.

FAMILY-FRIENDLY DINING

EXPENSIVE

Ickworth Hotel

Horringer, Bury St Edmonds, Suffolk, 📞 *01284 735350, www.ickworth hotel.co.uk*

A beautiful country-house hotel with a restaurant providing a free (if not too busy) crèche (maximum stay two hours) as well as PlayStations for older children unable to withstand adult family chatter between courses. There is a Fairy Garden for toddlers with slides and swings and a lawn for games of football. Diners are also able to use the hotel's swimming pool and trampoline. The food is classic English cooked with fresh ingredients.

Open daily 6pm–8.30pm. **Main Course** £15–£20. **Amenities** highchairs, baby-changing, children's menu. **Credit Cards** all except DC.

MODERATE

Ask ★

9-10 St Johns Street, Stamford, 📞 *01780 765455*

Children are given special napkin-land activity packs with colouring-in sheets and pens, although they may still prefer to run around the restaurant growling at other diners pretending to be Shere Khan from *The Jungle Book* while insisting their oblivious younger brother quietly eating his pizza is Baloo. Staff are friendly, the restaurant is smart and trendy and the only two small snags are parking in the centre of Stamford and an existential crisis triggered after unexpectedly seeing an old journalist colleague pop up out of nowhere reporting on CNN Live on our hotel TV before leaving for dinner. 'He's out there with a field camera reporting on the Columbian drug wars in a flak-jacket while I'm holding this Noddy car about to check the toilets for a baby-change mat. And I got better marks than him in the news reporting module'.

Open Mon–Fri, Sun 12pm–11pm, Sat 12pm–11.30pm. **Main Course** £5.95–£10. **Amenities** highchairs, baby-changing. **Credit Cards** all accepted.

The Lemon Tree ★

48 St John's Street, Colchester, 📞 *01206 765387, www.the-lemon-tree.com*

A smart restaurant where our children were served quickly, given drawing paper and pens and there was no fuss when our son's glass of water was accidentally/deliberately, with the cry of 'No. I finished', pushed to the floor and smashed. We ate on a small terrace at the front of the restaurant and the pasta sauce went down well with our youngsters. While in Colchester check out The Town to Sea Trail, a short, two and a half mile, journey from Colchester's town centre through to the historic part of Hythe. Other top attractions include Rollerworld's massive rollerskating rink, IndieKart's go-cart track, the Natural History Museum, Colchester Zoo and the East Anglian Railway Museum. (*www.visitcolchester.com*).

Open Mon–Sat 10am–10pm. **Main Course** £6–£15. **Amenities** highchairs, baby-changing, children's menu. **Credit Cards** all accepted.

The Lord Nelson ★★

Walsingham Road, Burnham Thorpe, Kings Lynn, Norfolk, ☎ *01328 738241, www.nelsonslocal.co.uk*

We suggest immediately on arrival here that you sit in the high-backed settle that was Lord Nelson's (see box) favourite drinking spot, push one arm under your jacket and say, in a dying swoon, 'Thank God I did my duty'. Once this is out of the way you can retire to the garden where there is an adventure playground for children to clamber around. There is no bar in this great little pub and instead you order your pub grub direct from the taproom. After you have been warned not to buy any more Nelson's Blood (a delicious unique rum-based concoction) you can hand your wife the car keys, and on the way back to the hotel, slumped in the passenger seat, tell her all about the political significance of the English defeat of the French at the Battle of Trafalgar that you read about on the pub wall.

Open Mon 12pm–2.30pm, Tues–Sun 12pm–2.30pm, 6pm–9pm. **Main Course** £8–£15. **Amenities** highchairs, booster seats, baby-changing, children's menu, colouring-in books and pens, toys. **Credit Cards** all except DC.

The Wheatsheaf Inn

45 Chapel Street, Exning, Newmarket, ☎ *01638 577237, www.wheatsheafexning.co.uk*

We had been told there were so many horses in Newmarket that there were more vets than doctors and that pelican crossings were set at an elevated height for mounted jockeys to press. We half expected the high street to look like something out of the Wild West, but a 10-minute cruise up and down turned up absolutely nothing equine except some larger-than-normal teeth in the mouth of a woman outside Curry's, so we came here. The pub was one of the most geared up for children we encountered, with a playground outside, and inside, a selection of toys including a chalkboard. They have children's menus and also do smaller portions for half the price of adult versions. Newmarket itself is a good base to explore surrounding family attractions including the National Horse Racing Museum (*www.newmarket.org.uk*), the city of Ely and two good festivals for all ages: Cambridge Folk Festival (late July) and Ely Folk Weekend (start July). Cambridge Folk Festival is a laid back affair with ceilidhs for children, music workshops and tons of cool stuff for youngsters and teenagers alike.

Open Mon–Fri 11am–2.30pm, all day at weekends. **Main Course** £10–£15. **Amenities** highchairs, plastic cutlery and cups for children, toys, children's menus. **Credit Cards** V, MC and Maestro.

FUN FACT ▶ Valiant Young Man ◀

Lord Nelson lived down the road from The Lord Nelson pub in the parsonage and legend has it he'd come here to drown his sorrows between ship commands. The day before he took charge of *The Agamemnon* he treated the entire village to a meal save one boy too young to take part, who was mercilessly teased by other villagers for his exclusion. He got into a fight and Nelson so admired his pluck that he called him a valiant young man. The boy was promptly rechristened Valiant in All Souls Church.

Boardwalk Restaurant ★

Southwold Pier, North Parade, Southwold, 📞 01502 722105, www. southwold.pier.co.uk

The original Southwold Pier was built as a landing stage for the Belle steamships that travelled from London Bridge. Rebuilt in 2001, it is now surely the only pier in England where you can buy a Roquefort salad, attend a Farmer's Market and watch an ironic Punch and Judy show. Our children were given books to read and sea-themed colouring-in sheets to work on while my wife and I discussed excitedly actress Juliet Stephenson, who we'd spotted thorough the window. You must visit the Under the Pier Show arcade afterwards where hand-built machines include, I kid you not, the auto-frisk robot, where my wife was so expertly felt she broke into a £5 note in the Mermaid toy shop to go back for more.

Open summer 10am–8.30pm, winter 10am–4pm. Main Course £8. Amenities highchairs, children's menu, baby-changing. Credit Cards all except AX.

Essex Rose Tea House ★

High Street, Dedham, 📞 01206 323101, www.trooms.com

Nevermind the Met Bar, this tea shop is where it's at. Celebrities who have hung out here amongst the cream teas and Tiptree jams include Sting, Griff Rhys-Jones, Dave Hill from Slade and Frank Lampard who pops in for a tuna jacket potato with no tomatoes (he doesn't like tomatoes – you heard it here first). Staff in the tearooms, set in a half-timbered 15th-century building with rustic wonky floorboards, handed out pens and paper for our children to

The Lord Nelson, Burnham Thorpe

93

draw on. They serve light lunches like lasagne and sandwiches, with half-portions at half-price for children. Order some Little Scarlet jam with your scones and they'll tell you it's the condiment of choice of James Bond. 'Do you expect me to talk, Blofield? No, Mr Bond, I expect you to order your favourite preserve'.

Open summer 10am–5.30pm, winter until 4.30pm. **Main Course** £4–£6.50. **Amenities** highchairs. **Credit Cards** all except AX and DC.

The Farmers Arms Inn

Grimston Road, Kings Lynn 01553 676220, www.thefarmersarmsinn. co.uk

Brisk service, no-nonsense fish finger and chip options, and paper and pens for the children to draw the Hunstanton Wash Monster (see p 185) on were provided at this friendly pub where they didn't mind having their menu chalkboard knocked over, sat on and the entire day's specials rubbed off by the seat of our son's jeans.

Open Mon–Fri 12pm–9.30pm, Sat until 10pm and Sun until 9pm. **Main Course** £7.50. **Amenities** highchairs, baby-changing, children's menu, parking. **Credit Cards** all except AX.

The Hampton

5 Ashbourne Road, Off London Road, Hampton, Peterborough, 08701 977206, www.brewersfayre.co.uk

After getting lost, we finally arrived at this Beefeater-style chain restaurant close to 9pm. In the fun-factory play area, our daughter rode on Dougal from the *Magic Roundabout* while I had a beer and my wife a glass of wine. The food was served quickly and our daughter got to hug Brewster Bear (a man in a bear costume), there for someone else's birthday. Then my son hugged Brewster bear. Wrung out and exhausted I wanted to hug Brewster bear. So did my wife. Our children were given stickers, crayons and some minisaurus quiz cards. We drove back to the hotel vowing never to eat out again.

Open daily 12pm–10pm. **Main Course** £5.95–£11. **Amenities** children's menu, highchairs, baby-changing. **Credit Cards** all accepted.

5 Shakespeare Country & Heart of England

HEART OF ENGLAND

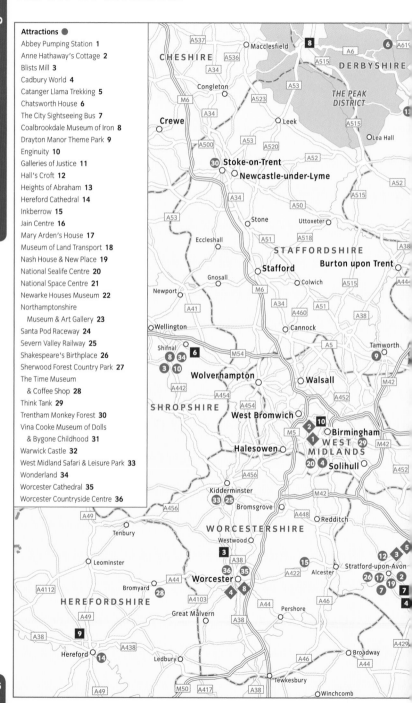

Attractions ●
Abbey Pumping Station **1**
Anne Hathaway's Cottage **2**
Blists Mill **3**
Cadbury World **4**
Catanger Llama Trekking **5**
Chatsworth House **6**
The City Sightseeing Bus **7**
Coalbrookdale Museum of Iron **8**
Drayton Manor Theme Park **9**
Enginuity **10**
Galleries of Justice **11**
Hall's Croft **12**
Heights of Abraham **13**
Hereford Cathedral **14**
Inkberrow **15**
Jain Centre **16**
Mary Arden's House **17**
Museum of Land Transport **18**
Nash House & New Place **19**
National Sealife Centre **20**
National Space Centre **21**
Newarke Houses Museum **22**
Northamptonshire
  Museum & Art Gallery **23**
Santa Pod Raceway **24**
Severn Valley Railway **25**
Shakespeare's Birthplace **26**
Sherwood Forest Country Park **27**
The Time Museum
  & Coffee Shop **28**
Think Tank **29**
Trentham Monkey Forest **30**
Vina Cooke Museum of Dolls
  & Bygone Childhood **31**
Warwick Castle **32**
West Midland Safari & Leisure Park **33**
Wonderland **34**
Worcester Cathedral **35**
Worcester Countryside Centre **36**

Accommodation ■
Belmont House Hotel **1**
City Pads **2**
The Elms **3**
Ettington Park **4**
Hellidon Lakes Golf & Spa Hotel **5**
The Holiday Inn **6**
Macdonald Alveston Manor **7**
The Old Hall Hotel **8**
The Stables **9**
Staying Cool **10**

Dining ◆
Aria **1**
Bank **2**
Hathaway's Tea Room & Bakery **3**
Little Venice **4**
Marlowes **5**
Old Orleans **6**
Pizza Express **7**
The Three Pears **8**
Wagamama **9**
Ye Olde Trip to Jerusalem **10**

OK, we have given this chapter a fancy-sounding name because frankly we were worried if we called it by its real name – the Midlands – then you might skip over it and go straight to the North-West. If you did this, and we realize you might, now we have let you in on our trick, you'd be missing out because the Midlands – basically as the name suggests a huge swathe of England round the country's waist – has much more going for it than a few museums dedicated to the smelting process. For instance, did you know the Midlands' village of Inkberrow is where the radio series *The Archers* is based, that Midlanders play host to the country's National Space Centre in Leicester and that Shakespeare was in fact more or less a Brummie? Other well-kept secrets include the beautiful countryside of Northamptonshire not to mention that of the hugely underrated Worcestershire. There is a unique monkey forest in Trentham and a fabulous cable-car ride in the spa town of Matlock Bath.

That's not to say the whole bashing out of rivets side of things isn't well catered for. It is. In Ironbridge Gorge in Telford there are more than 10 separate attractions dedicated in such detail to the Midlands' pivotal role in the Industrial Revolution and there is actually a whole museum about tar. There are the usual theme parks too, including two that especially appealed to our children – Drayton Manor and the peculiarly fascinating Wonderland in Telford, which is to toddlers what Ironbridge Gorge is to engineering buffs. And while not officially classed as one, the town of Stratford-upon-Avon is effectively, in all but name, a theme park dedicated to William Shakespeare. There are a rash of properties his name was associated with to visit, a bus tour and a river trip on the Avon not to mention the theatres where his works are performed all year around. The big cities here are Birmingham, with its aquarium and Think Tank science museum, Leicester, which in addition to the Space Centre has the quirky Jain Centre as well as the only museum I know of dedicated to our daughter's greatest interest in the world – poo. Coventry meanwhile has the largest transport museum in Europe while Nottingham will bombard you with its many Robin Hood attractions.

CHILDREN'S TOP 10 ATTRACTIONS

❶ **Receive large** choccy hand-outs during a tour of the Cadbury World chocolate factory. See p 105.

❷ **Watch a mediaeval** trebuchet fire 150mph cannon balls at Warwick Castle. See p 102.

❸ **Talk to the lions** in a Brummie accent at West Midland Safari Park. See p 110.

❹ **Wander amongst** costumed characters from the Industrial Revolution occasionally wondering if they actually are in costume because this is Shropshire at Blists Mill museum in Ironbridge Gorge. See p 106.

⑤ Relax in a rainforest shower at magnificent former stately home The Elms, one of the country's most child-friendly hotels. See p 125.

⑥ Learn about wildlife on a trek with llamas from the Catanger herd near Towcester. For older children. See p 113.

⑦ See nursery rhyme characters brought to life at Wonderland fun-park in Telford. See p 111.

⑧ Play at being a doctor at interactive science museum, Think Tank, in Birmingham. See p 110.

⑨ Follow the progress of human waste down a sewage pipe from a Leicester toilet like our poo-gripped daughter at the Abbey Pumping Station in Leicester. See p 115.

⑩ Take a children's assault course to see whether you would make a good astronaut at the National Space Centre in Leicester. See p 118.

STRATFORD-UPON-AVON & AROUND

The home town of William Shakespeare is pretty much a theme park to the bard. A market town full of half-timbered buildings, it attracts four million tourists a year eager to walk in the footsteps of their quill-scratching hero, and shop, sleep and eat at venues with titles like the As You Like It coffee shop and the Twelfth Night guesthouse. The town, easily walkable and alive with costumed street performers forsoothing at the drop of a feathered hat, has scores of family-friendly restaurants and cafés from which to observe foreign-language students leafing through Penguin copies of *Hamlet* and *Macbeth* in oversized cardigans.

Essentials

Getting There

By Train From London (Marylebone) every two hours there are direct trains to Stratford. The journey takes two hours 15 minutes. For more information contact Chiltern Railways (℡ 08456 005 165, *www.chilternrailways. co.uk*). From Birmingham (Snow Hill) there are direct hourly services that take 54 minutes. For more information contact London Midland (℡ 0844 811 01330, *www.londonmidland. com*). From Worcester (Foregate Street) there are London Midland indirect services going every hour that take between two and two and a half hours.

By Bus From London four National Express (℡ 0870 5808080, *www.nationalexpress.co.uk*) coaches leave a day. The journey takes around three and a quarter hours. From Birmingham two buses from the same company leave a day for Stratford-upon-Avon and the journey takes around 45 minutes. The same is true from Manchester although the journey takes four hours.

By Car From London take the M40 towards Oxford and then the A34 to Stratford-upon-Avon.

Visitor Information

Stratford-upon-Avon Tourist Information Centre (☎ *0870 1607930, www.shakeapearecountry. co.uk*) is at Bridgefoot, Stratford-upon-Avon and open Mon–Sat 9am–5pm (Sunday 10am–5pm); Warwick Tourist Information Centre (☎ *01926 492212, www. warwick-uk.co.uk*) is at The Court House, Jury Street, Warwick and open daily 9.30am–4.30pm.

What to See & Do

> **INSIDER TIP** ➤
> Prices are 10 per cent cheaper online.

Anne Hathaway's Cottage
ALL AGES

Cottage Lane, Shottery, ☎ 01789 292100, www.houses.shakpeare. org.uk

A picture-perfect thatched cottage that's home to the 'courting chair' upon which Shakespeare is reputed to have wooed Anne. The house also contains an Elizabethan maze. Be careful crossing the roads with little ones. There are no pavements.

Open *Apr–Oct (and Feb half-term) 9am–5pm and Nov–Mar 10am–4pm.* **Adm** *adults £6, children £6, conc £5, families £15.50.* **Amenities** *parking, garden.* **Credit Cards** *all except DC and AX.*

Hall's Croft ALL AGES

Old Town, Stratford-upon-Avon, ☎ 01789 92107, www.houses. shakpeare.org.uk

The 17th Century home of Shakespeare's eldest daughter, Susanna, and her husband Dr. John Hall. You can see Hall's consulting room, with interesting medical artifacts in the first edition of his medical notes published in 1657. There's also a children's trail.

Open *Apr–Oct (and Feb half-term) 10am–5pm and Nov–Mar 11am–4pm.*

Mary Arden's House ALL AGES

Station Road, Wilmcote, Stratford-upon-Avon, ☎ 01789 293455, www. houses.shakpeare.org.uk

At the former home of Shakespeare's mum, watch sheep being sheared and bread and candles being made. There is a wild flower meadow and a nature trail where children meet rare breeds such as Gloucester Old Spot pigs and can learn something very

Mary Arden's House, Wilmcote

A Shakespeare Pilgrimage

There are five properties owned by the Shakespeare Trust that you must visit. Do not skimp and only go to the Birthplace Museum. Do not think you can whip around Ann Hathaway's Cottage, poke your nose in Mary Arden's House, and then tell everyone you've done Stratford-upon-Avon. Get in there and go to all the attractions; even Hall's Croft, owned by a friend of a friend of Shakespeare's uncle who wasn't really even his uncle but a family friend who once bought a glove from his dad. Best for families is Mary Arden's House and if you must visit only one other, make it the Birthplace Museum. The cheapest way to see the properties is with the Five Houses ticket (adults £15, children £7.50, conc £13, families £39.50) or the Town Houses Ticket, which includes Shakespeare's Birthplace, Nash's House, New Place and Hall's Croft (adults £9, children £4.50, conc £8, families £24).

disgusting about how farmers wipe the bottoms of Cotswold sheep (we know and now so must you too so brace yourself. Because of their thick fur they 'dab').

Open *Apr–Oct (and Feb half-term) 10am–5pm and Nov–March 10am–4pm.* **Adm** *adults £8, children £4, conc £7, families £21.* **Amenities** *parking, café.* **Credit Cards** *all except DC and AX.*

Nash House and New Place
ALL AGES

Chapel Street, Stratford-upon-Avon, 📞 *01789 292325, www.houses. shakpeare.org.uk*

More period costumes.
Open *Apr–Oct (and Feb half-term) 10am–5pm and Nov–Mar 11am–4pm.*

Shakespeare's Birthplace
ALL AGES

Henley Street, Stratford-upon-Avon, 📞 *01789 204016, www.houses. shakpeare.org.uk*

The half-timbered house of the bard has been visited by generations of writers including

Tennyson, Keats, Scott and Dickens but isn't particularly child-friendly and we were nearly turfed out when our son climbed on to Shakespeare's second-best bed. The grounds are home to Shakespeare Aloud events, which see period costumed actors suddenly jumping out of nowhere and launching into Shakespeare plays. These actors will happily pose for snaps and pretend not to mind having their tights wiped with the luminous orange residue from your son's Hipp Organic spaghetti bolognaise.

Open *Apr–Oct (and Feb half-term) 9am–5pm and Nov–Mar 10am–4pm.*

The City Sightseeing Bus ★
ALL AGES

📞 *01789 412680, www.cityseeing. com*

This 12-stop tour of the town includes all the major Shakespeare attractions – the five houses, Holy Trinity Church, where Shakespeare was buried, the grammar school he was educated at as well as a short hop out to the countryside to see Mary Arden's House and Anne Hathaway's Cottage. The buses run every 20 minutes in the summer (every 30 minutes in the winter) and children are given goodie bags containing felt-tips (moderately washable) and a packet of Haribo Starmix sweets so sticky I used one to fasten back on the loose flapping sole of my left trainer. The bus ticket (valid for 24 hours) comes with pre-recorded commentary teaching you all about the bard's life. It can be combined with a boat tour along the River Avon with Bancroft Cruises that lasts about 40 minutes and can be a relaxing end to a fretful day of family sightseeing, or else can take the fretting to new heights as you struggle to control your boisterous one year old who wants to run about/fall overboard and scratch other toddling boat trippers. Our son did, however, make amends – he said his first ever

word on this cruise – duck (admittedly while staring at a swan).

Adm adults £11, children £5.50, conc £9, families (two adults and up to three children) £27. Combined with a boat tour: adults £15, children £8, conc £13, families £36.

Warwick Castle ★★ ALL AGES

Warwick, Warwickshire, 📞 *0870 4422000, www.warwick-castle.co.uk*

Our favourite moment here was either watching a medieval trebuchet fire a huge cannonball into a surprised flock of birds or, our (possibly weird) one year old in the Kingmaker Exhibition lifting his arms up for a cuddle from a not-that-realistic wax model of a long bowman playing a game called Nine Mans Morris. The castle is a fabulous family outing that includes archery and falconry demonstrations all perfectly timed so if you rush between activities alternatively bribing and scolding your children to hurry up, you can still almost miss every single thing. For an extra £2.75 (not for under eights) in

---

FUN FACT ▶ **Shakespeare Facts** ◀

1. No-one knows what the bard looked like.
2. The most hurtful insult used by Shakespeare, who'd clearly never attended a West Ham match, was: 'You Bull's Pizzle'.
3. Shakespeare's family were all illiterate.
4. The bard coined the sexual term, 'The beast with two backs' in his play *Othello*.
5. Many academics don't believe Shakespeare wrote his plays. Theories about the real author have focused on Christopher Marlowe, Ben Jonson, Francis Bacon, Queen Elizabeth I, and an infinite number of monkeys each with their own typewriter.
6. When reading vertically from Shakespeare's original published copy of *Hamlet*, the furthest left-hand side reads 'I am a homosexual' in the last 14 lines of the book.

Inkberrow

You cannot, if you are nearby, miss a chance to visit the village of Inkberrow, famous as the setting for the (unmissable if you are my wife) radio series *The Archers* about everyday country folk who drink a lot of tea and speak more loudly than normal because of the loud birdsong permanently in the background, which has been running since approximately Roman times on Radio 4. To add to the thrill, time your arrival to coincide with the show actually playing on the radio so you can listen to it in the car feeling slightly surreal and that you might suddenly feature in the very episode you are listening to. More fun still is winding down the window and shouting Archerisms at passing locals. They will think you cheery if you bellow any of the following:

'Thinks he can tell me how to run my farm,'

'I've made a nice pot of tea'.

And, 'I see Woolmere cottage is up for sale again'. After this take a little drive to The Old Bull (two-course lunches £8.95). It's where the actors regularly meet up for reunions. Here my wife, before I sedated her and locked her in the roof box for her own safety, thought she saw Flora Linley.

the Ghosts Alive Exhibition actors in period garb will jump out at you when you least (most) expect it shouting chilling words like 'murder,' and 'killed' and 'sir, can you move your bag – we need the thoroughfare clear'.

Open *daily 10am–5pm 3rd Nov–20th Mar, 1st–24th Oct; 10am–6pm 21st Mar–30th Sept, from 25th Oct–2nd*

Warwick Castle

Nov. **Adm** adults £17.95 (off peak £15.95), children (4–16) £10.95 (off peak £10.45). Ghosts Alive an extra £2.75. **Amenities** car park, restaurant (with Annabel Kamel children's meals). **Credit Cards** all accepted.

> **INSIDER TIP** »
> Prices are up to £3.60 per ticket cheaper online.

BIRMINGHAM & AROUND

Springing to prominence during the Industrial Revolution, Birmingham – the city of a 1,000 trades – was where the famous Lunar Society was founded, including among its members pioneers Josiah Wedgwood, who revolutionized tableware, James Watt of steam engine fame, and Noddy Holder, who wore a silly mirrored top hat (not really). Birmingham, however, now prefers to remind visitors that far from being the concrete jungle of common perception it has more canal miles than Venice, more trees than Paris and is home to one of the finest concert halls in the world. Redeveloped, particularly around the Bull Ring, Brindley Place, in the restored canal area, is where most tourists head for, although Cadbury World is worth a look, as is the science museum, Think Tank.

Essentials

Getting There

By Air There are domestic flights from Inverness, Glasgow, Newquay, Belfast and Aberdeen from Birmingham Airport (℡ *0844 576 6000, www.bhx.co.uk*) and international services to more than 100 destinations. Main operators include Ryanair (℡ *0871 2460000, www.ryanair.com*), KLM (℡ *0871 2227474, www.klm.com*), Flybe (℡ *0871 7002000, www.flybe.com*), Lufthansa (℡ *0871 9459747, www.lufthansa.co.uk*) and bmi baby (℡ *0771 2240224, www.bmibaby.com*).

By Train From London Euston to Birmingham (New Street) there are three direct Virgin Trains (℡ *0845 0008000, www.virgintrains.co.uk*) per hour. The journey time is one hour and 24 minutes. From Stoke-on-Trent to Birmingham (New Street) there are two Cross Country trains (℡ *0844 811 0124, www.crosscountrytrains.co.uk*) per hour. The journey lasts 50 minutes.

From Manchester (Piccadilly) there are two Cross Country Trains (℡ *0844 811 0124, www.crosscountrytrains.co.uk*) per hour. The journey lasts an hour and a half.

By Bus Services from National Express (℡ *08705 808080, www.nationalexpress.com*) go from London Victoria's coach Station for Birmingham Digbeth coach station every half-hour to an hour throughout the day. The trip takes two hours and 40 minutes. From Manchester buses from the same company leave throughout the day, the journey taking between two and three hours

By Car Birmingham is two hours from London on the M40.

Visitor Information

There are tourist information centres at The International Convention Centre at the Mall on Broad Street, and at The Atrium, The National Exhibition Centre. They are both on ☎ *0121 2025099*. There is another office at The Rotunda on 150 New Street (☎ *0870 2250127*). The Ironbridge Gorge Tourist Information Centre (☎ *01952 884391*, *www.shropshiretourism.info/ironbridge*) is at The Toll House, Bower Yard.

What to See & Do

Cadbury World ★ ALL AGES

Linden Road, Bournville, Birmingham, ☎ *0845 4503599, www.cadburyworld.co.uk*

Tens of thousands of Aztecs died at the hands of brutal Spanish conquistadors in the 16th century, although on the upside their defeat and extinction as a people led ultimately to the Curly Wurly. There are three attractions at this working chocolate factory, not one of which sadly is a room full of orange-faced ompah-lumpahs. The Cadbury Exhibition tells the story of chocolate from its origins as a cocoa drink favoured by the Aztecs to the present day and includes regular handouts to keep youngsters interested. There are interactive gizmos including a talking hologram of conquistador, Hernán Cortés, speaking in a terribill Sapanish acceent, and the Cadabra Ride – a strange monorail journey through a kingdom of cocoa beans that read newspapers, ski and communicate in high-pitched voices. Elsewhere, expect to see a giant Cadbury chocolate, be rained on by Cadbury chocolate, and have the chance to write your name in Cadbury

Malverns

In this chapter you can visit the beautiful and historic Malvern Hills, once part of the ancient and formidable kingdom of Mercia that lie just west of Worcester, rising suddenly from the Severn Valley and stretching for 14km (9 miles). This tranquil area offers 13km (8 miles) of hiking and trails providing a breathtaking backdrop with immense views, eastward to the Cotswolds and westward to the Wye Valley and the Welsh Mountains. The towns meanwhile are especially famous for their healing waters, refreshing air and beautiful countryside vistas. One great walk begins directly to the south of Great Malvern. As you leave town, you'll see the ruins of an Iron Age fort high on a ridge. This has magnificent views, with the Black Mountains looming to the west. A hike along this ridge, starting at Chase End Hill, with a return trip takes 4.5 hours but the trail is well maintained and you'll have experienced some of the best scenery the Malverns has to offer.
www.malvernhills.gov.uk

chocolate, and in fact become so brainwashed by Cadbury chocolate that when opening a Kit Kat (Nestlé manufactured) for lunch, we were scared a hooter would sound and we'd be swooped on by security men in purple and white uniforms and dunked in a tempering vat. Essence concentrates on the perfection of the Cadbury Dairy Milk bar and the restraint Mr Cadbury showed in not sullying his recipe by adding brick dust. Its highlight is an opportunity to mix chocolate with random sweetie concoctions in a small cup to make your own delicacy.

Open daily 10am–3pm (4pm weekends). **Adm** adults £13.45, children and conc £10.30, under fours free. **Amenities** play-park, parking, baby-changing. **Credit Cards** all except DC and AX.

Ironbridge Gorge World Heritage Site

There are 10 Industrial Revolution-themed museums here (including, I kid you not, the Museum of Tar). The most child-friendly is Blists Mill – a recreation of an industrial street from 100 years ago, thankfully minus the chance of developing TB.

Blists Mill ★ ALL AGES

Coalport Road, Ironbridge, ☎ *01952 884391, www.ironbridge.org.uk*

Children are able to change their real money into shillings and farthings that they can then spend on bonbons at Mrs A. Earps retro sweetshop. Full of older schoolchildren that our three year old was so enthralled with that she rebelliously climbed on a governess cart and began wearing her coat by just the hood. Highlights include trying wooden coffins out for size in the carpenter's shop and hanging about in a 19th-century-style pub (full of costumed actors in 19th-century garb). Our one year old had great fun (and irritated everyone else) infiltrating a Shakespeare play being staged in an impromptu fashion by the Prince Albert players near the stables. In 1986, the Ironbridge Gorge became one of the first group of 7 UK sites awarded UNESCO World Heritage status. The designation as a World Heritage Site recognised the area's unique contribution to the birth of the Industrial Revolution in the 18th century.

Open 10am–5pm Apr–Oct, 10am–4pm Nov–Mar. **Adm** adults £10.50, children £7.50; conc £9.50.

FUN FACT ⟩⟩ **I Should Cocoa** ⟨⟨

The Aztecs first cultivated a cocoa drink. They believed it to be a gift from the god, Quetzalcoatl, who, their legends foretold would return in 1519, unfortunately for them, the exact year that Spanish conquistador Hernán Cortés landed in the New World. It meant that Aztec emperor Montezuma (great name for a chocolate bar) mistook Cortés for Quetzalcoatl (bad name for a chocolate bar), and caved into the Spanish with little resistance.

Blists Mill, Ironbridge

Amenities café. **Credit Cards** all except DC.

INSIDER TIP ≫

If you plan to see more than one museum it is cheaper to buy a Passport ticket. They are valid for 12 months, allowing multiple visits to all museums. Price: adults £14.95, children £9.95, families (two adults and three children) £48. For more information on Ironbridge Gorge Museums: (📞 01952 884391, **www.iron bridge.org.uk**).

And if you have more time:

Enginuity AGES 3 AND UP

Coach Road, Coalbrookdale, Telford, 📞 01952 884391, **www.ironbridge. org.uk**

This is a museum full of distracting and interactive gizmos for children to press the buttons of and then, sometimes frustratingly, move on to press other buttons before the results of pressing the original buttons are known. You can build things from Meccano, manage a large dam and design an environmentally friendly car for the future or build an earthquake proof tower and look at familiar objects with new eyes using the giant X ray machine.

Open daily 10am–5pm. *Adm* adults £6.25, children and conc £5.25. *Amenities* soft-play area. **Credit Cards** all except DC.

And if you are obsessed with steam, cast iron machines and loud clanking noises also try:

Coalbrookdale Museum of Iron ALL AGES

Coalbrookdale, Telford, 📞 01952 884391, **www.ironbridge.org.uk**

It was here in 1709 that Abraham Darby first successfully smelted iron with coke instead of charcoal providing the basis for the Industrial Revolution and many dull school history lessons. It is also here where our daughter, tired now of things not in bright-enough pastel colours, sulked in a whaling pot. Check out the film of Darby with a Brummie accent boasting about his work and coming within an ace surely of using the word 'it were right bostin'.

Open 10am–5pm Apr–Oct, 10am–4pm Nov–Mar. *Adm* adults £5.95, children £4.25, conc £5.45. *Amenities* toilets. *Credit Cards* all except DC.

> **INSIDER TIP**
> The yellow signs directing you here are not very good –follow signs for the Iron Museum and it's a little way past here.

National Sealife Centre ALL AGES

3a Brindley Place, Birmingham,
0121 6403 6777, www.sealife europe.com

There are 60 varied and intriguing displays at this attraction, with plenty of sea curiosities for youngsters to touch and feel in the Discovery pool encounter, plus a soft play area. Older children will be interested in the 'Think Tanks' and many talks such as at the Shark lagoon or getting close with crabs, starfish and anemones. There is even an otter demonstration (about what species they are and how they differ to other species of otter, rather than striking, unruly otters). There are feeding sessions at 11pm, 1pm and at weekends 2pm. Otter feeding is at 11.30am, 1.30pm and 3pm, while sharks get their scram (Thurs and Sat only) at 2pm. In

addition there are seahorses, ray talks, a one-million litre ocean tunnel featuring sharks and the Atlantis Mirror Maze where I bumped my head so many times I came out with a face shaped like a 50 pence piece.

Open daily 10am–4pm (5pm weekends and holidays). *Adm* adults £10.95, children (3–14) £5.95, conc £9.50. There are sometimes discounts if you book online. *Amenities* café, buggy-friendly route. *Credit Cards* all except DC.

Severn Valley Railway ALL AGES

Comberton Hill, Kidderminster,
01299 403816, www.svr.co.uk

On this steam train ride we became concerned (and our daughter delighted) about the affects of global warning on the West Midlands when we spotted elephants and a herd of bison grazing in fields passing by the train window. Just as we were considering ringing John Craven, it was pointed out by a guard that it was the West Midland Safari Park. For the best free view of the wild animals sit in right-hand seats leaving Kidderminster. If you have toddlers the journey time (one hour or so) can be quite long. *Steam Days* magazine isn't a great distraction and waving at old ladies eating gammon on a passing buffet car only quells the boredom for so long. The best bet is to buy colouring-in books and pens beforehand, and failing that, to lie outrageously about what other wild animals you just saw out of the window when your children weren't looking. I

The Severn Valley Railway

got away with a gnu. The Engine House in Highley, further up the line, is a brand-new museum that tells the story of the Severn Valley Railway with lots of interactive gizmos including a surprisingly entertaining exhibit on tapping the stays on a boiler to find the broken ones. There's also dressing up as a mail train man, a frame trolley to (illegally) climb on, a toddler play park, and fun to be had competing to overhear the most boring railway question asked of an SVR volunteer ('So tell me about the vacuum brake system').

Open every weekend, daily May–Sep and during school holidays Feb, Easter and Oct. First train departs Kidderminster 10.25am and leaves Bridgnorth 5pm (3.55pm off peak). Adm Day Rover adults £14, children (4–15) £7, families (two adults and up to four children) £37. Engine House Museum adults £4 (£3 if bought with Day Rover), children £2.50 (£2 with Day Rover), families £12 (£8.50 with Day Rover). Amenities restaurants (with highchairs and children's menus) at Kidderminster and Engine House, baby-changing. Credit Cards all except AX.

Think Tank ★ ALL AGES

Curzon St, Birmingham, ☏ 0121 202 2222, www.thinktank.ac

A science place for children that includes a special toddler area where our daughter treated me in a mocked-up doctor's surgery for a poorly tummy by listening for a heartbeat in my leg and putting a dolly on my head. Four floors of hands-on galleries feature zones on Birmingham's industrial past, medicinal breakthroughs and displays on how the body works. There's also a wildlife room where you can hear the various calls of the urban fox including hunger, fear and, 'yippee, I just found a whole zinger burger in the bin outside Moor Street

Subway'. There is also a planetarium (separate charge, often nothing suitable for youngsters) and an Imax theatre on the floor below, where during the film *Wildlife Safari*, our daughter refused to wear the 3D glasses after a rhino came out of nowhere.

Open daily 10am–5pm. **Adm** Think Tank only adults £9, children (3–15) and conc £7.15, families (two adults, two children) £27.40. Imax £8, children £6.15, families £25.40. Planetarium £1.95. Combined tickets for Think Tank and Imax adults £15.90, children and conc £12, families £48. **Amenities** baby-changing, parking, café. **Credit Cards** all accepted.

West Midland Safari and Leisure Park ★★ ALL AGES

Spring Grove, Bewdley, Worcestershire, 📞 *01299 402114,* **www.wmsp.co.uk**

Before getting to the fantastic Big Game it's worth mentioning the variety here. The park has 30 high adrenalin rides, a Cubs Kingdom with nine attractions for young adventurers, a £1m Wild River Rafting course and an all-weather Discovery Trail with reptiles, seals and creepy crawlies. On the bigger animal side, in my day winding your window down in a safari park meant men in stripy Landrovers with tranquilizer guns all over you issuing dire warnings about maulings, yet here we watched amazed as a llama leant so casually into the driver's side window of the car in front that you'd be forgiven for thinking it was giving the family directions to the Discovery Trail. This is a fantastic safari park

with elephants, rhino, wolves and camels and big cats that has the added bonus of being in Kidderminster. If you're a misguided and daft southern softie, this allows you to use a Brummie accent when doing impressions of the animals for your children. ('Somewhere 'otter would 'ave been noyse, but act-shull-eee its roit bostin in Kidderminster'). That was, of course, a lion. Other highlights here included a giraffe eating a chocolate cracklet from our dashboard, the sea-lion show (1pm and 5pm) and reptile encounters at 12.30pm, 1.30pm and 3.30pm. There's also a climbing wall (£3 for three minutes), face-painting and a fun-park for which you can buy a multi-ride wristband for £9.75.

Giraffe at the West Midland Safari and Leisure Park

Open summer and peak period daily 10am–5pm, off peak 10am–4pm). *Adm* adults £8.99, children (3–16) £7.99, under threes free, conc £1 off. *Amenities* café, shops. *Credit Cards* all except DC.

Wonderland AGES 6 AND UNDER

Telford Town Park, Telford, Shropshire, 📞 *01952 591633, www.wonderlandtelford.com*

Our children had a field day at this toddler heaven, where fairy-tales and nursery rhymes are brought to life though animatronic models, many of whom move their arms about almost exactly like Harry Enfield scousers pleading, 'Cahm down, cahm down'. The dense tree canopy blocking all natural light gives a weird underground alternative-world feel on a summer's day, which made my wife and I go slightly berserk beside the Snow White and the Seven Dwarfs exhibit when *Hi Ho* began screaming so loudly from speakers we stumbled over a security net into a pond that garden gnomes were fishing in. In Winter Wonderland, our daughter, in what proved to be a complicated procedure, wrote a letter in the Mail Room to her favourite Wonderland character that, as we understood from the postal system here, was to be delivered by an elf to a rabbit in the Arctic Room, who would by means unknown grant her wish to make her 'Cinderella, but with lots of sweets'. There are great storytelling sessions at peak times (11am and 2pm), where your children can plug their

Fun at Wonderland, Telford

thumbs in and listen to an in-costume *Red Riding Hood* or *Snow White*. For younger ones, be warned there are a few witch-related alarms notably around Hansel and Gretel's house. Dribble Dragon's Café has a ball pit for youngsters, where you can overhear fraught teachers say wonderful things like this to each other, 'I'm afraid Mrs Clack hasn't risk-assessed the ball pit so they gotter come out'.

Open daily 10.30am–6pm at peak times (Jul–Aug and every weekend in May, Apr, June) and until 4pm all other times except Jan and Feb when the park is closed. *Adm* under twos free all year, peak times adults/children £5.75, off peak £4.95. *Amenities* baby-changing, tea shop, restaurant (with highchairs and children's menus), pushchair/wheelchair access route. *Credit Cards* all cards accepted.

NORTHAMPTON & AROUND

'Car smashes into house. Man saved by sofa'. This was the headline in the *Northampton*

Chronicle and Echo the day we arrived, which from our own days working as newshounds on this very local newspaper demonstrated clearly that very little still happens in Northampton. Claims to fame? It was once the shoe capital of England and Des O'Connor was born here. That said, this area has some of the loveliest countryside in England. There are peaceful places around the Rockingham Forest and the River Nene where you'll see thatch cottages, lakes and woods. At Thrapston Lakes and Titchmarsh Nature Reserve near Aldwincle village, for example, there's around 178 acres of what is now a designated a Site of Special Scientific Interest with more than 120 species of birds and 20 species of butterfly. You can follow this with a walk on the Nene way by the river with views of St. Nicholas Church and the village of Islip.

Essentials

Getting There

By Train There are regular London Midland (📞 *0121 6342040*, *www.londonmidland.com*) services from London Euston to Northampton. The journey takes 54 minutes. From Birmingham International the same company has regular services to Northampton that take 49 minutes. From Manchester take a Virgin (📞 *0845 0008000*, *www.virgintrains.co.uk*) service to Milton Keynes (every 30 minutes) and then change onto a London Midland service onto to Northampton. The journey takes two hours.

By Bus There are regular National Express (📞 *0870 5808080*, *www.nationalexpress.co.uk*) services from London's Victoria coach station. The journey takes about two hours. The same company has a two-a-day service from Birmingham to Northampton that takes one hour and 45 minutes and a five-a-day service from Manchester that takes about five hours

By Car Northampton is about one hour from London on the M1.

Visitor Information

Northampton Tourist Information Centre (📞 *01604 838800* or *01604 838801*), The Guildhall, St Giles Square, Northampton; **Rushden Tourist Information Centre** (📞 *01832 742189*), Newton Road, Rushden, Northamptonshire.

What to See & Do

Catanger Llama Trekking
AGES 4 AND UP

18 High Street, Weston, Near Towcester, 📞 *01295 768676, www.llamatrekking.co.uk*

Llama trekking is not like pony trekking, let's get this out of the way straight away. When you llama trek you do not, as my wife thought we could, ride on top of the llama. You walk with the llama by your side on the end of a rope. Aimed at those aged eight to 88 (under eights not allowed,

89 year olds probably not that interested) the Catanger herd, owned by Mary and David Pryse, numbers almost 80. Trekking requires no previous handling experience, although it's advisable not to be as jumpy as my wife, who panicked she might be savaged (llamas do not savage) if she tugged too hard on the rope and/or accidentally stroked the chin of her llama, Spinach. As part of the trek across fields, down bridleways and through what we can only think to call 'some mud' Mary will point out badger holes, talk about the difference between haylige and silage and make townies feel inadequate for not knowing the difference between wheat and barley. If you're lucky you might see muntjac deer, foxes, hares and hear David back at the paddock tell you about his scary-sounding friend with a fully armed attack helicopter. There are plans for an education centre, and an opportunity to buy itchy-looking/incredibly right-on llama fibre hats for £30.

Half-day trekking (two hours, two adults, two llamas, covering four miles) £85 includes (one 8–12year old child free per adult). Full-day picnic trek (two adults, two llamas, six and half miles, three hours with a picnic break in a log cabin) £150 (one 8–12year old child free per adult). This trek is a lot of fun but only available Apr–Oct. On-farm trek (two llamas, two people, one hour) £50.

Northamptonshire Museum and Art Gallery ALL AGES

Guildhall Road, Northampton, ☎ 01604 838111, www.northampton.gov.uk

Everybody in Northampton knows this as the Shoe Museum although for some reason it is called Northamptonshire Museum and Art Gallery as if Northampton is embarrassed about its shoe past. It should not be. There are 12,000 shoes in this world-famous collection (actually 12,001 – our one year old lost one of his here). The story of the shoe is told wittily from Neolithic times and includes a scary shoe fact about how a Japanese girl fell to her death from a pair of 13cm heels, and more mundanely one about a Spice Girl spraining her ankle in the same fashion, or as I rather wittily put it to my wife, 'I tell you what I want, what I really want …a surgical ankle sock support'. There are activities for children in most rooms and at the end you can make a recording for the Northampton Borough Council's Youth Forum on a videolink TV of your daughter singing 'Cobbler, cobbler mend my shoe, I'll pick it up at half past two'.

Open 10am–5pm Mon–Sat (Sun 2pm–5pm). Adm free. Amenities baby-changing.

Santa Pod Raceway AGES 8 AND UP

Airfield Road, Podington, Wellingborough, ☎ 01234 782828, www.santapod.co.uk

If you don't mind your children possibly being deafened while at the same time enjoy mixing with men in oily boiler suits wearing Throttle in a Bottle T-shirts, eating chip cobs and talking about

Santa Pod Raceway

LEICESTER & AROUND

We lived here for two years during our reporting days on the *Leicester Mercury* and have to say it is not only the friendliest city in the East Midlands (ask for directions and locals call you 'ma duck' and often walk you there) but it has the most to offer families, including an award-winning space centre and more importantly, if you are there, a museum dedicated to poo. The city is also famous for producing the one-time fattest man in the world, the ugliest man in the world, *Elephant Man* John Merrick and the smuggest man in the world ex-England striker, football pundit and crisps thief, Gary Lineker. The first package holiday was devised by Thomas Cook here in 1841 so the locals could escape the fug created by the booming textile industry while famous residents include authors Julian Barnes, Sue Townsend of *Adrian Mole* fame and the singer Englebert Humperdinck. Coventry has the best transport museum in Europe.

torque and nitrous fuel a lot, then the Santa Pod raceway is a great place to spend an afternoon. They have races featuring souped-up cars and monster truck events. We came here, for the Summer Nationals, something we do not fully understand because we could not hear a word anyone said to us for the entire day owing to the revving engines of dragsters and the men in oily overalls shouting loudly things like: 'I lent her too far over'. There is a children's caravan where children complaining of tinnitus can draw pictures of cars with ear muffs (available from the Motor Shack for a fiver) and also some Pod Racer dodgems to work out the aggression you have so far only experienced vicariously watching racing drivers in the stands with your wife's hands over your bleeding ears.

Open check for events. **Adm** Adults £17–£32, under 16s free. **Credit Cards** all except AX.

Essentials

Getting There

By Train Services from East Midland Trains (☎ *08457 125678*, *www.eastmidlandtrains.co.uk*) go from London St Pancras station every 25 minutes. The journey takes one hour and 10 minutes. From Birmingham every hour there are services from Cross Country Trains (☎ 0870 0100084, *www.crosscountrytrains.co.uk*). The journey takes just under an hour. From Manchester take a Virgin (☎ 0845 0008000, *www.virgintrains.co.uk*) service to Nuneaton and change to a Cross Country service onto Leicester. The journey takes one and half hours.

By Bus Around 15 National Express (☎ 0870 5808080, *www.nationalexpress.com*) buses a day leave from London Victoria's coach station to Leicester. The journey time is around two and half hours. From Birmingham the same company has six buses to Leicester a day and the journey is an hour while from Manchester there are around eight services taking three to four hours.

By Car From London take the M1 north to junction 21. The drive takes around two hours.

Visitor Information

Hinckley Tourist Information Centre (☎ 01455 635106), Hinckley Library, Lancaster Road, Hinckley, Leicestershire; Leicester Tourist Information Centre (☎ 0844 8885181), 7/9 Every Street, Town Hall Square, Leicester; Market Harborough Tourist Information Centre (☎ 01858 8282820 Council Offices, Adam and Eve Street, Market Harborough, Leicestershire.

What to See & Do

Abbey Pumping Station ALL AGES

Corporation Road, Leicester, ☎ 0116 2995111, www.leicester.gov.uk

'And now we're going to a museum, Phoebe, where they tell you what happens to poo'. 'Hooray!'

It was here at this station, used in the 19th century to pump Leicester sewerage to a treatment works in Beaumont Leys, that our son was confusingly allowed to put his hand down a toilet without being told off. Meanwhile our daughter watched, enthralled, the progress of poo from a Leicester toilet along a see-through pipe heading to Wanlip sewage works ('Look daddy – there it goes'). It's not just for children either. What self-respecting adult cannot fall hopelessly in love with a museum that informs you matronly that 'The escaping spray from a toilet flush will spread germs over four cubic metres'. Then there's the least likely museum exhibit in England: 'Stand or crouch – how posture assists bowel movement'. There are some beam engines made child-friendly by adding random teddy bears amongst their machinery for children to find.

Open daily 11am–4.30pm Feb–Oct. *Adm* free. *Amenities* toilets, lots of them.

Drayton Manor Theme Park ★
ALL AGES

Drayton Manor, near Tamworth, Staffordshire, ☎ 0844 47221960, www.draytonmanor.co.uk

Basically Alton Towers for toddlers. We spent five hours here in the newly opened Thomas Land trying out the Lady Carousel, the Sodor Classic Car, Berti's Crazy Bus and Crank's Drop Tower. Be warned parents: the Thomas-land gift-shop is so extensive and includes every item of merchandise you can imagine branded with a Thomas face and it will cost you a fortune going near it. In fact, waiting for the Rockin' Bulstrode revolving boat to start up, my wife and I supposed if a tragedy befell the nation and we were swept back to the Stone Age through some apocalyptic accident we could survive comfortably in Thomas Land – we would sleep on Thomas mats, under Thomas duvets, eat Thomas pork chops and occasionally fire out Thomas signal flares to let other mini-communities know we were here. When you need a break from the Thomas theme tune, there is a small zoo, which includes leopards, tigers, reptiles, monkeys and a possibly made-up animal called the Fishing Cat. For older children there are roller-coaster-type rides. Apocalypse is the world's first stand up tower drop, Shockwave is Europe's only stand up roller-coaster, while Maelstrom is the only gyro swing to make you face outwards. If that's not enough, the £3 million G-Force rollercoaster turns at speeds of up to 70 kph at 4.3 G's, whilst hanging by the hip.

Open daily 9.30am–5pm 21st Mar–1st Nov (Thomas Land reopens for the festive season on 28th Nov). The zoo is open all year round. *Adm* adults £25.00, children (4–11) £21.00, seniors £12, conc £19, under fours free, families (four members) £80.00. *Amenities* cafés, parking, highchairs, children's menus. *Credit Cards* all major cards except DC.

Drayton Manor Theme Park

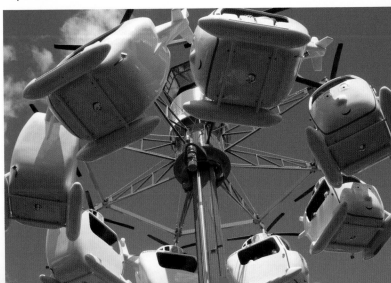

Jain Centre AGES 11 AND UP

32 Oxford Street, Leicester, 📞 *0116 2541150, www.jaincentre.com*

This temple – the most significant of its kind in Europe – doesn't look much on the outside, but inside there are 44 hand-carved sandstone pillars weighing over 250 tons, which took over 100,000 hours to complete. Just off a busy Leicester ring road this place somehow makes you feel you're in a peaceful forest clearing. The tranquillity even permeated our children, who amazingly only whined a little when asked to leave their Quavers behind as food is not allowed in the place of worship. The relaxed attitude to children meant our one year old was only slightly put off the devotees by trying to pull down images of the 16th and 23rd tirthankaras. Dr Ramesh Mehta, who took us around – ring ahead for a personal tour – even took time out to teach us the main tenets of his religion: non-violence (both in word and deed), multiplicity of viewpoint and the careful limiting of your possessions. Buggy-pushers beware: there is no lift. Menstruating women beware – you cannot go upstairs.

Open Mon–Fri 2pm–5pm. Adm free.

Museum of Land Transport ★
ALL AGES

Millennium Place, Hale Street, Coventry, 📞 *024 76234270, www.transport-museum.com*

This is one of the largest museums of its kind in Europe presenting many opportunities to get separated from your family enabling you to sneak back to the stimulator for the Thrust-SSC, the car in which Richard Noble broke the landspeed record in 1997. In fact, it wasn't until my third ride (no children under 1.15m) travelling over the Black Rock Nevada dessert at 750mph that I received the text message from my wife ('I know what you're doing. Get back this minute'). Other highpoints include a display about the Michael Cain movie, *The Italian Job*, which was partly filmed (and not a lot of people know this) near Coventry. Elsewhere in the museum our son had fun crawling into an Anderson shelter until the air raid siren started, while our daughter's highlight was a demonstration by a period-costumed member of staff of various bygone bicycles including a hayfork tricycle from 1880 that she perched on top of. Children get to draw their own cars at a circular table with crayons and there's a lift for buggy-pushers.

Open daily 10am–5pm. Adm free. Amenities café, shop, parent and baby room.

National Space Centre
★ ALL AGES

Exploration Drive, Leicester, 📞 *0116 2610261, www.spacecentre.co.uk*

Full of raucous school parties screaming and pinching each other's bottoms in the darkness of the stellarium room showing a 3D map of the nearest stars to earth, there's interactivity galore here. A bombardment of science facts will frazzle all but the largest young minds although our daughter most enjoyed crawling through a black-hole and emerging not in another space dimension but with wet tights as she'd had 'a little accident, daddy'. There's a Sunshine Theatre for the under fives, where you can marvel at the fact, surrounded by the secrets of the known universe, your children still prefer to play with an alphabet jigsaw. Highlights include operating a Martian rover and a weather studio where children can make their own forecasts. Elsewhere you can make postcards of yourself jumping on the moon and take part in a kind of NASA physical and mental assault course to see what sort of astronaut you'd

National Space Centre, Leicester

make. Entrance includes a show in the Space Theatre narrated by Ewan McGregor.

Open (term-time) Tues–Fri 10am–4pm and Sat–Sun 10am–5pm; (school holidays) Mon–Sun 10am–5pm. *Adm* off peak adults £11.74, children £9.17, families (two adults, two children) £37.19; peak adults £13.70, children £11.74, families £14.03. *Amenities* café, shop, baby-changing, lifts to all floors. *Credit Cards* all except DC.

Newarke Houses Museum
ALL AGES

The Newarke, Leicester, ☎ 0116 2254980, www.leciester.gov.uk

Telling the story of Leicester through the ages, this museum has a collection of Tudor toys for children to play with although is mainly worth visiting to learn about the one-time fattest man in the world, Leicester's Daniel Lambert. Weighing a massive 52st 11lbs Lambert, who died in 1891, was so famous in his day he was introduced to King George III, and mentioned in the works of Dickens, Melville and Thackeray. He became a symbol for the strength of the English during the Napoleonic wars and was so large he'd float down the River Soar with up to six children on his stomach. Here you can see his waistcoat, stockings and a portrait of him by Ben Marshall, although be careful – our amazed daughter set off an alarm trying to get too close to the outsized mementoes of this prodigy of nature.

Open daily Mon–Sat 10am–5pm, Sun 11am–5pm. **Adm** free. **Amenities** baby-changing, gardens.

NOTTINGHAM & AROUND

The city is principally known for its connection to the evil medieval sheriff of Robin Hood fame. Many attractions in the city are geared around him, and the men in Lincoln green he hunted down, with roads, cafés and shops successfully piggy-backing the theme to sell amongst other things gold Robin Hood pens and teddy bears with jointed limbs and detachable tunic and hat (we bought one). Nottingham, which was at the forefront of the Industrial Revolution is, of course, now better known as the gun capital of Britain. In fact from reading about Nottingham we expected to be ducking volleys of machine-gun fire every few minutes and we can only assume from wandering around getting smiled at mainly, that the newspapers have got this wrong or else it all happens at night when parents with small children are safely inside drinking wine and watching box sets.

Essentials

Getting There

By Train There are regular services from East Midland Trains

(📞 08457 125678, *www.eastmidland trains.co.uk*) from London St Pancras. The trip takes one hour and forty-five minutes. The same company operates services every hour to Nottingham. The journey takes one hour 50 minutes From Birmingham New Street there are Cross Country (📞 0844 811 0124, *www.cross countrytrains.co.uk*) services very 15 minutes to Nottingham. The journey takes one hour and 20 minutes.

By Bus There are regular National Express (📞 0870 5808080, *www.nationalexpress. com*) services from London's Victoria coach station. The journey takes about three and half hours. From Birmingham the same company has coaches that take an hour and 20 minutes to Nottingham while from Manchester the trip takes between three and four hours.

By Car The M1 from London runs a few miles west of Nottingham. The best bet into the city from here is the A453. The drive takes between two and two and a half hours.

Visitor Information

Nottingham Tourist Information (📞 08447 75678 or 01159 155330) 1–4 Smithy Row, Nottingham; **Bakewell Tourist Information** (📞 01629 813227), Old Market Hall, Bridge Street, Bakewell, Derbyshire; **Buxton Tourist Information** (📞 01298 25106); The Crescent, Buxton, Derbyshire; **Matlock Bath**

Tourist Information Centre
(📞 *01629 55082*), The Pavilion, Matlock Bath, Derbyshire.

What to See & Do

Chatsworth House ★ ALL AGES
Bakewell, Derbyshire, 📞 *01246 565300, www.chatsworth.org*

Instantly recognizable as the famous setting for many period movies including *Pride and Prejudice* starring Keira Knightley, and more importantly for my wife, Matthew Macfayden, Chatsworth has been owned by the dukes of Devonshire for 450 years. While wives can thrill to memories of Macfayden in tights and even stroke a statue of him towards the end of the tour, there's plenty for normal family members as well. There are extensive art works, four royal thrones and Harry Potter's firebolt broomstick given to the Duke in 2002. Our daughter enjoyed some old baby carriages from the 18th century, and our son had fun breaking free from our arms and attempting to wipe Marmite on the original silk damask of the first duke's state bed. There are beautiful and extensive grounds including a yew maze, while for children there is a farmyard with animal-handling sessions and

an adventure playground with commando wires and a rope walk. Picnic boxes are also available from the farmyard café, where children can make up their own ice cream.

Open daily (house) 11am–5.30pm, (garden) 11am–6pm, farmyard and adventure playground 10.30am–5.30pm. **Adm** *Discovery pass for all attractions: adults £16, children £10, conc £12.40, families £48. House and Gardens: adults £11.50, children £6.25, conc £9.50, families £30. Garden only: adults £7.50, children £4.50, conc £6, families £21. Farmyard and adventure playground; adults £5, children £5.25, conc £4, families £19.50.* **Amenities** *shop, café.* **Credit Cards** *all except AE.*

Galleries of Justice
The Lace Market, Nottingham, 📞 *0115 952 0555, www.galleriesofjustice.org.uk*

During a mock trial with audience participation in the courts where former train robber Buster Edwards was sentenced, we were asked by our role-playing guide in the manner of a judge: "And what is the name of your daughter?"

"Phoebe."

"And what is the name of her teddy?"

"It's not a teddy it's a hitato-pamus," Phoebe whispered to gales of laughter, and a stern rebuke, "Silence in court."

FUN FACT ≫ **Silver Service**

Chatsworth, one of Britain's most famous stately homes, was built in 1694 and included exceptionally lavish royal apartments because the first Duke of Devonshire hoped newly crowned King William and Queen Mary would visit. They never did – instead sending the heartbroken Duke a silver toiletry set.

As well as participating (my wife and I were solicitors) in the trial of an 18th century arsonist all visitors are given tickets with a real former convict's number on it. As you progress through the tour of the courts and the former county jail you become this convict. I was Henry Elliott, here for stealing seven yards of linen and three yards of purple ribbon in 1736, while my wife was transported, quite rightly, to Australia for thieving a shawl. For toddlers there are a few slightly grisly sections along the way - including the recreation of woman burning to death. Although that said our normally quite jumpy daughter didn't bat an eyelid at any of this, and towards the end after the bathhouse tour (where we were all fumigated) even began dancing quite morbidly, we felt, to her own internal medley made up of the sounds of prison doors banging shut and the groans of inmates ("Shall we stop for another little dance here, dad?") Elsewhere my wife cowered at the ghost stories relating to former inmates hung here while our son had fun playing with a sloping-out bucket. You must book performance tours unavailable on Mondays in advance.

Open 15 Mar–10 Sept daily 10.30am–5pm and 11 Sept–14 Mar Mon–Fri 10.30am–7pm (Sat/Sun 11am–5pm). *Adm* Tues–Sat adults £8.75, children/conc £6.80. Mon (audio tours) adults £4.85, children/conc £3.85. *Amenities* shop, safe. *Credit Cards* All except AE.

Heights of Abraham ★ ALL AGES

Matlock Bath, Derbyshire, ☎ 01629 582365, www.heightsofabraham. com

The Heights of Abraham, 1,000 feet above the town of Matlock Bath on Masson Hill, is accessed via an alpine-style cable car fully buggy accessible unless you're my wife, who managed to jam our son's pushchair under a rotating pod causing the entire system to shut down. At the top there are two underground caverns (easiest with a buggy is the Rutland Cavern), although if you have youngsters be warned it gets particularly dark when they turn the lights out to recreate 17th-century mining conditions. Alarmingly, our son disappeared for a moment with the lights down to turn up right next to me, chewing a Haribo sweet. The miners tales are brought to life by a series of animatronics to give a feeling of life underground in the large network of naturally formed caverns and passageways. Tours last about half an hour.

Open daily during Feb half-term 10am–4.30pm, weekends only 28th Feb–14th Mar 10am–4.30pm, daily 14th Mar –30th Sept 10am–5pm (Oct–1st Nov 10am–4.30pm). *Adm* adults £10.80, children (5–15) and conc £7.80, under fives free. *Amenities* café, shop, playground. *Credit Cards* all except AX and DC.

INSIDER TIP ≫

Don't skimp on the pay-and-display car park to access the cable car. We meanly put in £1.50 instead of £2.50 and spent the entire outing having this conversation: 'What's the time?' … '2pm'… 'What time's the next pod?' … 'Ten minutes'…. 'How long did we have on the ticket?' … 'two hours'…. 'What time did we buy it?'

Sherwood Forest Country Park ALL AGES

Edwinstowe, Near Mansfied, ☎ 01623 823202, www.nottinghamshire. gov.uk

Here the Major Oak, the tree that Robin Hood supposedly hid in to escape the Sheriff of Nottingham, is a 20-minute walk from the visitor centre, although more like an hour when you've a one-year-old who's just learnt to walk. The tree, voted Britain's favourite we are not sure by who, is disappointingly fenced off, its major branches supported by scaffolding props. Watch out for the tourists sporting green felt feather-adorned spiky Robin Hood hats having their photos taken here in jaunty outlaw poses. They are available for £1 from the visitor centre, where in an exhibition about Robin Hood, we discovered he preyed on travellers on the great north road (now the A1), was first mentioned in 1261 and that stories about him spread when villagers came together to celebrate May Day. We also learned while walking through a mocked-up forest in a dangerously inaccurate interactive display that it was perfectly safe to eat deadly nightshade. Instead of going 'yuk', the misfiring machine triggered by pressing a picture of deadly nightshade, went 'yum'. The visitor centre is full of semi-boring detail about preserving heathland and managing forests that really needn't concern you unless you're either John Craven or a vole.

Matlock Bath

Built alongside the River Derwent in a steep gorge and created as a spa town in the 19th century, Matlock Bath was once extremely fashionable attracting the then Princess Victoria in 1832 and again in 1844. Other famous visitors included Lord Byron and Mary Shelley, who mentions the town in her novel, *Frankenstein*. The coming of the railway brought in day-trippers so that Matlock Bath developed the inland 'seaside' resort image it still carries today. Nowadays what strikes you about the town is the sheer number of powerful motorbikes parked alongside the quaint tea-shops. Donington Park is nearby and revved-up petrol heads like to risk their lives weaving in and out of traffic on the bendy A6 on their way home, stopping here for a slice a Bakewell tart and to plug a few pound coins into the slot machine arcades before racing home in time for their dinner and *Top Gear*.

Open daily 10am–5pm May–Sept (weekends 5.30pm), 10am–4.30pm Oct–Apr. *Adm* free (£3 parking on weekends Apr–Nov and during school holidays. *Amenities* restaurant with highchairs, baby-changing, children's meals.

Trentham Monkey Forest
ALL AGES

Stone Road, Trentham, Stoke-on-Trent, 📞 01782 659845, *www.trenthamleisure.co.uk*

This 60-acre reserve of 140 monkeys, mainly from Algeria and Morocco, is a fun place to spend a few hours, although be warned, they roam at will among you so keep close to your possessions and your children lest they be kidnapped, assumed into the monkey troupe and taught to come running for melon rind at 15 minutes past every hour. At the Banana Café children's meals are £2.40.

Open 14th Feb–March 10am–4pm, April–17th Jul 10am–5pm, 18th Jul–6th Sept 10am–6pm, 7th Sept–24th Oct 10am–5pm, 25th Oct–15th Nov 10am–4pm, closed 16th Nov–13th Feb. *Adm* adults £6, children (3–14) £4.50, under threes free. *Amenities* baby-changing, café. *Credit Cards* all except DC and AX.

INSIDER TIP »
Baby monkeys are born between May and July.

Vina Cooke Museum of Dolls and Bygone Childhood **ALL AGES**

The Old Rectory, Great North Road, Cromwell, Newark, 📞01636 821364, *www.vinasdolls.co.uk*

Containing the largest collection of dolls anywhere in Britain (3,000), this weird museum is also a doll's hospital and it's worth popping in just to see the eerie workroom. When we visited a large plastic dolly was laid out face down on a lace-draped

The Peak District

To the north of Derbyshire, The Peak District National Park, contains waterfalls, hills, moors, green valleys, and dales. It covers some 1,404 sq. km (542 sq. miles), most of it in Derbyshire, but some spilling over into South Yorkshire and Staffordshire. The park has some 4,000 walking trails that cover some of the most beautiful hill country in England. The southern portion of the park, called White Peak, is filled with limestone hills, tiny villages, old stone walls, and hidden valleys. In the north, called Dark Peak, the scenery changes to rugged moors and deep gullies, best visited in spring when the purple heather comes into bloom. The best place to overnight is Buxton, which also has one of the best walks between villages (Buxton-Bakewell) for older children, the Monsal Trail. Bike hire is also widely available with centres at Ashbourne, Derwent and Parsley Hay. Buxton itself is a beautiful old spa town that once rivalled Bath and now has many elegant 1700s buildings. Sites worth visiting include the large Pavillion Garden and Poole's Cavern (a cave with a natural vaulted roof bedecked with stalactites).
www.peakdistrict.org

dining-room table with both arms detached and an ominous pair of sharp scissors beside her. There are dolls made from all manner of things from many time periods scattered about in a seemingly random order, and if its quiet, the eponymous Vina conducts you around personally, although the place isn't quite as child-friendly as you'd expect with lots of 'don't touch' signs and areas screened off. The scariest room (and maybe the scariest thing in the Midlands) is the not-to-be-missed 'room upstairs' featuring hundreds of dolls all turned to face you as you enter; there is even a ventriloquist's dummy whose head has been known, according to Vina, 'to move of its own accord'. Check out the room containing two letters from Shirley Temple in the 1940s, where I realised I was being referred to by Vina as 'the man' when she thought I was out of earshot. As in, 'the man is asking about the Beatles dolls'. On your way out try not to imagine what a doll museum curator would be like as a Royston Vasey character. 'Silence, dollies. We agreed that would never happen again'. 'I am sorry, you have upset the dollies. You will have to go'.

Open Mar–Oct 10.30am–4.30pm, Mon, Thurs, Sat and Sun (Wed and Fri by appointment). Nov–Feb ring ahead. *Adm* adults £3, children £1.50, conc £2.50. *Amenities* car park. *Credit Cards* cash and cheques only.

THE WELSH BORDER & AROUND

With some wonderful scenery and a sleepy pace of life, Worcestershire is a bit like Cornwall or Devon without the sea. Built around the River Severn,

Vina Cooke Museum of Dolls and Bygone Childhood, Cromwell

Worcester is famous for glove making, wool, porcelain and as the home of the composer Sir Edward Elgar, whose image was recently removed to much angst in the city from the new £20 note and replaced with that of a Scottish financier. Hereford-shire, meanwhile, over the Malvern Hills is dominated by Hereford, based along the banks of the River Wye. The city is slightly old fashioned and down at heel but worth a visit for its famous cathedral and also the strangest museum we visited in England – the Time Museum and Coffee Shop in Bromyard.

Essentials

Getting There

By Train To Worcester (Foregate Street) from London (Paddington) there are direct **First Great Western** (☎ 08457 000125, **www.firstgreatwestern.co.uk**) trains every two hours. The journey takes two and a half hours. From Birmingham (New Street) there are direct services every hour with **London Midland** (☎ 0844 8110133 **www.london midland.com**). The journey takes around 50 minutes. To Hereford there are First Great Western from London (Paddington) every 30 minutes, mostly with a change at Newport. The journey takes around two hours 50 minutes. There are direct **Arriva** trains (☎ 0845 6061660, **www.arrivatrainswales.co.uk**) from Manchester (Piccadilly) that go hourly to Hereford. Journey time is two hours 20 minutes.

From Bristol (Parkway) there are indirect services around every hour, with a change at Newport to Hereford. The journey is one hour 18 minutes. For more information call First Great Western (☎ 08457 000125, **www.firstgreatwestern.co.uk**).

By Bus To Hereford there are three direct buses from London's Victoria coach station. The journey takes about four hours. For more information call National Express (☎ 0870 5808080, **www.nationalexpress.com**). To Worcester, National Express buses leave with roughly the same frequency and the journey time is the same.

By Road From Birmingham to Hereford the quickest route is the M5 south to A4103, which then leads west into the city. From London to Hereford take the M5 to Ledbury or Rompon-Wye then use the A9. Driving to Worcester from London takes about three hours. Take the M5 to junction 7.

Visitor Information

Hereford Tourist Information Centre (☎ 01432 268430 or 01432 260701) is at 1 King Street, Hereford. The **Kington Tourist Information Centre** (☎ 01544 230778) is at 2 Mill Street, Kington, Herefordshire. The Bromyard Tourist Information Centre (☎ 01432 260280 or ☎ 01432 261845) is at The Bromyard Centre, Cruxwell Street, Bromyard. The **Bewdley** Tourist Information Centre (☎ 01299 404740) is at Load Street,

Bewdley, Worcestershire. **The Bromsgrove Tourist Information Centre** (📞 *01527 831809*) is at The Bromsgrove Museum, 26 Birmingham Road, Bromsgrove, Worcestershire. The **Malvern Tourist Information Centre** (📞 *01684 892289* or *01684 862345*) is at 21 Church Street, Malvern, Worcestershire. The **Worcester Tourist Information Centre** (📞 *01905 726311* or *01905 722480*) is at The Guildhall, High Street, Worcester.

Hereford Cathedral ALL AGES

5 College Cloisters, Cathedral Close, Hereford, 📞 *01432 374200, www. herefordvathedral.org*

Claim to fame: here is the Mappa Mundi, a rare and priceless 13th-century medieval map of the world, which my heathen wife thought looked like a Twister board.

Good if you like that kind of thing: the cathedral contains the Chained Library, so named because 1,500 rare antiquated vellum books are chained up like those pens you get in banks so nobody steals them.

Best hiding place: between the north choir aisle and the eastern aisle of the transept behind the tomb of Bishop Aquablanca.

When the children get bored: there is brass rubbing available and a quiz.

Associated with: St Ethelbert, who was beheaded by King Offa of Mercia in 792 because he thought Ethelbert fancied his daughter.

Open 7.30am–6pm. ***Adm*** donation.

The Time Machine Museum and Coffee Shop

★ FIND ALL AGES

The Old Bakery, 12 The Square, Bromyard, Herefordshire, 📞 *01885 488329, www.timemachineuk.com*

This museum is great. Or should we say F.A.B. We were supposed to be visiting the Mappa Mundi, the 13th-century map of the world and treasure of medieval England in Hereford Cathedral but we came here instead because it had *Thunderbirds* puppets in 'realistic studio settings'. Here you can see Captain Scarlet's Spectrum patrol car, and life-size models of R2D2, David Tennant, a Dalek and a six-feet Cyberman. You enter the museum through Tardis double doors, the *Dr Who* theme blarring out, and descend into labyrinth of underground rooms stuffed with sci-fi memorabilia collected over 40 years by two middle-aged owner-brothers,

Elgar statue in front of Hereford Cathedral

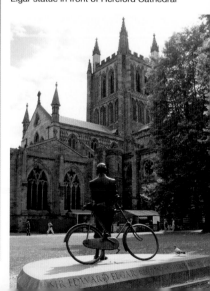

who run a coffee shop on the upper floor. Also in the low-ceilinged museum is a 'sexed doll' from 1860, and a scary looking Armand Marseille bride doll with fangs that made me momemtarily (and unjustifiably) concerned that the owners were evil, had lured us to their basement museum and intended to bolt the Tardis door shut and dress up as Cybermen to torture us. Upstairs we chatted to the brothers in their coffee shop (no highchairs or children's menu) where they were evasive about the BBC contacts that enabled them to acquire a genuine *Dr Who* Dalek.

Open daily 10.30am–5pm Apr–Sept, 11am–4pm Wed–Sun Oct–Mar. **Adm** adults £4.50, children £2.50. **Amenities** coffee shop. **Credit Cards** cash and cheques only.

Worcester Cathedral ALL AGES

8 College Yard, Worcester, 📞 *01905 28854, www.worcestercathedral. co.uk*

Claim to fame: it appears on the reverse of the old £20 note. A Viking was killed and his skin nailed to the church door to ward off future raiders although disappointingly it's not on show, but stored in the by-appointment-only library.
Good if you like that kind of thing: the first performance of Elgar's *Enigma Variations* took place at the cathedral during the 1899 Three Choirs Festival.
Best hiding place: the crypt.
When the children get bored: get them to find an image of a pink giraffe in the cathedral's west window. According to legend when the images were crafted the animal's shape was known but not its colour so they took a (very bad) guess. It's in the bottom right of the two centre panels of stained glass.
Associated with: King John, who famously signed the Magna Carta in 1215 and then died the following year from a 'surfeit of peaches'. Former Prime Minister Sir Stanley Baldwin is also buried here.
Be wary of: the narrow door to the cloisters if you have a huge double buggy. We spent five minutes forcing our way through it and in the crush lost a precious child's shoe. Financial cost £30. Emotional cost: incalculable.

Open 7.30am–6pm. **Adm** free.

Worcester Countryside Centre GREEN ALL AGES

Wildwood Drive, Worcester, 📞 *01905 766943, www.worcestershire. whub.org.uk*

A good place for a woodland ramble, we took a 45-minute trail in Nunnery Wood, a designated local nature reserve of thick ancient semi-natural woodland with cherry, pear and crab apple trees. Outdoor activities include guided bird-watching, fungal forays, orienteering and for the youngsters - a junior rangers club. Pick up an event sheet for details. We saw squirrels, various birds and a foxglove our daughter couldn't grasp wasn't an actual glove.

Worcester Countryside

Open *daily 24 hours, car park 5am–9pm and countryside centre 10am–5pm.* **Adm** *Free.* **Amenities** *café (highchairs, children menus), baby-changing.*

FAMILY-FRIENDLY ACCOMMODATION

EXPENSIVE

The Elms ★★★

Abberley, Worcester, ☎ *01299 896666, www.theelmshotel.co.uk*

Effortlessly welcoming and child-friendly, this beautiful 18th-century hotel was so like arriving at a best friend's house after a long journey, I half expected staff to insist on helping to bath and put our children to bed while I drank a glass of wine downstairs and put my feet up watching *Final Score*. With views on a clear day across Herefordshire, Worcestershire, Shropshire and Powys, and children's toys under the stairs along with a friendly cat and dog, Tickle and George, the idyllic setting makes an Enid Blyton backdrop seem gritty. There is a free children's nursery (the Bear Den) emphasizing creative arts like T-shirt printing, cooking and mask-making. There are ample grounds and in the health club a whacky 'experience shower' that mimics a tropical storm (expect to hear birds, changes in water temperature, lightning effects, thunder, and your wife banging on the door shouting, 'I know you can hear me. I want you to help me feed the children'). Famous guests have included Greg Rusedski and Lee Evans and all the chefs are parents so expect great children's meals.

Rates *family room (sleeping up to four) £295–£395.* **Amenities**

swimming pool, trampoline, tennis courts, croquet lawn, air hockey, Xbox, adventure playground, outside table tennis. *In Room* baby-bottle warmers, sterilizers, baby-listening. *Credit Cards* all except DC.

MODERATE

Belmont House Hotel

De Montfort Street, Leicester, ☎ *0116 2544773, www.belmonthotel.co.uk*

Best for families is the suite with two bedrooms, although be warned, the second one (with bunk beds) is so small we couldn't get our one-year-old's travel cot in it so in the end my wife and I slept in the bunk-beds ourselves. Cherries Restaurant is a good place to eavesdrop on professors from Leicester University discussing students' work and to have an argument with your wife over some excellent fillet of scotch beef and pork with apricot mint and chorizo about who is the most Jainist (me – she sent back a stale bread roll). Children can eat in Jamies' Bar from 6.30pm and at Cherries from 7pm. There are no children's menus but half-portions are available at half-price. Nearby, Leicester's state of the art theatre, designed by world renowned architect Rafael Viñoly is in the heart of the new 'cultural quarter' on Rutland Street. Curve features two auditoria and has children shows such as Peter Pan as well as a strong comedy, dance and theatre programme. (*www.curveonline. co.uk*).

Rates double room £125, family room £140. *Amenities* mini-gym, wifi (but expensive at £9.95 for 24 hours and £5.95 for three hours), free broadband. *In Room* cots, phone, TV. *Credit Cards* all except DC.

Ettington Park ★★

Alderminster, Stratford-upon-Avon, ☎ *0845 077454, www.handpicked hotels.co.uk*

I had been looking forward to luxuriating at this former home of the great Shirley family, where Shakespeare reputedly drew inspiration for his balcony scene in *Romeo and Juliet*, but alas I had to spring from the still-moving car on our arrival to be sick ignominiously behind a tree. It's sometimes not easy to rate a hotel – there's so much to judge: the service, the room, the food and drink, how flexible they are. I have a new rating – how staff handle an ashen-faced guest checking in looking very worse for wear. On this rating system,

Ettington Park Hotel, Stratford-upon-Avon

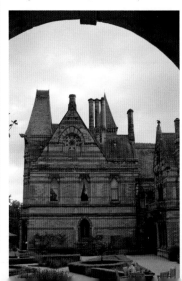

and indeed on any of the others, this hotel does well. I was nursed back to health from my food poisoning through pints of Coca-Cola that Damon the porter brought me, by reading about new jams in *Cotswold Life* magazine and through hearing my three-year old daughter telling room service, 'Daddy ate somefink bad. I am making him feel better by stroking his head' (really just staring at me). The hotel is part of a 40-acre estate, and it is believed the term Toad in the Hole was first coined here (see box). The Neo-Gothic mansion is in a very peaceful spot, just five miles from Stratford-uopn-Avon, in a verdant valley with the River Stour meandering through it.

Rates per night per room £130–£230, interconnecting rooms £260–£280. *Amenities* board games, croquet, tennis, swimming, jogging routes, wellies for walks, bike hire (£15), drying room. *In Room* TV, phone, travel cots, babysitting (through Safe Hands). *Credit Cards* all except DC.

Hellidon Lakes Golf and Spa Hotel

Hellidon, Daventry, Northampton-shire, 01327 262550, *www.qhotels.co.uk*

On the border of Northampton-shire and Warwickshire, you can hook a tee shot on the golf course here and amuse your family with the quip that the ball just landed in another county. The hotel has slightly dated business-style rooms with its own bowling alley that has a special metal frame for youngsters to roll heavy balls down (or drop on their toes as our daughter did because she picked the really heavy 8kg pink one). Children's meals are available, nobody minded when we made lunch rolls from those left at breakfast and if you're coming down for dinner and using a baby monitor, sit near the buffet table overlooking the golf course. It's the only spot with mobile reception. The highlight for our children was finding two baby swans down by Swanson Lake, while ours was the great sunsets at dinner. Children under 14 sharing with parents are free, while children in separate rooms pay half-price and eat for free.

Rates double room £80–£140, a suite with two bedrooms and a lounge £130–£190. *Amenities* highchairs, steam room, Jacuzzi, sauna, two golf courses (nine and 18-holer), walks, swimming pool. *In Room* cots, TV, phone, tea and coffee making. *Credit Cards* all accepted.

Swans at Hellidon Lakes Golf and Spa Hotel

Toad in the Hole was named after an incident in 1859 when workmen found a live toad in a wall cavity. With no access to air or food they concluded the toad had survived in suspended animation since 1740, when work was last carried out on the wall. There is a toad engraving on the outside wall of the library in recognition of the tale.

Macdonald Alveston Manor ★

Clopton Bridge, Stratford-upon-Avon, 📞 *0844 8799138, www.macdonaldhotels.co.uk*

Handily placed for Shakespeare attractions, the first-ever performance of the bard's *Midsummer Night's Dream* was performed under the cedar tree of the grounds here. A deceptively huge hotel with more than 113 rooms, ask for one in the older section of the house. They are closer to the oak-panelled manor bar with its roaring all-year-round log fire. At dinner, you might overhear some wonderful family conversations, our favourite of which was this line from an incensed Lancastrian boy aged nine talking to his mother and father about the tomato bread he'd just been served: 'Tomato in bread. Dad, that's messing bread about'.

Rates double room £119 (B&B) per night. Amenities swimming pool (open to children from 8am to 7pm). In Room TV, phone, tea and coffee making. Credit Cards all accepted.

Staying Cool ★

150 New Street, 📞 *0121 6430815, www.stayingcool.com*

Based on the 20th floor of the Rotunda building next door to the Bull Ring in Birmingham,

we hated the pretentious swank of this apartment at first. Open-plan and thus noisy when the children went to bed, we watched the widescreen telly sat in a designer chair next to a flimsy stylish tripod lamp that Charlie knocked over within seconds of our arrival and it seemed impractical for a family stay. The tap handle in the kitchen fell off and the apartment shook so violently when we had the washing machine on we thought we were in the launch capsule of a space ship preparing for take off. There were trendy design books lying around about modern living and a book called *21 Stories* (the number of floors in the Rotunda) containing this sentence: 'The rotunda has become a constant, sometimes subliminal presence in my life. It lived in the psyche of the city and its innate congenital knowledge…' 'Yeah', we screamed, 'but the curtains are too thin in Charlie's bedroom'. But slowly we started to understand what the fuss was about. We had balcony views overlooking the city. The children loved tearing around the open-plan space. Soon we noticed ourselves conversing about clustered pendant lights and the playful design of Peckham library.

Rates double room apartment £139, two-bed apartment £185–£275. *Amenities* travel cots, tea, coffee, orange for juicer, milk. *Credit Cards* all except DC.

The Stables ★

Canon Pyon, Hereford, ☎ 01432 760022 or 07974 353172, www. hermitholiday.co.uk

A homely cottage set in 12 acres of gardens, visitors can pick raspberries from the kitchen garden while children are invited to feed organic feed pellets to black Welsh mountain sheep (watch out for Betsy). Opposite the former home of the Bishop of Hereford, and with sweeping views towards Hereford, the house has a log fire along with games for children. The cottage with three bedrooms is owned by Ron and Ritsuko, who will cook you a Japanese meal (£24.50 per head, £18.50 for European-style alternative) that even our fussy children ate. The kitchen has a fridge freezer, a microwave and outside there's a very basic games room/shed, where our daughter nearly ripped the baize on a pool table launching her cue at the ball like she was Ray Mears trying to skewer a rockpool fish. The local shop for supplies is in Canon Pyon about 1.5km away.

Rates £100 a night or £395–£640 per week, apartments £80 per night, and £295 per week. *Amenities* 350 acres of woodland. *Credit Cards* cash and cheques only.

City Pads

111 The Ropewalk, Nottingham, ☎ 0870 8507995, www.citypads servicedapartments.co.uk

These apartments, in an old eye hospital, are close to Robin Hood attractions although watch out for the sharp low-level cutlery drawer, which if opened in bare feet will shear off about a centimetre of your foot. With a modern open-plan kitchen and living room (laminate floor, shiny sofas) the apartment has a dishwasher, a washing machine, two bedrooms (one with en suite shower room) and a removable glass top on the coffee table for children to toboggan off the sofa on. The apartment is a few minutes' walk to Tesco Express towards Market Square and Budgens on Derby Road.

Rates one-bed apartment £105 per night, two-bed apartments £135. *Amenities* TV (with Cbeebies), washer-dryer, microwave, oven, dishwasher, car parking (£5 per night). *Credit Cards* all except DC.

The Holiday Inn

St Quentin Gate, Telford, ☎ 01952 527000, www.ichotelgroup.com

A budget option with family perks including free entry to Wonderland (see p 133). Other benefits include 10 per cent off admission prices to Ironbridge Gorge museums, Cadbury World and the West Midland Safari Park. Dinner in the restaurant took a frustratingly long time coming although that said nobody seemed to mind our baby son messily massaging his omelet like he was a coronary specialist trying to restart a heart. The rooms were clean and smart, although slightly on the small side.

Rates *double room £65–£70, inter-connecting room £120.* **Amenities** *swimming pool, gym, sauna, steam room, games room with pool tables and a quiet lounge where, if there are a lot of children, they put on movies, swimming pool (open for children until 8.30pm).* **In Room** *phone, TV, tea and coffee making.* **Credit Cards** *all accepted.*

The Old Hall Hotel

The Square, Buxton, Derbyshire, 📞 *01298 22841, www.oldhallhotel buxton.co.uk*

This hotel claims to be the country's oldest owing to the fact Mary Queen of Scots stayed here in the 16th century under house arrest, which is dubious reasoning that would make Wormword Scrubs the biggest hotel in London. The Old Hall was, however, regularly visited by nobility including the Earl of Leicester and Lord Burghley and at one time was so synonymous as a centre for royal intrigue it was said that the future of England was determined more in Buxton than in London. The hotel has characterful uneven floors to disorientate you when returning to your room from the George Potter bar after a few drinks and possibly the smallest lift in the world, which is so jerky we felt we had been physically thrown upstairs. If you fancy a peak, Mary Queen of Scots stayed in room 26, while if you need to tire

the children out the Pavilion Gardens opposite has two play parks and is home to strange red-billed ducks that nobody knew the name of and which looked, my wife thought 'a bit like dodos, although before you make a fool of me in the guide-book, I DO know the dodo is extinct'.

Rates *double room (B&B) £130, family appartment (two adults, two children) £90 per night, £400 a week.* **Amenities** *car parking (£3 a day), restaurant.* **In Room** *TV, phone, tea and coffee making.* **Credit Cards** *all except DC.*

FAMILY-FRIENDLY DINING

EXPENSIVE

Aria

2 Bridge Street, Birmingham, 📞 *0121 6431234, www.birmingham. regency.hyatt.co.uk*

This is the perfect place on a Sunday for a family-friendly lunch and if your daughter will pipe down for one minute about the removal of the 'horrible tomato bits' from her pizza, a listen to some restful jazz. The restaurant, based at the palatial Hyatt Hotel with Roman pillars and a water feature, has a children's menu although staff will cook pretty much anything and kids get crayons and colouring-in books, while under threes eat free. The food is modern European with some British classics such as the trio of Shropshire lamb, char-grilled cutlets, lamb shoulder boulangere and sautéed sweet breads all sourced from quality, local producers. The service is good and flexible, even when your daughter is throwing a wobbler ordering dessert, 'Can you tell the people that I want lots of chocolate ice cream. Not a little bit this time. A lot'.

Open daily 12pm–2pm and 5.30pm–10.30pm (5.30pm–7.30pm fixed pre-theatre menu). *Main Course* £11.50–£30 (jazz Sundays £21, children £10.50). *Amenities* highchairs, children's menu, baby-changing. *Credit Cards* all accepted.

Bank

4 Brindley Place, Birmingham, ☎ 011 6334466, *www.bankrestaurants. com/birmingham*

Handily placed for the Sealife Centre (see p 108) this place is frequented by Birmingham City and Aston Villa footballers as well as pop stars like Jamelia. The restaurant has a great children's menu serving solid basics like sausage and mash, spaghetti and fish and chips. Affiliated to its more famous sibling in Westminster, London, staff are friendly and the children's menu comes with a colouring-in page and crayons.

Open Mon–Fri 12pm–11pm, Sat 11.30am–11.30pm, Sun 11.30am–10pm. *Main Course* £11–£22. *Amenities* highchairs, baby-changing, children's menu. *Credit Cards* all except DC.

Marlowes ★

Floor, 18 High Street, Stratford-upon-Avon, ☎ 01789 204999, *www. marlowes.biz*

A favourite haunt of Shakespearean actors such as Ben Kinglsey, Vanessa Redgrave and Donald Sinden, this restaurant in a 500-year-old half-timbered building has no children's menu but half-portions of adult choices are available. Colouring-in books and crayons are provided and co-proprietor Diane Carver has been known to double as an impromptu nanny and supervise children's games to give parents time to scare their wives with the poltergeist stories associated with the restaurant.

Open Mon–Thurs 5.30pm–10pm, Fri 5.30pm–10.30pm, Sat 5.30pm–11pm, daily for lunch 12pm– 2.15pm. *Main Course* £10–£17. *Amenities* highchairs. *Credit Cards* all except DC.

MODERATE

Old Orleans

Walter Tull Way, Sixfields, Northampton, ☎ 01604 757536, *www. oldorleans.com*

Children under 12 eat for free here (provided they're with an adult). The portions are generous and you can eat in the jazz, New Orleans (voodoo dominated) section. Children are given a goody bag containing crayons and colouring books. A sneaky treat for parents who have lost an expensive children's shoe in the Northampton Shoe Museum is the cocktail bar. Try the Alligator Cooler.

Open Mon–Sat, 12pm–11pm, Sun 12pm–10.30pm. *Main Course* £7–£14. *Amenities* highchairs, baby-changing, a plastic crocodile on the wall for use in frightening your one year old into eating his homemade fish-fingers. *Credit Cards* all except DC.

Wagamama ★

6 Highcross Lane, Leciester, 📞 *0116 2530046, www.wagamama.com*

A chic but friendly minimalistic-looking Japanese-style restaurant where everyone eats at long benches meaning our daughter got to peer into the bowls of other diners and exclaim in a loud voice: 'Daddy – why's that funny man eating with his fingers. He should use a fork. I use a fork, don't I?' Children's food is served promptly, staff are friendly and youngsters are given colouring-in pads and crayons when they tire of commenting on the chicken katsu the same man is by now consuming more self-consciously.

Open Mon–Sat 12pm–11pm, Sun 12pm–10pm. Main Course £6.50–£12.50. Amenities highchairs, baby-changing, children's menus. Credit Cards all except DC.

Hathaway's Tea Room and Bakery

19 High Street, Stratford-upon-Avon, 📞 *01789 292404*

A quaint spot for a late lunch or a cream tea (£1.65) and, gadzooks, the scones are lovely.

Open Mon–Sat 8.30am–5pm, Sun 9am–5pm. Main Course £6. Amenities highchairs, baby-changing, children's menu. Credit Cards cash and cheques only.

Little Venice

1–3 St Nicholas Street, Worcester, 📞 *01905 76126, www.littlevenice.uk.com*

Specializing in homemade pizzas, pasta and lasagnas, this Italian is a good bet for children who, for £3.25, get a main course and an ice cream plus a chance to shout: 'Hello Mr Chef. Can I have my dinner now please?' into the open kitchen. There are no colouring in books and pens for youngsters but a great little bit of theatre from the frenetic chefs spinning and rolling their specialities to keep everyone amused.

Open daily 12pm–10.30pm. Main Course £7. Amenities highchairs, baby-changing, children's menu. Credit Cards all except DC.

Pizza Express ★

3-5 St Martin's Square, Leicester, 📞 *0116 262 1995, www.pizzaexpress.com*

Children are handed balloons, puzzle books and stickers and our daughter loved her pizza so much here that afterwards she told us on the way home, 'I love pizza, don't I? I would take some pizza to my bed to sleep with me and my teddies but it would get all over the sheets'. Pizza Express is a chain that consistently gets it right for families of all ages.

Open Sun–Thurs 12pm–10pm, Fri- and Sat 12pm–11pm. Main Course £6. Amenities highchairs, baby-changing, children's menus. Credit Cards all except DC.

The Three Pears

Wainwright Way, Warndon, Worcester, 📞 *01905 45140, www.beefeater.co.uk*

This Beefeater provided exactly what we wanted. Before the food

Older Children

Although the incredible imaginations of the under 5s mean they'll get something out of virtually any attraction however dull they seem even if its only a carpet burn playing "I be the snake and you be the person", you'll not get the same leeway with a more savvy 9-year-old. For older pre-teens the most diverting attractions tend to involve those with the highest amount of inter-activity and rides. Good bets for this include Drayton Manor Theme Park, Think Tank and The National Space Centre. Five to ten year-olds like to assert their independence too wherever possible and many of the bigger London attractions (The Natural History Museum and The Science Museum in London, for example) have special age-specific rucksacks its worth looking out for full of games and quizzes that can make your kids feel they are really going it alone.

arrived the children were given goody bags that included a colouring-in competition, balloons to accidentally release in the pay-and-display car park and various stickers, crayons and a special felt tip shaped like a space rocket although I did get in trouble for saying in the car as we left, 'Good ordinary food. That's exactly want I wanted. Just the sort of meal we get at home'.

Open Sun–Thurs 12pm–10pm, Fri–Sat 12pm–11pm. *Main Course* £5.99 if ordered before 6.30pm (£7.99 for two courses). Under fives – a main and dessert for £3.75. *Amenities* highchairs, children's menu, baby-changing. *Credit Cards* all except DC.

Ye Olde Trip to Jerusalem

Brewhouse Yard, Nottingham, ☎ *0115 947 3171, www.triptojerusalem.com*

This, the oldest pub in Britain (AD 1189), was where the Knights Templar (see box, p 78) in King Richard I's day met for a drink and a rest before embarking on the Crusades. The pub, built into the walls of Nottingham Castle, has no children's menu, highchairs or baby-changing and children are actually barred after 7pm but it's just about worth having lunch here to read all the history on the walls.

Open Sun–Fri 11.30am–12am, Sat 10.30am–12am. *Main Course* £6. *Amenities* not really. *Credit Cards* all except DC.

6 The Southwest

SOUTHWEST ENGLAND

Attractions ●
Arthurian Centre **1**
Berkeley Castle **2**
Blue Reef Aquarium **3**
Bristol Zoo Gardens **4**
Brownsea Island **5**
Dinosaur Land & Fossil Museum **6**
The Donkey Sanctuary **7**
The Eden Project **8**
Edward Jenner Birthplace Museum **9**
Flambards Theme Park **10**
FutureWorld@Goonhilly **11**
Glastonbury Abbey **12**
Glastonbury Tor **13**
Gloucester Cathedral **14**
Living Coasts **15**
National Marine Aquarium **16**
Newquay Zoo **17**
Pecorama Gardens & Grotto **18**
Pendennis Castle **19**
Roman Baths & Pump Room **20**
Slimbridge Wetland Centre **21**
SS Great Britain **22**
Sudeley Castle **23**
Tank Museum **24**
Teddy Bear Museum & The
  Museum of Terracotta Warriors **25**
Tintagel Castle **26**
Watermouth Castle **27**
Wookey Hole & Papermill **28**

Accommodation ■
Cheltenham Chase Hotel **1**
The Esplanade Hotel **2**
Falmouth Hotel **3**
The Grand Hotel **4**
Hotel du Vin **5**
Knoll House **6**
Mercure Holland House Hotel & Spa **7**
The Sandy Cove Hotel **8**
Soar Mill Cove Hotel **9**
The St Enodoc **10**
Trehellas Hotel **11**
Waterside Holiday Park **12**

Dining ◆
The Bistro **1**
Dukes **2**
Fowey Hall **3**
Gylly Beach Café Bar **4**
Harbour Restaurant at
  the Red Lion Hotel **5**
Mother Meldrum's Tearoom &
  Restaurant **6**
Old Manor Restaurant **7**
The Regency Tearooms at
  the Jane Austen Centre **8**
Stein's Fish & Chips **9**
Venus Café **10**

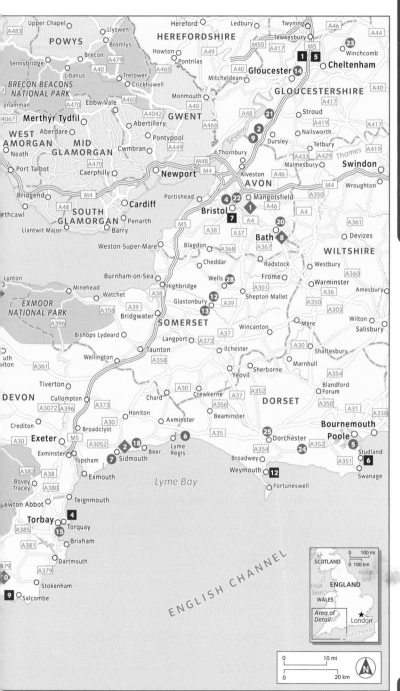

Cornwall, often seen as a backwater by Blackberry-wielding metropoles, is a fiercely proud county shaped like an elephant's trunk, which demonstrates its fierce independence from the rest of the country mainly by voting Lib Dem and getting cross when it's suggested its pasties aren't as good as those from Devon. One of the most beautiful counties in England, it has miles of unspoilt sandy beaches ideal for surfing and sandcastles. While still vying with Devon to be the undisputed king of bucket-and-spade country, over recent years Cornwall has reinvented itself as something of a boutique destination with towns like Rock now popular, with among other others, Princes William and Harry. Next door's Padstow, with its Rick Stein restaurants, attracts discerning gastro-tourists looking for something a little more sophisticated than a well-crimped pasty. The county also abounds in Arthurian folklore and boasts one of the boldest and best-received new large-scale attractions in the country – the homage to the environment that is the quirky, fun but ever-so right-on, Eden Project. Devon, meanwhile, warmed by the Gulf Stream, has the mildest climate in the country, and along with Cornwall the longest hours of sunshine too. The vast area encompasses Dartmoor and boasts majestic cliffs, the English Riviera, centred on Torquay, as well as the historic town of Plymouth with the best aquarium in the country. Dorset, further east along the coast, is forever associated with Enid Blyton, who holidayed and based many of her children's stories on this area dominated by the county's natural harbour at Poole. Dorset, like Devon and Cornwall, is packed with family-friendly attractions that range from tank museums to dinosaur exhibitions. Completely distinct again is the area around the city of Bristol, home to the great engineering feats of the Clifton Suspension Bridge and Isambard Kingdom Brunel's *SS Great Britain*. The time capsule that is Georgian Bath is a short drive from here while elsewhere great days out include visits to Wookey Hole Papermill, Glastonbury Abbey and the Slimbridge Wetland Centre.

CHILDREN'S TOP 10 ATTRACTIONS

❶ **Feel like a traveller** from the 22nd century riding around Futureworld@Goonhilly on a Segway transporter. See p 153.

❷ **Test your gulping** reactions against those of the Australian long-necked turtle at Bristol Zoo Gardens. See p 143.

❸ **Visit Gloucester Cathedral**, where Harry Potter was partly filmed. See p 145.

❹ **Watch a beautiful** sunset at the Esplanade Hotel after a day's surfing on Fistral Beach in Cornwall. See p 168.

❺ **Play deck quoits** on the world's one-time fastest ship, the *SS Great Britain*. See p 148.

6 **Stay in the** St Enodoc Hotel overlooking the beautiful Camel estuary, and have pictures of four-eared cats shown to you at breakfast. See p 166.

7 **Canoe through** the Slimbridge Wetland Centre handling ducklings and feeding birds. See p 147.

8 **Learn about** everyday life 2,000 years ago in the Discovery Centre at the Roman Baths and Pump Room in Bath. See p 146.

9 **Learn to communicate** with naval flags and watch medieval knights jousting at the spectacular Pendennis Castle in Falmouth. See p 154.

10 **Have a slice of** Mrs Bennet's Lemon Drizzle cake in the Regency Tea rooms at the Jane Austen Centre. See p 173.

BRISTOL, BATH & AROUND

Bristol, or Brissle, as it is pronounced in these parts, is famous for many things, including the Clifton Suspension Bridge, as well as being the birthplace of Archibald Leach (Cary Grant) and *all* the members of Bananarama. It is also where the Plimsoll line, Ribena, Tarmac, Wallace and Gromit and Little Britain's Vicky ('I am so not last in this list') Pollard are from. Its main family attractions include the *SS Great Britain* and the zoo gardens, while not far away are the Slimbridge Wetland Centre, Gloucester's famous cathedral as well as the castles at Sudeley and Berkeley and the Edward Jenner Museum. A popular retreat in Georgian times, Bath's chocolate-box beauty hasn't altered much in 200 years, and probably never will with planners so mindful of it they have actually built a shopping centre here with an entire mock Georgian façade and car parking for up to 850 hansom cabs (OK, we made that last bit up). Home to Jane Austen and that 18th-century arbiter of manners, Beau Nash, you can still expect to be tutted at politely here for eating with your elbows on the table. The Roman Baths are its chief draw (although the MacDonald Bath Spa Hotel is not very child-friendly) and within striking distance are the Wookey Hole caves and Glastonbury.

Essentials

Getting There

By Air There are flights from Bristol Airport (📞 *0871 3344344*, *www.bristolairport.co.uk*) to more than 100 national and international destinations including Leeds Bradford, Manchester, Europe, the US and Canada. The Bristol International Flyer express coach service picks up passengers outside the airport up to every 15 minutes, and drops off at Bristol Temple Meads train station, where you can catch a train service into Bath. The complete journey time from Bristol International Airport to Bath is approximately 60 minutes.

By Train There are every-half-hour services from London Paddington to Bristol Parkway from First Great Western (📞 *0845 7000125, www.firstgreatwestern. co.uk*). The journey takes around one hour 45 minutes. From Manchester catch the Cross Country (📞 *0870 0100084, www. crosscountrytrains,co.uk*) service to Bristol Meads, which includes a change at Birmingham New Street. The whole journey takes three and a quarter hours. From Birmingham New Street, using Cross Country trains, it takes one and a half hours to Bristol Temple Meads. To Bath there are also regular services from London Waterloo and Paddington. The journey is around one and a half hours.

By Bus National Express (📞 *08705 808080, www.nationalexpress.com*) has hourly services from London Victoria coach station to Bristol, the trip around two and half hours long. The same company has six services a day from Manchester to Bristol, the journey time around five and a half hours, and seven buses a day from Birmingham, the journey taking about two hours 15 minutes. There are also frequent services to Bath from London Victoria, Heathrow and Gatwick.

First (*www.firstgroup.com*) operate over 500 bus services in the area while Bath is a very compact city so transport isn't really needed to see all the main sights, but there is a hop on/hop off City Sightseeing Bus Tour (*www.bathbuscompany.com*).

By Car To get to Bath from London it is pretty much the M4 the whole way, with a short section on the M32. From the north you will come in on the M5 as you will from the southwest. Bath is a short drive from Bristol on the A4 and then the A36.

Visitor Information

www.visitbath.co.uk is worth a look and the Bath Tourist Information Centre (📞 *0844 8475256*) is at Abbey Chambers, Abbey Churchyard, Bath open Oct–May Mon–Sat 9.30am–5pm (Sun 10am–4pm) and June–Sept Mon–Sat 9.30am–6pm (Sun 10am–4pm). The Cheltenham Tourist Information Centre (📞 *01242 522878, www.visit cheltenham.info*) is at Municipal Offices, 77 Promenade, Cheltenham, Gloucestershire. The Gloucester Tourist Information Centre (📞 *01452 396572* or *01452 396576, www.gloucester.gov.uk/ tourism*) is at 28 Southgate Street, Gloucester and the Bristol Tourist Information Centre (📞 *0906 7112191*) is at the Wildwalk@Bristol, Harbourside, Bristol.

What to See & Do

Berkeley Castle ALL AGES

Berkeley, Gloucestershire, 📞 01453 810332, www.berkeley-castle.com

Tours of this 900-year-old castle tell the story of the unfortunate King Edward II, killed here in a dungeon on the orders of his wife's ambitious lover, Roger

Berkeley Castle

Mortimer. Unpopular because he wasn't as hard as his dad Edward I (Hammer of the Scots) and was gay, the final straw was when he gave his wife Isabella's jewels away to one of his man favourites. Edward II was dispatched with a red-hot poker shoved up his rear. On the more romantic side, Shakespeare's *Midsummer Night's Dream* was written for a Berkeley (the castle's owners) family wedding. For children, there's a brilliant medieval festival of jousting the last two weekends in July. If you want to get active, cycle the castle way which is on National Cycle Network 41 or for a more exotic experience try the Butterfly House here that has 42 species, the world's largest moth plus you can observe the life cycle up-close with displays of caterpillars and chrysalises.

Open Apr–May and Sept–Oct every Sun 11am–5.30pm, May–Aug Sun–Thurs11am–5.30pm. Adm adults £7.50, children (5–16) £4.50, families (two adults, two children) £21. Amenities parking, café. Credit Cards All except AX.

> **INSIDER TIP**
>
> Between Berkeley Castle and the Edward Jenner Museum in the remembrance garden of the graveyard of St Mary's Church, there is a tomb to the last jester in England, The Earl of Suffolk's fool, Dick Pearce, who died in 1727.

Bristol Zoo Gardens
★★ **AGES 11 AND UNDER**

Clifton, Bristol, ☎ 0117 9747399, www.bristolzoo.org.uk

A small, pretty zoo featuring interesting animal talks, it was here my wife revealed if she were to marry a fish it would be the porcupine puffer fish 'for its beautiful blue eyes'. The lemurs are good value, and Twilight World, a darkened area full of nocturnals, was fun until we lost our one year old near the owl monkeys. There's also a gorilla island, a new butterfly forest and

Residents of Bristol Zoo

various interactive gizmos, where you can, for instance, test your gulping reactions against that of a long-necked Australian turtle. For the record if push came to shove, I myself would marry a giant gourami fish.

Open daily 9am–5.30pm (5pm off peak). **Adm** adults £11.36, children (3–14) £7.04, under threes free, conc £9.98. **Amenities** wheelchairs, café. **Credit Cards** All except AX.

Edward Jenner Birthplace Museum ALL AGES

Church La, Berkeley, Gloucester, ☎ 01453 810631, www.jenner museum.com

It was in this house, where Jenner first inoculated against smallpox. Jenner, who had survived smallpox as an eight-year-old boy, was so scared by the experience he spent years researching the disease before he finally found the answer – injecting sufferers with cowpox.

His discovery made him a member of the Royal Society and respected throughout the world (even Napoleon was a fan). The Jenner Museum has become pro-active in promoting a public understanding of immunology, the science underlying Jenner's work and developed from it. It's a fitting way to document and preserve the knowledge of a man who as a boy collected birds' eggs and visited the shores of the River Severn (only a mile to the west of Berkeley) to collect fossils and anything of interest that might have been washed ashore. There is a film about Jenner, who actually injected pox into his own children, that helps put his discovery into child-friendly language, kids explorer bags and a varied programme of talks for children and adults year round. There's also an I-spy trail and tranquil gardens for complicated games of 'I am Mowgli and you are King Louie. You grab me and I escape and mummy comes along and she's Baloo. And Charlie's … what's the snake called again daddy?…'

Open daily 1st Apr–30th Sept, June–Aug 12.30pm–5.30pm (Sun 1pm–5.30pm), closed Mon Apr–May, Sept. Oct 1pm–5.30pm (Sun only). **Adm** adults £4.80, children (5–15) £2.50 and conc £4. **Amenities** parking. **Credit Cards** all except AX and DC.

Glastonbury Abbey ★ ALL AGES

Magdalene Street, Glastonbury, 📞 01458 832267, www.glastonbury abbey.com

The mythical spot at this seventh-century ruined abbey where King Arthur and Queen Guinevere are supposedly buried and Jesus came on his holidays with his Great Uncle Joseph of Arimathea, is a great place to people watch. Hari Krishnas process up and down nearby streets ringing bells, lending a restive backdrop to your observations of the hippies in floaty clothes wandering about humming the lyrics to John Lennon's Number 9 dream. There is a children's trail, and, at the back of the visitor centre, a dig pit to find pottery in. Costumed actors invite youngsters to retrieve swords from lumps of stone to prove they are the rightful King of England, while twice a day there's a re-enactment of Excalibur being pulled from a duck pond behind the abbey.

Open Jan and Dec 10am–4.30pm, Feb 10am–5pm, Mar 9.30am–5.30pm, April, May and Sept 9.30am–6pm, June–Aug 9am–6pm, Oct 9.30am–5pm. Nov 9.30am–4.30pm. **Adm** adults £5, children (5–15) £3, under fives free, conc £4.50, families (two adults, two children) £14.50. **Amenities** ice-cream kiosk, baby-changing. **Credit Cards** all accepted.

Glastonbury Tor AGES 4 AND OVER

For those who haven't had enough legend, there is a shuttle bus (blue – you can't miss it) from the Pay and Display car park at the front of the Abbey (see p 145) to Glastonbury Tor (£2.50 for adults). Do not attempt to drive there. You can't park anywhere near it and police are hot on ticketing those who run the double yellow line gauntlet. The bus ride is about 10 minutes, the walk to the top of the hill about five minutes. The Tor, from the top of which you can see across the counties of Somerset, Wiltshire and Devon, is steep so no buggies. St Michael's church, now no more than ruins, was destroyed by an earthquake in 1275 and is believed (by people probably with enormous beards and bells on their toes) to be the opening to a fairy kingdom. Expect to hear excitable chatter at the top about ley lines from grown men in grey ponytails carrying books with wizardy-style lettering on the front.

Gloucester Cathedral ALL AGES

2 College Green, Gloucester, www.glouceastercathedral.org.uk

Claim to fame: when the cloisters were used during the filming of three Potter movies, they covered the stain glass depicting

Arthurian Legends

Legend has it the boy Jesus together with his great-uncle, Joseph of Arimathea, built Glastonbury's first wattle-and-daub church on a visit to Britain. After the crucifixion of Jesus, Joseph returned bearing the Holy Grail – the cup used by Christ at the Last Supper. When Joseph landed on the island of Avalon, he set foot on Wearyall Hill – just below Glastbury Tor. Exhausted, he dug his staff into the ground and rested. By morning, his staff had taken root – leaving a strange thorn bush – the sacred Glastonbury Thorn. For safe-keeping – as we all do with our most treasured possessions – Joseph then buried the Holy Grail just below the Tor. Shortly after this, a spring, Chalice Well, flowed forth and the water that emerged brought eternal youth to whosoever drank it. Years later, finding the Holy Grail was the purpose behind the quests of King Arthur.

religious scenes with wizard figures with big hats. Henry III, aged only nine, was crowned here with his mum's bracelet as they'd lost the Crown Jewels.

Be wary of: volunteer staff, who have been banned by Warner Bros from conducting Potter tours and answer questions about the teenage magician furtively as if convinced Warner Bros supreme Jeffrey Schlesinger himself will emerge from behind the organ casing with a copyright infringement writ.

Good, if you like that kind of thing: the cathedral has the largest stained glass window in the country, made in 1350.

Best hiding place: behind Edward II's tomb.

When the children get bored: get them to try and find the 40 green men that are dotted about; no-one really knows the provenance of them. There's a quiz too.

Associated with: Edward II (1284–132?), who is buried here. He was murdered at Berkeley Castle (see p 142) for favouring homosexual lovers. It was meant to be a quiet burial but when word got out everybody started flocking to Gloucester feeling tearful about what had happened, a bit like when Princess Diana died. In the end they had to build a special tomb and redesign part of the cathedral to make it appropriately grand.
Open 7.30am–6pm. *Adm* free.

Roman Baths and Pump Room ★ ALL AGES

Abbey Church Yard, Bath, ☎ 01225 477785, www.romanbaths.co.uk

Discovered in Victorian times buried beneath the town when a drain flooded, the wonderfully restored baths – a temple to the Roman God Sulis Minerva – are a spectacular sight that it's tricky enjoying with a one year old strapped to your back in a harness going at your neck with his fingernails because 'I wanna walk'. There is, however, a great children's activity centre where children (banned from travelling in buggies, hence the harness) can learn about the Romans while colouring in characters such as the dimwitted-sounding Flavia, wife of Gaius ('We have two houses in Acquae Sulis and I love beautiful and fashionable things. This is Apulla, my slave'). There is an audio guide pitched at adults and another for children, who are given a trail sheet with stickers, which on completion leads to a certificate they can lose instantly whilst petting a small terrier in the square outside the baths.

Roman Baths and Pump Room

Open Jan–Feb 9.30am–4.30pm, Mar–Jun 9am–5pm, July–Aug 9am–9pm, Sept–Oct 9am–5pm and Nov–Dec 9.30am–4.30pm. Adm adults £11, children (6–16) £7.20, under fives free, conc £9.50, families (two adults, up to four children) £32. Amenities baby-changing, pump-room restaurant. Credit Cards All except AX.

Slimbridge Wetland Centre
⭐ **ALL AGES**

Slimbridge, Gloucester, ☎ 01453 891900, www.wwt.org.uk

Our children handled ducklings and fed wild fowl ('There's some for you, swan. And you, goose. No! You've had yours you naughty, naughty heron') at this nature reserve, which is home to some 30,000 birds. There are flamingo and crane talks, canoe and safari jeep rides and guided one-hour walks through the site at 11am and 2pm. A cinema shows wildlife films and in an arts and crafts room our daughter made a crocodile mask ('Snap, snap I eat your head') to scare her brother with. The observation tower has great views across the River Severn to the Forest of Dean and there is a great children's play park – Welly Boot Land – with an artificial stream running through it that our children attempted fully clothed to swim up like salmons running to their native breeding grounds – except with a lot more telling off.

Open Nov–Mar 9.30am–5pm, Apr–Oct 9.30am–5pm. Adm adults £8.75, children (4–16) £4.80, conc £6.75. Amenities café, parking, buggy and disabled friendly access. Credit Cards All except AX.

Aboard the SS Great Britain

SS Great Britain ★ ALL AGES

Great Western Dockyard, Bristol,
📞 *0117 9260680, www.ssgreat
britain.org*

The one-time fastest ship in the world and the first to be made of iron, Isambard Kingdom Brunel's (see box) *SS Great Britain* sailed more than one million ocean miles before it ended its seafaring days in the Falklands. The ship, whose passengers have included gold diggers, consumptives, magicians, bishops, nuns, an organ grinder, soldiers and the England cricket team, was also where Anthony Trollope wrote his novel *Lady Anna*. The *SS Great Britain*, or Grand Old Lady as it is nicknamed, was returned to Bristol by tug in 1970 to wild jubilation from locals. There is an audio guide (a separate one for children) for your tour of the ship (not buggy friendly), which also includes the chance to

play quoits on the weather deck. In the Dockyard museum there is a children's quiz, and a video about the ship's history.

Open daily Jan, Nov, Dec 10am–4pm, Feb–Mar 10am–4.30pm, Apr–23rd Oct 10am–5.30pm, 24th Oct–31st Oct 10am–4.30pm. **Adm** *adults £10.95, children (5–16) £5.95, under fives free, conc £3.50. families (two adults, up to three children) £30.* **Amenities** *parking, café, baby-changing.* **Credit Cards** *All except AX.*

Sudeley Castle ALL AGES

Winchcombe, Gloucestershire,
📞 *01242 604244 or 01242 602308,*
www.sudeleycastle.co.uk

A former castle of Henry VIII's, where Liz Hurley was married and Catherine Parr buried. For children there's dressing up and woody grounds. Other bonuses include seeing an incisor that once sat in the jawbone of Henry VIII's kindest wife (she let him rest his ulcerated leg on her lap)

Catherine Parr, letters from Robert E. Lee and Andrew Jackson during the American Civil War, paintings by Turner and Van Dyke and some fully dressed models of Henry's VIII's wives left over from a David Starkey documentary. In the café (with highchairs) over a flapjack while you read in the guidebook about all the monarchs who have lived and stayed in this countryside castle – Lady Jane Grey, Charles I and Elizabeth I among them – you can also check out the year round events such as easter egg trails, 'Halloween Happenings', lace making demonstrations and Rose week. There's also a pheasantry and wildfowl area here with a collection of 15 rare and endangered species of birds from around the world. The secret garden is worth a peek, too.

Open daily 10.30am–5pm 30th Mar–1st Nov. **Adm** adults £7.20, children (5–15) £4.20, conc £6.20, families (two adults, two children) £20.80. **Amenities** café, parking. **Credit Cards** All except AX and DC.

Wookey Hole and Papermill AGES 4 AND UP

Wells, Somerset, (*01749 672243,* *www.wookey.co.uk*

The bones of a mammoth were discovered in these caves and if we hadn't been on our metal those of our family might well have joined them. Deep underground, the limestone floors here are wet and slippery, so do yourself a favour and hire one of the lightweight buggies available. We didn't, which meant because our double buggy was too unwieldy for the steps, we had to carry our tantruming toddler (no sleep, dirty nappy) as he bucked and jack-knifed in fury that he wasn't allowed to wander into the blackness of the cave system. Our son's commotion meant the guide asked/suggested/beseeched us, to skip the commentary and go on alone. What followed made *The Poseidon Adventure* seem like a Sunday picnic. Let's just say the nightmare culminated in my holding our one year old in one arm and the heavy

Isambard Kingdom Brunel

Isambard Kingdom Brunel (1806–1859), as well as designing the *SS Great Britain* and the Clifton Suspension Bridge, the longest spanned bridge in the world at the time, was also famous for creating the Great Western Railway. Coming second in a 2002 poll for the greatest Britons, Brunel died aged 53 of a stroke, having slept an average of less than four hours a night his whole life and smoked upwards of 40 cigars a day. Britain's greatest engineer had almost died twice before this – once when he was miraculously rescued from a tunnel collapse digging under the River Thames and another time demonstrating a magic trick for his three children when a half sovereign coin became lodged in his windpipe.

buggy in the other as we crossed a one-person wide bridge over a 20-feet drop into a dark, seemingly bottomless underwater lake, my wife meanwhile holding our daughter, ramping up the pressure chorusing, 'one wriggle and that's it. No more Charlie. Remember Ben. One wriggle and he is gone'. The mammoth bone find is the basis for the dinosaur park afterwards, while in the papermill children get a chance to make a slice of A4 in a shallow tray. There are soft-play areas and a children's show in the Wookey Theatre, where children are dragged up on stage to make a racket with a clown. As we were still traumatized from the caves earlier, we sat catatonically through this, gently dribbling down the fronts of our shirts.

Open *summer Apr–Oct 10am–5pm, winter Nov–Mar 10am–4pm.* **Adm** *adults £15, children (3–14) £10, family (two adults, two children) £45.* **Amenities** *baby-changing, cafés, car park.* **Credit Cards** *All except AX.*

DEVON & CORNWALL

These two counties represent the summer holiday capital of England. In addition to the great beaches, fine food now served in this increasingly sophisticated region, and the chance of seeing Prince Harry in a brandy-coloured striped rugby shirt, there are numerous zoos in Devon and Cornwall as well as animal sanctuaries and aquaria.

The up-to-the minute modern Eden Project is based here, along with numerous theme parks and the Goonhilly attraction in Helston, where you get the chance to ride a futuristic Segway transporter.

Essentials

Getting There

The huge majority of holidaymakers to Devon and Cornwall come by car but for train and bus information within these two counties contact Traveline (📞 *0871 2002233*, *www.traveline.org.uk*).

By Car During the busy holiday season driving to and from the southwest via the M5 and A303 can be hell on wheels. Once you're off the A roads the pace of life slows with B roads and some A roads having long single-lane stretches.

By Train London and Southeast: First Great Western Trains (📞 *08457 000125*, *www.firstgreatwestern.co.uk*) have services to the Southwest from South Wales and the South of England from among others Bristol (Temple Meads and Parkway), Swindon, Reading and London. Southwest Trains (📞 *08456 000650*, *www.southwesttrains.co.uk*) have services from Brighton, Southampton, Guilford and Bournemouth as well as from London Waterloo.

Virgin Cross-Country Trains (📞 *08457 222333*, *www.virgintrains.co.uk*) have services to the Southwest from Derby, York,

Newcastle, Edinburgh and Glasgow.

By Bus National Express (📞 08705 808080, *www.nationalexpress.com*) has a network of services between major towns across the country. For bus rides within Devon, Stagecoach (*www.stagecoachbus. com/devon*) has services mainly originating from Exeter to Axminster, Tiverton, South Molton, Dartmouth, Torbay, Plymouth and Barnstaple. First (*www.first group.com*) provide services to the North Devon coast.

By Air Exeter Airport (📞 0871 80990, *www.exter-airport.co.uk*) has internal flights to among others Aberdeen, Belfast City, Dublin, Edinburgh, Glasgow, Guernsey, Jersey, Leeds Bradford, Manchester, Newcastle, Norwich and international flights to over a dozen destinations including Spain, Portugal, France and Italy. Its main operator is Flybe (📞 0871 5226100, *www.flybe.com*).

The main domestic operator at Plymouth Airport (📞 01752 204090, *www.plymouthairport. com*) is Air South West (📞 0870 241 820, *www.airsouthwest.com*). It has internal flights to Bristol, Jersey, Leeds Bradford, London (Gatwick) and Manchester.

At Newquay Airport (📞 01637 860600, *www.newquaycornwall. com*) Air South West (📞 0870 241 820, *www.airsouthwest.com*) has flights to among other destinations Bristol, Leeds Bradford, London (Gatwick) and Manchester.

Visitor Information: Cornwall

Useful sites include North Cornwall Tourism's *www.visitcornwall. com*, *www.visit-westcornwall.com*, *www.landsendarea.co.uk* and *www.thelizard.co.uk*. While *Coast Lines and Countryside News* (a free annual paper) has good tips. *King Harry's Cornwall Guidebook* published annually is a useful source about the Falmouth area.

Information centres are found at: Fowey, South Street (📞 01726 833616, *www.fowey.co.uk*); Looe, The Guildhall, East Looe (📞 01503 262072, *www.caradon.gov.uk*); Bodmin, Shire Hall (📞 01288 354240, *www.bodminlive.com*); Boscastle, Cobweb Car Park (📞 01840 250010, *www.visitboscastle andtintagel.com*; Bude, The Crescent (📞 01288 354240, *www.visit bude.info*); Padstow, North Quay (📞 01841 533449, *www.padstowlive. com*); Tintagel, Bossiney Road (📞 01840 779084, *www.visitboscastle andtintagel.com*); Wadebridge, Town Hall (📞 01208 813715, *www. visitwadebridge.com*); Falmouth, Markey Strand, Prince of Wales Pier (📞 01326 312300, *www.acornish river.co.uk*).

What to See & Do in Cornwall

Arthurian Centre ALL AGES

Slaughterbridge, Camelford, 📞 01840 213947, www.arthur-online.co.uk

A short, fairly uninspiring walk under some electricity pylons from the centre (children given a trail sheet) is the site of the sixth-century Camlann battlefield where King Arthur was mortally wounded by Mordred. There isn't much to see apart from a stone that may date to the time of the battle, although our children had fun splashing through muddy puddles, waving the plastic swords we brought them in Tintagel and filling in their activity sheets. More fun is the centre itself, where there is a children's play area, some castle-themed toys and the chance to speak to knowledgeable owner Joe. He informed me my surname was very common in Cornwall, that he knew another Ben Hatch who lived across a nearby field, and that more than likely I was a Celt like King Arthur. This fact led me to refer irritatingly to all Cornish people as 'we' and anything in the county as 'our' for the rest of our time in Cornwall, as in, 'Dinah, have you tried some of our clotted cream?'

Open Easter–late Oct daily 10am–5pm. *Adm* £3, conc £2. Families £8.50. *Amenities* microwave to heat up baby bottles. *Credit Cards* all except AX.

Blue Reef Aquarium ALL AGES

Town Promenade, Newquay, ☎ 01637 878134, www. buereefaquarium. co.uk

A short walk from the beach, the aquarium has a shark tank, a re-created turtle creek, and an area dedicated to predators including jellyfish and the lion fish our son was disappointed wasn't 'roaring, daddy'. There are fish talks and a detailed exhibition about the rescue of a loggerhead turtle. Home to more than 3,000 tropical fish, there are regular feeding sessions here throughout the day as well as shark talks. To see one of the most intelligent inhabitants of the big blue make your way to the Octopus exhibition. These 'Einsteins of the deep' are capable of solving complex puzzles and tests of memory, including unscrewing jam jars to get at the food inside. You can also discover their close cousins the squid, cuttlefish and nautilus. In over 40 naturally themed habitats you'll see some truly bizarre species such as rescued Mud turtles, Mata Mata turtles from Brazil and the endangered Pig-nosed turtle from Australia.

Open 10am–5pm daily. *Adm* adults £8.95, children (3–14) £6.95, conc £7.95, families (two adults, two children) £26. *Amenities* café with high-chairs, baby-changing, baby-food warming, buggy friendly, beach wheelchair hire. *Credit Cards* all except AX.

Flambards Theme Park ALL AGES

Helston, Cornwall, ☎ 01326 573404, www.flambards.co.uk

In Ferdi's Funland, at the largest theme park in Cornwall, I got my own back on our daughter whilst riding on a small bubble car on the Kiddies' Animal Express. In the back as she sat at the wheel I huffed in intimation of her when *I* drive: 'Ooooow. It's takin' a long time. Are we nearly there yet? Put Jungle Book on and press play'. There are lots of toddler rides here although our highlight was the Wonderful World of Gus Honeybun, based around a defunct 1960s' rabbit character from local Southwest

TV rehomed here in a glass box, and still trotting out his woeful wink and low-tech ear waggle. Our one-year-old Charlie, meanwhile, who wore a Hawaiian shirt and shorts all day, which made him look, when he walked, from the rear, like some eccentric ball-busting American called J. Peabody III, enjoyed the pirate ship. There are shoot-'em-up games for older children, a circus and also regular meet and greets with children's TV characters like Shaun the Sheep. Other attractions include a recreated Victorian street and a joke shop where I bought a 99p plastic turd that caused great uproar at breakfast in the Falmouth Hotel a few days later.

Open *4th Apr–21st May daily 10.30am–5pm, 23rd May–31st May daily 10.30am–5.30pm, 1st Jun–19th July daily 10.30am–5pm, 20th July–31st Aug daily 10.15am–5.45pm and 1st Sep–31st Oct daily 10.30am–4.30pm.* **Adm** *adults £16.50, children (3–15) £11.50, conc £11.50.* **Amenities** *café, baby-changing.* **Credit Cards** *all except AX.*

FutureWorld@Goonhilly

★ ALL AGES

Helston, Cornwall, 📞 *0800 679593, www.goonhilly.bt.com*

Telling the story of Cornwall's importance as a communications hub, here you see Britain's first working satellite dish, operate a robot and ride a futuristic Segway machine. The attraction starts with a film narrated by fictitious scientist Eric Dribble, who tells the story of the world's first parabolic satellite entertainingly enough for our baby son to lean so far forward on his bench he fell off it into a pensioner's sandwich box. A bus takes visitors to three futuristic rooms where the highlight is playing with Robin the Robot and the low point is a sanctimonious BT lecture about boiling less water to make a cup of tea. Elsewhere you can make a free international call to anywhere in the world, visit the fastest Internet café in the world (I couldn't get online when we visited), and walk round Arthur, the communication station (not for under fives) where the first satellite pictures were beamed to. I was paranoid I might slip, get my belt buckle caught in the gears and end up wiping *Hollyoaks* from two million homes. There is a play-park for children, free Xboxes for teens to play on and the Segway transporters. Like intuitive motorized bikes that you steer through moving your body weight, as you ride around it helps if you picture you're dressed from head to toe in silver. Children cannot ride them if they are under six stone.

Open *15th Mar–27th Jun daily 10am–5pm, 28th June–5th Sept daily 10am–6pm, 6th Sept–31st Oct daily 10am–5pm, and 1st Nov–14th Mar 11am–4pm.* **Adm** *adults £7.95, children (5–16) £5.50, conc £6.50, families (two adults, two children) £25.* **Amenities** *café, car parking.* **Credit Cards** *all accepted.*

Zebra at Newquay Zoo

Newquay Zoo ★ ALL AGES

Trenance Gardens, Newquay, Cornwall, 📞 *01637 873342, www. newquayzoo.org.uk*

This toddler-friendly zoo has regular animal-encounter sessions with snakes and talks on lemurs, penguins and otters. Children's activities include face-painting, a bouncy castle and an enclosure with piratical themed animals including the giant tortoise, nicknamed 'slow food' by buccaneers who carried them alive on board their ships for future meal times. For 8-11 year olds there's a Penguin Club for those interested in the Zoo, animals and conservation and for 12-16 year olds the Pride Club, which again educates on animal communication, behaviour and conservation. There's also a chance to become a Junior Keeper and work alongside the zoo presenter and keepers where you get souvenirs of photographs and a certificate. Café Lemur has highchairs, children's meals and an outdoor seating area.

Open 1st Apr–30th Sept daily 9.30am–6pm, 1st Oct–31st Mar daily 10am–5pm. Adm winter adults £6.90, children (3–15) £4.70, under threes free, conc £5.80, families (two adults and two children) £19.75; summer adults £10.95, children £8.20, under threes free, conc £8.25, families £32.90. Amenities baby-bottle warming, wheelchairs, café, parking (pay and display £3). Credit Cards all except AX.

Pendennis Castle ★★ ALL AGES

Falmouth, Cornwall, 📞 *01326 316594, www.english-heritage. org.uk*

Built in 1545 by Henry VIII to strengthen England's fortifications in the event of a Spanish invasion, this castle has a marvellous family-friendly Discovery Centre. Telling the story of the castle's strategic importance – it was still in use as a radar-spotting station in World War II – children can have a go at communicating/getting tangled up with flags, and learn how to work a radar. Outside there are cannons to climb on and regular special events including, when we visited, an excellent in-character falconry show ('Thou must subdue yonder bird') as well as a jousting competition between Sir Philippe Grenouille of France and Sir James of England. There are tearooms (with highchairs), where you can embarrass yourself by placing the pretend turd you bought in Flambards Theme Park on the counter as you are paying for the coffee.

Open *1st Apr–30th Jun daily 10am–5pm, 1st Jul–31st Aug daily 10am–6pm, 1st Sept–30th Sept daily 10am–5pm and 1st Oct–31st Mar 10am–4pm.* **Adm** *adults £5.40, children £2.70, conc £4.30, families £13.50.* **Amenities** *baby-changing, café, parking.* **Credit Cards** *all except AX and Solo.*

The Eden Project
★★★ GREEN ALL AGES

Bodelva, Cornwall, ☎ 01726 811911, www.edenproject.com

Looking more like a *Star Trek* backdrop with futuristic golf-ball shaped biomes full of plants from all over the world, our children had a great afternoon here flouting every conceived notion of health and safety constructing a huge shanty town with hundreds of other families from wooden posts, bamboo poles, carpet tubing and rags during a den-building day. Other children's activities include kite and flag-making as well as hand-printing. There is a land-train for the less mobile, a zip-wire over the entire former clay pit site, although be warned – some of the biomes are tropical and can be very humid, meaning your children might emerge from behind a banana tree like feral animals suddenly totally naked complaining, 'I was itchy and hot and I want to run about like this

The Eden Project

please', having thrown their clothes in a river. One more warning, as well as oldsters sniffing plants and declaring 'I think this is hibiscus, Daphne', there are also plenty here from the we're-more-right-on-than-you brigade sipping Fairtrade coffees, flicking through their copies of *The Green Food Bible* who, when you accidentally drop a packet of cheese-and-onion crisps near the land-train, will stare at you like you've just detonated a cluster bomb on an orphanage.

Open *23rd Feb–29th Mar daily 9.30am–4.30pm, 30th Mar–Oct daily 9.30am–6pm.* **Adm** *adults £16, children (under 16) £5, under fives free, conc £11, families (two adults and up to three children) £38. Entry tickets valid for the entire year.* **Amenities** *café, parking, baby-changing, microwaves to heat baby food and bottles.* **Credit Cards** *all accepted.*

Tintagel Castle AGES 4 AND UP

Tintagel, Cornwall, 📞 *01840 770328,* **www.english-heritage.org.uk**

A cave on the beach below is, according to legend, Merlin's home, while the castle above was where King Arthur was conceived. To get here, however, is an Arthurian quest in itself. You must park in the town's Pay and Display, walk past all the Arthur-dominated retail outlets, resisting the urge to open your wallet in Merlin Gifts and Confectionary or Camelot Amusements, to get to a spot behind Wootons Country Hotel, where Landrover taxis operate (adults £1.50, children

Walk up to Tintagel Castle

75p, under threes free) Easter–Oct until 6pm daily. The taxis save you a 30-minute walk but you still need the strength to marshal two under-fives up the hundred or so steps of the cliff-face to the 13th-century castle ruins at the top. The climb is worth it. Our children were given an activity sheet and the views from the summit were spectacular, while there was also a useful low-walled garden area to coral them into for a game of 'sticks and horses, daddy' (jousting) that helped prevent them wandering off towards the sheer drops. Merlin's cave below is accessed via the beach at low tide and is free.

Open *1st Apr–30th Sept daily 10am–6pm, Oct–1st Nov daily 10am–5pm and 2nd Nov–31st Mar daily 10am–4pm.* **Adm** *adults £4.60, children £2.30, conc £3.70, families £11.50.* **Amenities** *baby-changing in gents and ladies, beach café.* **Credit Cards** *all except AX.*

FUN FACT >> Devil May Care <<

It is said the devil – a very fussy eater – never crossed the river Tamar into Cornwall on account of his fear of having to eat a Cornish pasty. That is because Cornish women were in the habit of putting every leftover they could find into pasties. The pasty has a long association with Cornwall. It was basically fast food for miners. They would throw the last mouthful into the mine for the gremlins for good luck. Although this was not as crazy as it seems. The mines contained arsenic that often got onto a miner's hands. So they held the pasty by the crimp and chucked this away at the end.

Visitor Information: Devon

The free sheet *Essential Devon* (**www.essentialdevon.co.uk**) covering East Devon and part of Mid Devon is packed with useful information while *What's On Exeter* (**www.whatson-exter.co.uk**) is helpful about the city, as is *What's On South Hams* (**www.whatsonsouthhams.co.uk**) while the website **www.englishriviera.co.uk** covers Torquay, Paignton and Brixham. Worth a visit is **www.devonshireheartland.co.uk** for info on dining and accommodation. For Plymouth try **www.visitplymouth.co.uk**.

Information Centres

Exeter, Civic Centre, Paris Street (☎ *01392 265700*, *www.exeter.gov.uk/visiting*); Exeter Quay House Visitor Centre, Exeter Quay (☎ *0139 271611*); Sidmouth, Ham Lane (☎ *01395 516441*, *www.visit-sidmouth.co.uk*); Barnstaple, North Devon Museum, The Square (☎ *01271 375000*, *www.staynorthdevon.co.uk*); Bideford, Victoria Park (☎ *01237 477676*); Braunton, The Bakehouse Centre, Caen Street (☎ *01271 816400*, *www.braunton.co.uk*); Ilfracombe, The Landmark, The Seafront (☎ *01271 863001*, *www.visitilfracombe.co.uk*); Woolacombe, The Espanade (☎ *01271 870553*, *www.woolacombe.co.uk*); Crediton, The Old Town Hall, High Street (☎ *01363 772006*, *www.crediton.com*); Great Torrington, Castle Hill, South Street (☎ *01805 626140*, *www.great-torrington.com*); Tavistock, Bedford Square (☎ *01822 612938*, *www.tavistock-devon.co.uk*).

What to See & Do in Devon

Living Coasts ★ ALL AGES

Torquay Harbourside, Beacon Quay, Torquay, Devon, ☎ *01803 202470, www.livingcoasts.org.uk*

A conservation-themed attraction full of coastal creatures (seals, penguins, etc.) that also wittily tells the story via a puppet show (yes, really) of the extinction of the Great Auk. Our daughter loved the clumsy cormorants while our son had fun in the discovery centre falling repeatedly from the children's climbing wall. There is a dig pit

Best Beaches

Southeast Cornwall

Crinnis, East Looe – a wonderful 1.6km-long sandy beach. Car park.

Looe – Sandy and popular with families. Café and car park.

Polridmouth, Fowey – two sandy beaches that join at low tide. Walk from car park at Menabilly.

Whitsand Bay – the best and longest in the area at about 5km long.

North Cornwall

Boobys Bay, St Marryn – a great sandy beach with rock pools and surfing. Park at Constantine and walk.

Harlyn Bay, near Padstow – great, wide sandy beach with surfing. Café, car park.

Daymer Bay, Rock – also called Beaks' Beach because it was where public school headmasters used to retire to in such great numbers before house prices hit the roof, there are some great rock-pools here. They have a car park and shop selling buckets and spades.

Padstow (St George's Cove, Harbour Cove and Hawker's cove) – three lovely flat sandy beaches within walking distance on the Camel estuary. Car park.

Polzeath – large family beach, good for surfing. Café, car park.

Summerleaze Beach, Bude – sandy beach with tidal swimming pool. Surfing, café, car park.

Mid Cornwall

Crinnis, Caerleon Bay – good kite-flying beach that's for nudists at the far end.

Fistral Beach, Newquay – one of the best surfing beaches in the UK. Café, car park.

Porth, Newquay – wide sandy beach. Café, car park.

Porthpean, St Austell – small sheltered family beach with rock-pools and dinghies. Car park, shop and toilets.

Watergate Bay, Newquay – wonderful 4km sandy beach close to Jamie Oliver's 15 Restaurant, popular with surfers where we (well I, the children weren't interested) built some great drainage works. Café, car park.

and lots of lift-flap info exhibits as well as a soft-play room, and an interactive floor where children can stamp on pictures of oil to dispel it from the sea. 'Local Coasts' is an indoor area which gives you an insight into the wildlife and habitats found along the coast. There's a crawl-through tank to see an array of little creatures including spiny starfish, cuttlefish, mullet, pipe fish and seahorses within, while waves crash through the tank above you. It also has Britain's first major exhibit based on a

Living Coasts, Torquay

mangrove swamp habitat with an underground forest containing blue stringrays and dinosaur crabs.

Open daily 10am–5pm. *Adm* adults £7.95, children (3–15) £5.95, under threes free, conc £6.20, families (two adults, two children) £25. *Amenities* café, baby-changing. *Credit Cards* all except AX and DC.

National Marine Aquarium
★★ **ALL AGES**

Rope Walk, Coxside, Plymouth, 📞 *01752 600301, www.national-aquarium.co.uk*

This, the best aquarium in England we reckon, has a fantastic Discovery Centre where our daughter checked out a whale skull, completed a fish jigsaw and made an electric eel hat out of cardboard. It was also in here that I read the following poem on the whiteboard that I feel it is a duty to repeat in full:
If crabs could fly and fish could sing
Then why didn't they ping
And why don't they wear bling
My name is Karen-jeet Singh

There is also a 3D Story of the Turtle show (my wife's own personal *Room 101*) in the cinema that includes a few sensory surprises that we won't spoil, while in the aqua-theatre (a large tank of water) there is a chance to try out a remote-operated underwater vehicle and elsewhere, in a small booth, to hear sperm whales and dolphins communicating. The Ocean View café on deck 2 has highchairs and children's lunchboxes.

Open Oct–Mar 10am–5pm, Apr–Sept 10am–6pm. *Adm* adults £11, children (5–16) £6.50, under fivess free, conc £9. *Amenities* café, baby-changing, picnic area and sandpit. *Credit Cards* all except AX.

Pecorama Gardens and Grotto **ALL AGES**

Beer, Devon, 📞 *01297 21542, www.peco-uk.com*

There is a miniature train ride, children's shows, free face-painting and a model railway exhibition full of enthusiasts discussing the OO gauge and asking each other very, very seriously 'you have digital command control over your model?'

Open 6th Apr–31st Oct Mon–Fri 10am–5.30pm (Sat 10am–1pm). *Adm* adults £4.75, children (4–14) £2.80, conc £4.75, over 80s free. *Amenities* café, baby-changing. *Credit Cards* all except AX and DC.

The Donkey Sanctuary **ALL AGES**
Sidmouth, Devon, 📞 *01395 576222, www.thedonkeysanctuary.org.uk*

Here you can expect to find fields and fields of donkeys for

Best Beaches

East Devon

Beer – pebbly with a café and a car park.

Branscombe – a pebble beach with a café and a car park.

Exmouth – long sandy beach good for watersports. There is a fun-fair here but watch the strong tides. Plenty of cafés and car parks.

Jacob's Ladder, Sidmouth – has great sand when the tide is out. There is a café and a car park.

Sidmouth – long pebble beach in front of the regency seafront where I believe I ate 3,456 corned beef sandwiches on family holidays in the 1970s.

North Devon

Barricane Beach, Woolacombe – a sheltered cove with rock-pooling. Car park.

Combe Martin – sandy beach with rock-pools. Car park.

Croyde Bay – a 1.6km long sandy beach.

Hele Bay, Ilfracombe – small beach, sand and single with rock-pools, Café and car park.

Tunnels Beaches, Ilfracombe – accessed by exciting tunnels and popular with families, it has rock-pools and a tidal pool.

Westward Ho! Bideford – a sandy beach almost 3.5km long. Café, car park.

West Devon

Bigbury – a huge expanse of sand at low tide, this was where my wife told me to stop digging the moat for our sandcastle because 'Nobody is interested. You can just sit and do nothing. They're paddling now, Ben'. There are rock-pools, a café and a car park.

Blackpool Sands – an idyllic sandy cove set against conifers. Café, car park.

Hope Cove – we know several families who swear by this sheltered sandy cove with rock-pools and safe swimming.

Mill Bay, Salcombe – sheltered sandy bay.

your children to pat. They are everywhere. Donkeys with eye patches, limping donkeys, moulting donkeys, donkeys that are perfectly all right. There is a barn with pictures of each resident, giving their names and a brief summary of their lives including a few salient facts about their ability to, say, smell polo mints through a coat pocket, and also entertainingly who they hang out with at the sanctuary ('Nelly is big mates with Daisy and Teddy – they are quite a little clique'). The Haycroft restaurant is a good place afterwards for dinner and a debate about the mindset of old ladies who leave everything to donkeys they don't know. Basically, we believe, there is something piquantly hangdog about a donkey. That is how it happens. Donkeys barely ever lift their heads, look mostly at the ground and when they bray the noise seems to come less from aggression but more from a deep well of self-pitying hurt that more injustice has been heaped upon them. Unless the biddies who make their wills are just bonkers, of course. You can, if you like – and we didn't because we are not yet 78 – adopt a donkey here.

Open daily 9am–dusk. **Admn** free. **Amenities** café, parking.

Watermouth Castle ALL AGES

Ilfracombe, North Devon, ☎ *01271 867474, www.watermouthcastle. com*

A castle-based theme park with lots of rides (snake tube, steam carousel) that are ideal for toddlers, which also includes a separate gnomeland park where you can learn fascinating gnome facts such as this – they wear red hats to deter their enemies and women gnomes marry at midnight on their 100th birthdays. There are plenty of indoor activities as well and don't miss the strange water show accompanied by organ music to the patriotic tune of Land of Hope and Glory. Our son, scared of the dungeon labyrinth, loved the room full of coin-activated model railways.

Open off peak 10am–6.30pm, peak 10.30am–6.30pm. **Adm** adults £12,

under 14s £10, conc £8, children under 92cm high free. **Amenities** café, parking. **Credit Cards** all except AX and DC.

DORSET

We always assumed Dorset was for people who were too lazy to drive to Devon. It was like driving to London and giving up at Luton and kidding yourself you'd made it. Although that is unfair because Dorset has many worthy attributes. Its Jurassic Coast is fantastic for fossil hunting and the holiday resort of Lyme Regis has plenty to offer, while county town, Dorchester, is where Thomas Hardy was born and set many of his chunky novels. For families, Brownsea Island, where the first-ever scout camp was held, is a great day out and the nearby tank museum was a hit with our son. The county motto here is 'who's a'fear'd'. and although I have to say we were slightly a'fear'd in the Dorchester Teddy Bear Museum when a scary member of staff rounded on us, we fell so heavily in love with the rest of the county that we have been back twice since writing this book.

Essentials

Getting There

By Train From London Waterloo to Dorchester South Station, there are two South West trains (☎ *0845 600650, www.southwest trains.co.uk*) per hour on a weekday and Saturdays, and one train every hour on Sundays. The journey takes approximately two hours 40 minutes. From Bristol Parkway there are First Great Western (📞 0845 7000125, www.firstgreatwestern.co.uk) services each hour to Dorchester West station. The journey takes between two hours 30 minutes to three hours 30 minutes.

By Bus There is an average of three National Express (📞 0870 5808080, www.nationalexpress.co.uk) coaches a day from London to Dorchester. The journey takes approximately three hours 45 minutes. The same company has one service a day from Bristol bus station to Dorchester South. The journey takes two hours 15 minutes.

By Car From London take the M3 towards Southampton, then M27 and A31 and the A35 to Dorchester. The journey should take approximately 2 hours 15 minutes.

Visitor Information

The Dorchester Tourist Information Centre (📞 01305 267992, www.westdorset.com) is based at Unit 11, Antelope Walk, Dorchester, Mon–Sat 9am–5pm. The Lyme Regis Tourist Information Centre (📞 01297 442138, www.westdorset.com) is at the Guildhall Cottage, Church Street, Lyme Regis, Mon–Sat 10am–5pm and Sun 10am–4pm in the summer and Mon–Sat 10am–3pm in the winter.

Further information on Dorset can be found at www.visit-dorset.com.

What to See & Do

Brownsea Island ★ ALL AGES

Poole Harbour, Dorset, 📞 01202 707744, www.nationaltrust.org.uk

This island, which provided inspiration for Enid Blyton and was where Lord Baden Powell ran the world's first scout camp in 1907, is only accessible by boat. There are children's nature and smuggling trails and great walks through the red squirrel-rich woods, although our highlight was the two all-terrain buggies we were lent for free with enormous off-road tyres enabling us to abandon our monstrous double McLaren and feel like proper middle-class parents with a Phil and Ted buggy. The history of the island, just one and a half miles long, is told in the visitor centre and includes a strange previous owner William Bensen, who apparently used black magic on a servant girl to make her disappear in 1735, and Sir Augustus Foster, who, as intransigent minister plenipotentiary to the United States, helped cause the American War of Independence.

Part of the fun of a visit here is the boat ride. There are half-hourly sailings from Poole Quay or Sandbanks. We went from the former with Brownsea Ferries (📞 01929 462383, www.brownseaislandgferries.com) and our crossing including

Mary Anning

Born in 1799, her father Richard died from a cliff fall hunting for fossils but despite this, Mary resolved to follow in his footsteps. In 1811, aged just 12, she found the first ever ichthyosaurus. It was 17 feet long and had a four-feet skull. She also found the first plesiosaur in 1824 and in 1828 the first pterodactyl. She died in 1847 aged just 47 but is immortalized in the children's ditty 'She Sells Sea Shells on the Sea Shore'.

commentary about the area, its celebrity residents, which include Harry Redknapp and Eddie Jordan, and a jaunt around a few of the smaller islands nearby.

Open daily 14th Mar–27th Mar 10am–4pm, 28th Mar–17th July 10am–5pm, 18th Jul–31st Aug 10am–6pm, 1st–27th Sept 10am–5pm and 28th Sept–1st Nov 10am–4pm. *Adm* adults £5.20, children £2.60, families £13. *Amenities* café, picnic areas, baby-changing. *Credit Cards* all except AE.

Dinosaur Land and Fossil Museum ALL AGES

Coombe Street, Lyme Regis, ☏ *01297 443541, www.dinosaurland.co.uk*

This is a very good little museum where you can learn about the evolution and subsequent extinction of the dinosaurs and the famous local fossil-hunter Mary Anning (see box). They have children's quizzes and lots of lifelike fibre-glass dinosaurs to threaten your children with when they're not cooperating. The highlight for me was the mocked-up model of a saurian – a semi-human/lizard-like being that might have lived if the dinosaurs hadn't become extinct – with wetsuit-type skin,

webbed fingers and toes, who reminded us strongly of a man we bought roadside strawberries from in Norfolk.

Open daily 10am–5pm (check Nov–Feb as staff often close to go fossil hunting). *Adm* adults £4.50, children (5–16) £3.50, families (two adults, two children) £14. *Amenities* toilets. *Credit Cards* all except AX.

Tank Museum ★ ALL AGES

Bovington, Dorset, ☏ *01929 405096, www.tankmuseum.org*

Housing the world's largest collection of tanks and teeming with real-life squaddies on their days off, many with tattoos and shaven heads, assisting their youngsters in firing replicas of the Ben light machine gun, this place is a must for any serious, war-minded youngster. I, myself, got to fire an anti-tank gun launcher against Panzer IIIs and a Lee Enfield rifle at moving targets and, I have to admit, felt much better for it. This museum isn't, however, just a room full of military hardware – there are interesting and thought-provoking displays on the role of the tank as a symbol of state power, along with exhibits demonstrating the day-to-day trials of working inside a very large hollow piece of armoured metal (weeing into missile casings). There is a children's trail and a small war-table of plastic soldiers and tanks for children to make machine-gun noises and bomb blasts over. Or, in our daughter's case, to sit quietly watching a young lad holding a teddy bear under his arm, his thumb in his mouth and clearly uninterested in the Ferret Mk 5 scout car's amphibious operations his dad was loudly discussing.

Open *10am–5pm.* **Adm** *adults £11, children (5–16) £7.50, conc £9, families (two adults, two children) £30.* **Amenities** *café, parking.* **Credit Cards** *all except AX and DC.*

Teddy Bear Museum and the Museum of Terracotta Warriors ALL AGES

Eastgate, Dorchester, ☎ 01305 266040, www.teddybearhouse. co.uk

A peculiar museum, with the most unhelpful member of staff we met on our entire travels round England, purporting to be the home of a life-size teddy bear by the name of Mr Edward Bearidge. Inside Mr Bearidge's mocked-up home your children meet, hug and attempt to knock over many of Mr Edward Bearidge's relatives. There is a toy room full of books, a case full of celebrity bears including (hold your sides) Albear-t Einstein, while downstairs, strangely, there is a separate exhibition complimenting the teddy bear museum. And what would be the ultimate bedfellow

for a teddy bear museum? Why a museum, of course, dedicated to the famous terracotta warriors entombed with the ruthless Chinese megalomaniac first emperor, Chin Shi Huang Di. There is a film about the emperor but I never saw the end of it as the aforementioned staff member returned it to the beginning for another couple even though I was watching it, 'because you should have done your research beforehand'. She is right, it was unprofessional of us to roll up at an important teddy bear museum dedicated to a fictitious Mr Bearidge without having first thoroughly researched the terracotta warriors. We apologize.

Open *daily 10am–5pm (Nov–Mar 10am–4.30pm).* **Adm** *adults £5.75, children £4, conc £5, families (two adults, two children) £18.* **Amenities** *none.* **Credit Cards** *all except AX.*

FAMILY-FRIENDLY ACCOMMODATION

EXPENSIVE

Hotel du Vin ★

Parabola Road, Cheltenham, ☎ 01242 588450, www.hotelduvin.com

We had a family room here at this chain hotel with a bathroom so big we managed to secret our son to sleep in a travel cot in the walk-in shower (although every time he snored the echo made him sound like a gorgon). The hotel, which is the height of cool and located in the chic Montpelier district, has walkie-talkie baby alarms so you can come down to dinner. The

Cornish Fishing Villages

Encicled by coastline the ancient duchy of Cornwall abounds in rugged cliffs, hidden bays, fishing villages, sandy beaches and sheltered coves where smuggling was once rampant. We suggest basing yourself at one of the smaller fishing villages, such as East or West Looe, Polperro or Mousehole, to experience the true charm of the area. Many of the villages, such as St. Ives, are artists' colonies. The Isles of Scilly off the Cornish coast, have only five inhabited islands. Here you'll find the Abbey Gardens of Tresco, 297 hectares (735 acres) with 5,000 species of plants.

hotel bistro serves some delicious modern European cuisine and makes a good stab at having a real bistro feel, while there's also a Champagne bar and purpose-built Cigar Shack for smokers. The only bugbear – limited parking places. Norman Wisdom was billeted here during the war which made it almost impossible not to shout 'Mr Grimsdale' a lot.

Rates executive room (with space for extra children's bed) £180–£200 B&B. **Amenities** beauty treatment rooms, bistro. **In Room** phone, wide-screen TV, DVD player, tea and coffee making with fresh milk. **Credit Cards** all except DC.

Knoll House ★★★

Studland Bay, Dorset, ☏ 01929 450450, www.knollhouse.co.uk

The favourite hotel of Enid Blyton and also where Winston Churchill, King George VI and General Eisenhower sought refreshments during D-Day planning, this hotel has an old-world charm making it both the most relaxing, accommodating and friendliest place we stayed in England. Full of returning families – often with grandparents in tow – it felt like the clock had stopped during Blyton's time and we were back in the apple-cheeked 1950s, staying at Aunt Fanny's, about to have a spiffing adventure. During our whole stay we never once saw a child on a Nintendo DS or an adult on a laptop while the matronly kitchen staff wear what look like 50s' NHS-style uniforms. In the evening a baby-sitter already knew our children's names and ages and the 24-hour children's kitchen is full of everything you could possibly want. There's a children's den, packed with toys, while the lounge was full of families playing cards, dogs asleep in front of the log fire and chatter about shell hunts. There is a pirate ship for children, and a giant chess board I saw three children actually arguing over. Fantastic.

Rates £113 per person per night full board (under 13s pay a percentage of the full rate, five year olds 50 per cent, six year olds 60 per cent and so on while 10,11, and 12 year olds pay 90 per cent). **Amenities** swimming pool. **In Room** DAB radio. **Credit Cards** all except AX.

Dartmoor National Park

This national park lies northeast of Plymouth, stretching from Tavistock and Okehampton on the west to near Exeter in the east, a granite mass that sometimes rises to a height of 600m (1,968ft) above sea level. The landscape offers vistas of gorges with rushing water, spiny shrubs, and purple heather ranged over by Dartmoor ponies. This region is crisscrossed with about 805km (500 miles) of bridle paths and hiking trails. The Dartmoor National Park Authority (DNPA: *www.dartmoor-npa. gov.uk*) runs guided walks of varying difficulty, ranging from 1.5 to 6 hours for a trek of some 14 to 19km (9-12 miles). All you have to do is turn up but this country is rough, so you must have adequate clothing, footwear, and always carry good maps and a compass. You can also arrange a day's horseback riding across the moors. Two good operators are Skaigh Stables at Belstone (*01837 840917*) and Doone Valley Stables, Oare (*www.doonevalleytrekking.co.uk*).

Tourist Information Centre: Town Hall, Bedford Square, Tavistock. *0870 608 2608*.

Around the park

A good base to explore the park is the romantic, ancient town of Chagford in Sir Francis Drake country. It's well positioned to get out on to the enchanting north Dartmoor, overlooks the river Teign, which is overlooked by high granite tors and has good fishing. Some 21km (13 miles) west of Exeter, the peaceful little town of Moretonhampstead is perched on the edge of Dartmoor. Moretonhampstead contains several 17th-century colonnaded almshouses and a Market Cross, a carved stone structure used for centuries to mark the site of the local market, which is still around.

The St Enodoc ★★

Rock, Cornwall, 01208 863394, www.enodoc-hotel.co.uk

A reassuringly well-to-do hotel, with a well-stocked playroom for youngsters full of alarmingly posh children ('It was Martha's. And that's called stealing and I am telling my mummy'). The huge family suite came with baby bottle warmers, and a kitchenette with fridge and microwave, while every member of staff was relaxed around children. The same is also true of the other guests, one of whom at breakfast showed first his wife and then our daughter a picture of a four-eared cat from the *Daily Mail* ('Good Lord, darling, a four-eared cat. Young lady, would you like to see a four-eared cat?' She would). The hotel has wonderful views over the Camel estuary, and if you're here in August, the St Miniver's fete (check out the orange bomber) is a fun day out.

The estuary is a summertime mecca for sailing and water sports (Prince Harry sometimes attends) and for walkers there are miles of National Trust cliff paths and specially created cycle tracks nearby. For first-time surfers, there's Polzeath round the corner, separated by sandy beaches and rocky coves, where you can hit the waves.

Rates family double suites (with terrace, a bathroom and shower room) £210–£400 B&B per night. Standard family suites £155–£340. *Amenities* table tennis, PlayStations, swimming pool, restaurant. *In Room* TV, DVD, phone. *Credit Cards* all except DC.

MODERATE

Cheltenham Chase Hotel

Shurdington Road, Brockworth, Gloucester, 01452 519988, *www. qhotels.co.uk*

Within sight of the famously steep cheese-rolling Coopers Hill, this hotel has a children's play area outside and serves, in your room, a daily replenished packet of the best ginger biscuits I have ever not been allowed to eat because 'they're treats for the children, Ben'. Ostensibly a business hotel (you get short shrift turning over the news in the main lounge when *Chuggington* is on Cbeebies), families are well treated, with activity packs for children handed out on check-in. After the children are in bed and the Bebetel is rigged up, the restaurant is a good place to have a quiet meal alone with your spouse and to discuss after a good bottle of wine the possibility of trudging off to Coopers Hill to follow the Babybel from Charlie's packed lunch down to the bottom for a 'funny holiday snap'.

Rates double room (with extra bed) £64–£140 per night B&B. No charge for additional beds but over fives must pay for breakfast, interconnecting rooms £100–£140. *Amenities* spa and fitness centre, gym, swimming pool, travel cots. *In Room* TV, phone, CD player, tea and coffee making, bottled water, iron and ironing board. *Credit Cards* all accepted.

Falmouth Hotel

Castle Beach, Falmouth, Cornwall, 0844 5027587, *www.falmouth hotel.com*

A great option for families, these self catering cottages overlooking the sea have views of Pendennis Castle. The no-frills accommodation is a few yards from the beautiful Regency hotel (where you can use the restaurant, leisure club and pool), have their own kitchenettes with a fridge freezer, microwave, oven, dining table and chairs. Falmouth has lovely sandy beaches, excellent gardens (7 nearby), arts and crafts, dolphin spotting and lots of walking for all abilities. Seafood lovers should mark down October as a highlight of the year when the annual Falmouth Oyster Festival arrives.

Rates There are one-, two- and three-bed cottages ranging from £80 a night self-catering to £200. *Amenities* washing machine, parking *Credit Cards* all except DC.

Mercure Holland House Hotel and Spa ★

Redcliffe Hotel, Bristol, 📞 *0117 9689900, www.mercure.com*

Children are given so many toy boxes in this hotel ours refused to leave the room the next morning, our daughter pleading, 'You go to the zoo and me and Charlie will play Twister, Frustration and that other game with the plastic legs. Please'. Staff were accommodating when our baby monitor played up; the concierge went out for extra batteries, and at dinner I was treated to a free glass of rioja with my excellent cheese. The hotel, over the road from the church Samuel Coleridge was married in and next to where Blackbeard the pirate's house, has one drawback. The interconnecting rooms we stayed in had no bath but only two showers – a shock for our son who had never showered in his life and who showed all the signs (screaming until he was almost blue and banging his head on things) of never wanting to again.

Rates interconnecting rooms (no breakfast) £140–£159, family rooms £69. Amenities spa, swimming pool, gym. In Room TV, phone and tea and coffee making, iron. Credit Cards all accepted.

Soar Mill Cove Hotel ★★

Near Salcombe, South Devon, 📞 *01548 561566, www.soarmill cove.co.uk*

A luxury family hotel with a huge array of activities for children including a pirate treasure hunt at Soar Mill Cove, and a beach a short buggy-unfriendly yomp from the hotel. There are go-karts for children to use, a play park and every Sunday at teatime in the school holidays there is a chocolate fountain in the lounge. Owner Keith also conducts nature trail walks where children are encouraged to study shells and plant life and there is a weekly sandcastle building competition. The rooms are slightly tired and the food the same although the stay does comes with free tickets to the National Marine Aquarium (see p 159), while at the children's communal teatime in Castaways Coffee shop there is a children's menu and toys.

Rates family room per night (children stay free provided they have breakfast and high tea) £220 B&B. Amenities parking. In Room plasma TV, DVD player, phone, tea and coffee making. Credit Cards all except AX and DC.

The Esplanade Hotel

Esplanade Road, Newquay, Cornwall, 📞 *01637 873333, www.newquay-hotels.co.uk*

Overlooking Fistral Beach, this family-oriented hotel is a great place to watch a pinky sunset after a day of surfing. We stayed in an L-shaped family room at the back of the hotel that enabled us to hide our sleeping son in his cot round the corner. To get here, however, entailed an expedition so gruelling through countless doors, up flights of steps and lift rides to reach it, I wanted to lay down, give up the struggle for the night and press on in the morning.

Besides families, an older clientele is preferred, so expect the restaurant to close exceptionally early (8.30pm when we stayed), although once the guests are safely tucked up, staff let their beach-bum hair down, whack up the Robbie Williams, and will, if you ask them, pass on useful local information about where's currently best for dolphin spotting. Surfing lessons are available and your youngest child under 11 stays free while there are other offers worth checking on the hotel website.

Rates family room £40–£60 per person B&B per night. *Amenities* surfing lessons, swimming pool, soft-play area, sauna, Jacuzzi, pool table. *In Room* TV, phone, tea and coffee-making. *Credit Cards* all except AX.

The Grand Hotel ★

Torbay Road, Torquay, Devon, ☎ 0844 5027587, www.grandtorquay.co.uk

What do you expect to see out of a Torquay hotel room window, Madam? The hanging gardens of Babylon, wildebeests sweeping majestically across the plains? Actually we saw something even better – an exhilaratingly, perhaps rare, Red Arrows display from our balcony. A well-equipped hotel with gift bags handed out to children on check-in including colouring-in books, lollipops and cuddly rhinos, they also have a children's menu and highchairs at dinner. We slept in a one-bed sea-facing family room where an extra bed was laid on for our daughter and discovered, the next morning at breakfast, that we'd grown

inadvertently lazy, spoilt and over-accustomed to hotel living after I caught myself tutting inwardly about the watermelon, saying peevishly to myself, 'They haven't removed the pips'.

Rates sea-facing family room £120–£234 per night B&B. *Amenities* tennis courts, Jacuzzi, sauna, solarium, beauty centre, travel cots. *In Room* TV, phone, tea and coffee making. *Credit Cards* all accepted (three per cent surcharge for AX and DC).

The Sandy Cove Hotel

Old Coast Road, Combe Martin Bay, Berrynarnor, Near Ilfracombe, Devon, ☎ 01271 882243, www.sandycove-hotel.co.uk

I had high hopes for this hotel after spotting the Lotus Elise outside and seeing the stunning cliff-top views from the car park. But in actual fact it was one of the most disappointing we stayed in. Bulbs didn't work in our dark interconnecting rooms, while the many stiff fire doors in the narrow corridors not wide enough to walk through carrying a bag either side of you gave the inside an institutional feel – this was exacerbated by the old-style TV on wall brackets in the tiredly Artexed bedroom. There were baby monitors in the rooms although dinner was a low-key affair done and dusted by 9.30pm when all the oldsters – the mainstay here – had turned in to watch *Hetty Wainthrop Investigates*, a fact signified by a waitress ostentatiously dragging a bin-liner of rubbish through the dining room as we finished our wine.

Rates three nights £198 per person in the winter, per room (£210 in the summer), under fives free. **Amenities** covered swimming pool, steam room, sauna. **In Room** phone. **Credit Cards** all except DC and AX.

Trehellas Hotel ★

Washaway, Wadebridge, Near Bodmin, Devon, ☏ *01208 72700, www.trehellas.co.uk*

This Grade II listed hotel has in former times been a farm, a Chinese restaurant and a court. Staff are friendly, it was full of families and it's close to the Eden Project, the Lost Gardens of Heligan, Lanhydrock, Padstow, Rock, Wadebridge and just a short ride away from the Camel trail; over 17 miles of easy bike riding all the way to Padstow. We slept in the courtroom suite in a double bed on a dais that reminded my wife so much of being on stage she couldn't get to sleep because she felt like 'I'm being watched by an audience'. The room was big enough for one-year-old Charlie to sleep in a cot we cleverly hid behind a sofa bed and a chair.

Rates £100–£180 B&B per night. **Amenities** swimming pool, car parking, wifi, parking, restaurant. **In Room** TV, phone, chocolates, tea and coffee making. **Credit Cards** all except DC and JCB.

Waterside Holiday Park ★

Bowleaze Cove, Weymouth, Dorset, ☏ *01305 833103, www.watersideholidays.co.uk*

After showing initial reluctance to staying in a static caravan

following a run of classy hotels in Devon, our daughter ('What is this hotel, Daddy? I have never seen such a hotel') was soon fitting right in. Having inherited my wife's nosiness, she swivelled the armchair away from its TV position so it was overlooking the pathway between the rows of caravans so 'I can watch the people coming past and see who is nasty and nice'. It was lovely to wake up and hear the birds singing. There is a children's club called Boomers, you're close to the beach and the water park, and as you park right outside your front door, there is no lugging bags anywhere. The caravan has a large lounge, radiators, the carpets were thick and the only difference between here and in a house was the thinness of the walls, which didn't matter because everyone on the site seemed to be in bed by 9pm. You must bring your own towels and the only obvious bugbear was there was no room for a bath so we couldn't wash our shower-phobic one year old.

Rates cost for a week depending on berths £265–£1,085. **Amenities** swimming pool, takeaway restaurant, spa, children's entertainment in the Waves bar. **In Caravan** microwave, fridge freezer, cooker. **Credit Cards** all except AX and Electron.

FAMILY-FRIENDLY DINING

Fowey Hall

Hanson Drive, Fowey, ☏ *01726 833866, www.foweyhall.co.uk*

The inspiration for Toad Hall in Kenneth Graham's *Toad of Toad Hall* children's story, there is a children's crèche (£5 an hour) at this spectacularly grand hotel, which overlooks the sailing and fishing port of Fowey enabling parents to eat at the two AA Rosette award Hansom restaurant. Alternatively families can dine together in the conservatory. Not minimalist but comfy and relaxing throughout, the hotel's crèche, full of children's toys, is only open between 10am–4.45pm so would only work for a lunch. Activity packs are provided in the conservatory, which overlooks the hotel's croquet lawn.

Open *12pm–1.45pm and 6.45pm–9.30pm.* **Main Course** *£20.* **Amenities** *highchairs, children's menu, baby-changing.* **Credit Cards** *all except DC.*

Harbour Restaurant at the Red Lion Hotel

The Quay, Clovelly, 📞 *01237 431237, www.clovelly.co.uk*

If you can make it down the hundreds of cobbled steps to the foot of this privately owned fisherman's village, which has banned cars, you'll be treated to great ocean views. Staff are friendly and they have highchairs and a children's menu, but eat something substantial because it's such a long climb back up my knee started making funny popping noises close to the Charles Kinglsey exhibition. We recommend the sausages. To visit the village of Clovelly you have to pay £5.50.

Open *7pm–8.30pm.* **Main Course** *£18.50.* **Amenities** *baby-changing.* **Credit Cards** *all except DC.*

Old Manor Restaurant

The Bridge, Boscastle, Devon, 📞 *01840 250251*

Handily placed for visits to the Boscastle Visitor Centre, where you can learn about the famous flood, and also about The Rev Stephen Hawker (see box), the comfy restaurant has a safe garden and serves children's dishes like spaghetti bolognese and vegetarian options. Based next to the pay-and-display car park and specializing in British food, put enough change in the meter to visit the nearby Museum of Witchcraft, where you can learn how to make voodoo poppets to undermine your enemies and meet genuine witches, or cunning-men as they prefer to be known, who (we are not kidding) work behind the tills here.

Open *daily 11am–9pm.* **Main Course** *£10.* **Amenities** *high chairs, children's menus.* **Credit Cards** *all except DC.*

The Bistro

Hotel du Vin, The Sugar House, Narow Lewins Mead, Bristol, 📞 *0117 9255577, www.hotelduvin.com*

Based at the rejuvenated city waterfront, this restaurant serves excellent smaller-sized portions of adult meals for children, who eat free between 6pm and 7.30pm when dining with an adult. The staff are unsnooty and we suggest you wait until you're well into a bottle of South African red and

Reverend Robert Stephen Hawker

Parson Hawker (1803–1875), the quintessential English eccentric, won the Newdigate Prize for Poetry at Oxford but became famous after penning *The Song of the Western Men*, the unofficial Cornish anthem. Over the course of several moonlit nights, Hawker famously impersonated a mermaid on Bude Bay. Large crowds gathered to hear his wailing voice (favoured dress: a claret-coloured coat, a blue jersey and a yellow poncho) before, he disappeared beneath the waves on the final night of his stint singing *God Save the Queen*. Vicar of Morwenstow from 1834, Hawker kept a pig as a pet and nine cats, which accompanied him to church services. An opium smoker, he once painted a horse as a zebra and made a local doctor owner ride it through town on an appointment to see him. He also excommunicated his cat for mousing on Sundays.

the lemon-zingy mackerel before starting (apropos of your earlier remarks at the Edward Jenner Birthplace Museum, see p 144) the following conversation, 'So what do you really think about my idea. It is odd that I never get colds any more'.

'Ben, can we talk about something else?'

'I have a theory about how to cure the common cold that could prevent another swine flu pandemic and it doesn't interest you'.

'Not when it involves you sticking a finger up your nose'.

Open daily 12pm–1.45pm (Sun until 2.30pm), 6pm–9.45pm (Mon–Thurs), 6pm–10.30pm (Fri–Sun). **Main Course** £14. **Amenities** *highchairs, baby-changing.* **Credit Cards** *all accepted.*

Dukes ★

The Esplanade, Sidmouth, Devon, ☏ 01395 513320, www.hotels-sidmouth.co.uk

Just off Sidmouth's unspoilt stony seafront beach, where I spent almost every summer holiday as a small boy worrying needlessly about stinger fish, this hotel has friendly Antipodean staff who look after children with a Small Person's menu including plenty of healthy pasta-style options. It's popular with families and also, when we were here, two old ladies who said goodbye to each other very mysteriously with that sort of Miss Marple style of off-hand wisdom in the car park. 'So long Mrs Fartwhistle (we think we heard). It has been most enjoyable'.

Open Thurs–Sat 12pm-9pm. **Main Course** *from £7.95.* **Amenities** *highchairs, wifi.* **Credit Cards** *all except AX.*

Gylly Beach Café Bar

Cliff Road, Falmouth, Cornwall, ☏ 01326 312884, www.gyllybeach.com

Children are given colouring-in books and pens at this smart, busy but friendly beachfront restaurant. They have special offers (check the website) and regular live music for you to wax lyrical to your wife over the top of about how brilliant an idea the den-building day at the Eden Project was ('All those families building together. I felt part of a tribe. Everyone was helping each other. Well, actually it was quite competitive. I felt very competitive. That whole finish-your-den-then-sit-smugly- sipping-a Fairtrade-coffee vibe. But it was great. The children loved it. Until the den fell down and hurt them'. Serving Mediterranean food with an Asian influence the café overlooks Falmouth Bay and you can't go wrong with the Thai chicken.

Open Mon–Wed 10am–5pm, Thurs–Fri 10am–11pm and Sat–Sun 9am–11pm. **Main Course** £8. **Amenities** highchairs, children's menu. **Credit Cards** all except AX.

Mother Meldrum's Tearoom and Restaurant ★

Lee Road, Lynton, Devon, ☎ 01598 753667

A few minutes from the cable car separating Lynton from Lynmouth, the restaurant mentioned in the novel *Lorna Doone* (page 55 if you're interested) overlooks the Valley of the Rocks and Mother's Meldrum's caves, where the legendary witch Annie Norman lived in the 19th century. Staff serving mainly scones and light meals are very friendly and not at all witch-like and the café stays open for late supper in the holidays, while there are gardens with a Wishing

Tree and menu options that include 'wibble wobble jelly' and 'witch's fingers'.

Open daily 10am–5.30pm. **Main Course** £7. **Amenities** ad hoc baby-changing table as required, high-chairs, children's menu, Exmoor ponies and goats to look at. **Credit cards** cash and cheques only.

The Regency Tearooms at the Jane Austen Centre

40 Gay Street, Queen Square, Bath, ☎ 01225 443000, www.janeausten.co.uk

Based at the Jane Austen Centre, these Regency-style tearooms (free to enter) serve various *Pride and Prejudice* related cash-in dishes including a Mrs Bennett's Lemon Drizzle and Mr Darcy's Millionaire Shortbread. Full of women of a certain age declaiming and waitresses wearing traditional black and white uniforms. Without being warm, they're not overtly hostile to parents with two children under five who drag linen cloths off perfectly set tables to wipe their chocolatey faces. There are highchairs but no children's menu although staff will accommodate a request to cut a toastie up into soldiers. If you want to visit the museum (adults £6.95), there is a film about Jane Austen and a good display on the language of the fan although be warned by the sign in the gift-shop reading 'we welcome well-behaved children', which really means: we welcome *no* children.

Open summer daily 9.45am–5.30pm (July, Aug Thurs and Sat until 7pm), winter Sat only 11am–4.30pm. **Main**

Ride the Bristol & Bath Railway Path

Crossing the River Avon through ancient woodland you'll be treated to some great views of the Cotswold Hills on this 13-mile, flat, traffic-free, tarmaced cycle route along the track bed of the old Midland Railway between Bristol and Bath. Alive with birdsong and butterflies and passing beautifully colourful wild flower meadows, the route, dotted with sculptures by local artists, is also popular with walkers while you can expect to see blackberry pickers as well as other families foraging for the apples and plums that grow close to the path. The trail is part of National Cycle Network Route 4 and begins at St Philips Road in the centre of Bristol (follow the signs from Temple Meads Station) and it ends near Bath Spa railway station. It's ideal for buggy pushers and wheelchair users with only one quarter of a mile of its length forming a gentle gradient.
www.bristolbathrailwaypath.org.uk

*Course £5.95. **Amenities** highchairs. **Credit cards** all except AX.*

Stein's Fish and Chips ★

South Quay, Padstow, Cornwall, 📞 *01841 532700, www.rickstein.com*

Rick Stein has more business in Padstow than you can shake a crabbing net at. Our daughter had some excellent cod chunks with chips (£5.85) while our mackerel and chips were superb. You can't reserve a table and the only drawback is the queue to sit down although that does give you the time to envisage the town morphed 20 years from now into Padstein, when everything here and for miles around will be owned by Rick.

***Open** Mon–Sun 12pm–2.30pm and 5pm–8pm. **Main Course** £6.60–£10. **Amenities** baby-changing, high-chairs. **Credit Cards** all except AX.*

Venus Café ★

Lower Car Park, The Warren, Bigbury on Sea, Devon, 📞 *01803 712648*

Above the wonderful sandy beach, this award-winning self-service café offers outdoor Mediterranean-style organic food and children's lunchboxes (£3.99) that include activity packs. When the tide is out you can walk across the sand to the privately owned Burgh Island, the setting for many Agatha Christie mysteries. The pay-and-display car park here is roughly £1 an hour.

***Open** Apr–June Mon–Fri 10am–5pm (Sat–Sun 9am–5pm) July–Aug daily 8am–8pm, Sept–Oct Mon–Sun 10am–5pm, Nov–Mar 10am–4pm. **Main Course** £5.99. **Amenities** high-chairs, children's menu. **Credit Cards** all except AX.*

7 Northeast & Yorkshire

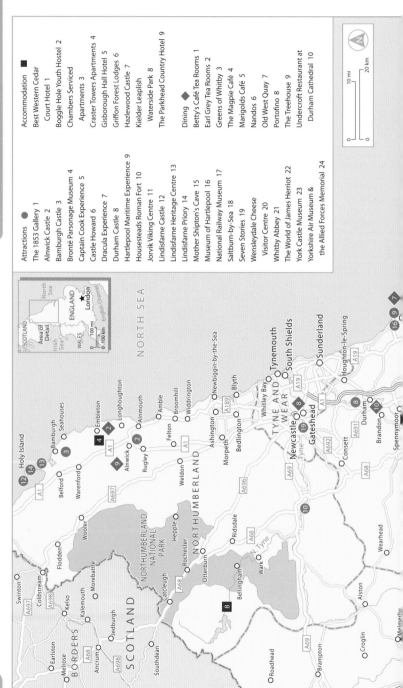

Accommodation
Best Western Cedar Court Hotel 1
Boggle Hole Youth Hostel 2
Chambers Serviced Apartments 3
Craster Towers Apartments 4
Gisborough Hall Hotel 5
Griffon Forest Lodges 6
Hazlewood Castle 7
Kielder Leaplish Waterside Park 8
The Parkhead Country Hotel 9

Dining
Betty's Café Tea Rooms 1
Earl Grey Tea Rooms 2
Greens of Whitby 3
The Magpie Café 4
Marigolds Café 5
Nandos 6
Old West Quay 7
Portofino 8
The Treehouse 9
Undercroft Restaurant at Durham Cathedral 10

Attractions
The 1853 Gallery 1
Alnwick Castle 2
Bamburgh Castle 3
Brontë Parsonage Museum 4
Captain Cook Experience 5
Castle Howard 6
Dracula Experience 7
Durham Castle 8
Hartlepool Maritime Experience 9
Housesteads Roman Fort 10
Jorvik Viking Centre 11
Lindisfarne Castle 12
Lindisfarne Heritage Centre 13
Lindisfarne Priory 14
Mother Shipton's Cave 15
Museum of Hartlepool 16
National Railway Museum 17
Saltburn-by-Sea 18
Seven Stories 19
Wensleydale Cheese Visitor Centre 20
Whitby Abbey 21
The World of James Herriot 22
York Castle Museum 23
Yorkshire Air Museum & the Allied Forces Memorial 24

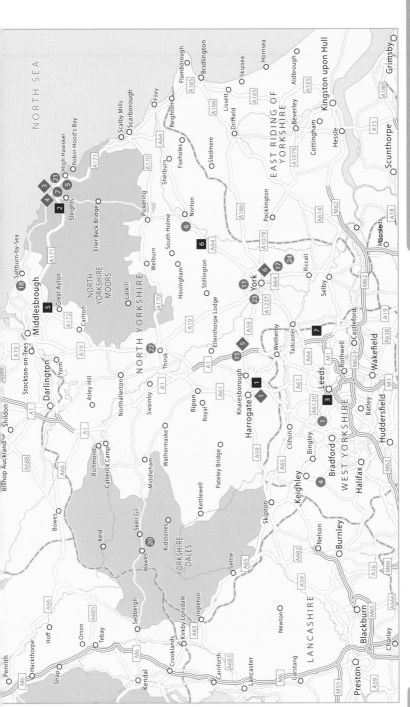

NORTH SEA

NORTH YORKSHIRE MOORS

NORTH YORKSHIRE

EAST RIDING OF YORKSHIRE

YORKSHIRE DALES

WEST YORKSHIRE

LANCASHIRE

Northumberland, our northernmost county and the former capital of England, was once a popular mediaeval dragon-slaying destination but is now such a sleepy region the barn owl was recently reintroduced just for something to talk about. It is, however, a hidden gem for family holidays, the county is basically a giant national park, with miles of deserted sandy beaches, wonderful castles and some of the most diverse wildlife in Britain. Meanwhile, the region named after the area's two main rivers, Tyne and Wear, contains the Northeast's major cities. One of these is Newcastle, where you'll find the magnificent Seven Stories children's attraction , the grand 19th century streets, the famous seven bridges that span the Tyne, the excellent Baltic centre for Contemporary Art and Life Science Centre (**www.life.org.uk**) and Discovery Centre (**www.twmuseums.org.uk**). Meanwhile, the UNESCO World Heritage Site of Durham grew up around its famous cathedral, and is so easily walkable and photogenic that in the eloquent words of songsmith Roger Whittaker 'leaving's gerner get you down', especially if you're heading towards the Tees Valley. This is, we have to say, one of the ugliest areas of the country, possibly of the world. Looking like the insides of a giant combi boiler, its power stations and smoking chimneys inspired Ridley Scott to create the cityscape in his doom-filled epic *Blade Runner*.

Yorkshire has a very different character. Our biggest county is the English Texas only with flat caps instead of stetsons and Yorkshire pudding and Parkin instead of oil and natural gas. Dynamic (well, they set up Asda), brash, and hugely sentimental about itself, Yorkshire is also the official nostalgia capital of Sunday night TV with *Heartbeat*, *All Creatures Great and Small* and *Last of the Summer Wine* all filmed here. This is a friendly place, although be warned Yorkshiremen are prone to bouts of self-aggrandizement, like to start sentences with the word ''Ark' and are extremely proud even if it's only about how it was tougher in their day 'when I had to sleep in't shoebox in't middle of t'road and be beaten t'death by me dad every night'. Often identifying more with their own county anthem 'On Ilka Moor Baht 'at' (a song about being outside without a hat on), than the country as a whole, the Yorkshireman will point his pipe towards the historic city of York and remind you that George VI famously said that 'the history of York is the history of England', although nowadays the history of York is more like the history of the mid-morning elevenses (Terry's, Thorntons and Rowntree's were all based here at one time). Easily doable on foot, full of beautiful old buildings and many parties of schoolchildren with their caps on sideways like Biggie Smalls, it's crammed with great family-friendly attractions, as is the bustling harbour town of Whitby, although Yorkshire's real highlight is the North York Moors. Why would anyone need t'travel anywhere else, our invented and heavily stereotyped Yorkshireman might ask, and for families holidaying here the answer is: they don't.

CHILDREN'S TOP 10 ATTRACTIONS

❶ Visit Alnwick Castle, the setting for the *quidditch* game in the Harry Potter movies. See p 181.

❷ Navigate using Polaris at the Hartlepool Maritime Experience. See p 183.

❸ Stay in a sea-view penthouse apartment at one of the country's oldest aristocratic homes in Craster, Northumberland. See p 200.

❹ Build sandcastles in front of the dramatic Bamburgh Castle. See p 181.

❺ Eat a family lunch in a treetop setting in spectacular Alnwick Gardens, full of children's water features, slightly worried that your wife has visited the Poison Garden and is talking about the deadliness of a tiny speck of Angel's Trumpet. See p 205.

Bamburgh Castle

❻ Test your sheep dog rounding-up skill at the James Herriot Experience in Thirsk. See p 196.

❼ Visit the dank cave where Old Mother Shipton, the world's most famous prophetess, was born. She predicted the Great Fire of London, the Plague and the use of Hotmail. See p 193.

❽ Sing sea shanties on a voyage beyond Whitby Harbour on a pint-sized replica of the famous *Endeavor*, on which Captain Cook sailed round the world. See p 191.

❾ Lie in a woodland hot-tub listening to the sounds of nature at Griffon Forest Lodges. See p 202.

❿ Fire at German fighter aircraft with a Lewis gun simulator at the Yorkshire Air Museum. See p 198.

THE NORTHEAST

The Northeast is home to two world heritage sites – Durham Cathedral and the greatest Roman monument in England, Hadrian's Wall. The largest shopping centre in Europe, The MetroCentre is in Gateshead while next door in Newcastle you'll find the award-winning children's attraction, Seven Stories. The Tees Valley boasts the child-friendly Hartlepool Maritime Experience, and a surprisingly wonderful sandy beach at Saltburn-by-Sea.

Northumberland, much of it a national park, has some of the finest unspoiled coastline in the country, not to mention magnificent Bamburgh Castle as well as the holy island of Lindisfarne, home to the world-famous priory that was the cradle of English Christianity. The town of Alnwick boasts the castle that Hogwarts was based on in the Harry Potter films, while Kielder Forest on the border with Scotland was recently voted the most tranquil place in England.

Essentials

By Train From London (Kings Cross) National Express East Coast trains (☏ 08457 225333, *www.nationalexpresseastcoast. com*) go every half-hour direct to Newcastle. The journey time is two and a half to three hours. The same company operates services from Edinburgh to Newcastle that run every half-hour with a journey time of around an hour and a half. From Leeds to Newcastle there are half-hourly direct Cross Country Trains (☏ 0844 8110124, *www. crosscountrytrains.co.uk*). The journey takes between one hour and one and a half hours.

By Bus There are four-a-day direct services to Newcastle by National Express (☏ 08705 808080, *www.nationalexpress. co.uk*) from London. Allow around eight hours for your journey. The same company operates a five-a-day service direct from Leeds with a journey

time of three hours, while from Edinburgh (three-a-day) direct services take three hours while the one-a day from Glasgow coach takes an extra hour.

By Road From London to Newcastle take the M1 and A1(M). The journey should take about five and a half hours. From Leeds to Newcastle it's the A58 and A1. Leave two hours for this at least. Meanwhile from Edinburgh it's the A1 all the way and this will take about three hours. Glasgow to Newcastle is slightly more complicated (M73, M74, M6 and A69) and will take as long.

By Air Newcastle Airport (☏ 0871 8821121, *www.newcastleairport. com*) has internal flights to all the UK's airports and international flights to destinations across Europe. Major operators include easyJet (*www.easyjet. com*), Air France (☏ 0871 6633777, *www.airfrance.co.uk*), Lufthansa (☏ 0871 9459747, *www. lufthansa.com*), flybe (☏ 0871 7000123, *www.flybe.com*), KLM (☏ 0870 5074074, *www.klm.com*), and Ryanair (☏ 0871 2460000, *www.ryanair.com*).

Visitor Information

Durham Tourist Information Centre (☏ 0191 3843720, *www. durhamtourism.co.uk*) is at 2 Millennium Place, Durham and is open daily 9.30am–5pm (Sun 11am–4pm). Hexham Tourist Information Centre (☏ 01434 652220) is at Wentworth Car Park, Wentworth Place,

Hexham and is open Mon–Sat 9am–5pm. Hartlepool Tourist Information Centre (☎ 01429 869706, *www.destinationhartlepool. com*) is at the Hartlepool Art Gallery and Information Centre in Church Square, Hartlepool, and is open daily 10am–5.30pm, (Sun 2pm–5pm). Newcastle Tourist Information Centre (☎ 0191 2778000, *www.newcastle gateshead.com*) at 8–9 Central Arcade, Newcastle is open Mon–Sat 9.30 am–5.30 pm.

What to See & Do

Alnwick Castle ★ ★ ALL AGES

Alnwick, Northumberland, ☎ 01665 511100, www.alnwickcastle.com

The seat of the ancient Percy family (now the duke and duchess of Northumberland), despite playing host to many great historical events, is now best known for being Hogwarts in the first two Harry Potter films. There is a Potter tour (called the Magical Tour for legal reasons), made challenging for us by the impenetrable Geordie accent of the guide, who spoke in incredibly fast short sentences like someone recovering from a near drowning. The tours start at the Lion Arch on the far side of the castle, where the Forbidden Forest started in the films but by the time we reached the courtyard the Italians in our party had broken away in frustration at the guide to stare at must-have Potter merchandise such as a Hagrid mask for £15.50 in the gift shop. The castle was where the

Hogwarts Express pulled into and the library scenes were filmed here along with the game of *quidditch*. For those whose lives are defined in non-boy-magician ways, there is The Knights Quest (full of rotating skulls, skeletons and other such stuff of toddler nightmares) and the chance to learn about the dragon-slaying first Earl of Northumbria, who carried a banner reading 'the raven of earthly terror'. Our daughter got to dress up as a court lady, decorated a shield with her very own colours ('a pink rabbit that is a really lovely one, dad') and on a State Room tour had fun finding fluffy white owls in each room while our son (our very own raven of earthly terror) tried to pull down a Louis IV pair of *pietra dura* cabinets from the Palace of Versailles.

*Open daily 1st Apr–30th Oct 10am–5pm. **Adm** adults £11.95, children (5–15) £4.95, under fives free, conc £9.95, families (two adults and up to four children) £29.95. **Amenities** restaurant with highchairs. **Credit Cards** all except DC.*

Bamburgh Castle ★ ★ ALL AGES

Bamburgh, Northumberland, ☎ 01668 214060, www.bamburghcastle.com

We have bored many people about this castle. I mean really, really bored them. This Norman castle is stunning. Built thrillingly into the cliff face over the fabulous sandy beach below, its spectacular location made it a contender a year or so ago in a poll to find the best view in Britain. Home to the kings of

Harry Hotspurs

Alnwick Castle's real history is about another Harry. The Harry Percy born here was the famous Harry Hotspurs, immortalized by Shakespeare, who fought his first battle aged eight, was knighted 10 years earlier than was commonly done aged 21 and died the day after losing his lucky sword in the Battle of Shrewsbury when he raised his visor to get some fresh air and was struck in the eye with an arrow. Hotspurs' body was impaled on a spear, and later cut up into quarters and sent around all of England. His head, meanwhile, was stuck on a pole at York's Gates. Sort of how we hoped Harry Potter might fare in the final film *The Deathly Hallows*.

Northumbria, the castle was the first in the world to fall to cannon fire while its illustrious former guests have included Queen Mary I and Henry VIII. Once owned in the 1800s by Lord Armstrong, who invented the first breach-loading cannon and the hydraulics on Tower Bridge in London, its exhibits include an Anglo-Saxon sword, two chairs from the coronation of Queen Elizabeth II and a curtain made from old Russian uniforms from the Crimean War. OK, fair enough there isn't as much inside this castle as you'd expect from its outside. That doesn't matter. The castle, used in the filming of *El Cid* and *Blake's 7*, isn't buggy friendly either, although children can have a go at being archaeologists in the free dig-pit of sand. But you must go. You must. We're boring ourselves now so we will shut up.

Durham Castle

Open 1st Mar–1st Nov 10am–5pm. Adm adults £7.50, children £3.50, seniors £6.50. Car park an extra £1. Amenities parking, baby-changing, café. Credit Cards All except AX and DC.

INSIDER TIP

To get to the unsignposted beach, drive down The Wyndings following signs to the golf course and pull in at any of the parking bays alongside the dunes. From there, walk down towards the castle.

Durham Castle AGES 16 AND UP

Palace Green, Durham, ☎ 0191 334 3800, www.dur.ac.uk

The only way to see the 11th-century Norman castle, still in use as a university halls of residence, is via a dry (if you aren't that interested in bishops' coats of arms) and also a strangely dimwitted student tour (we heard the parliamentary side in the English Civil War referred to throughout as the Republican Army). Basically there was just a child's suit of armour to point out to our children, who eventually went berserk in the dining room. Drunk with boredom, they started knocking cutlery off tables, forcing us to turn a bag of crisps on them like a water cannon to restore order.

Open daily during university holidays 10am–12.30pm and 2pm–5pm. **Adm** adults £5, children (up to 16) and conc £3.50, families £12. **Amenities** disabled toilet. **Credit Cards** cash only.

Hartlepool Maritime Experience and the Museum of Hartlepool ★ ALL AGES

Jackson Dock, Maritime Avenue, Hartlepool, 01429 860077, www. hartlepoolmaritimeexperience.com

You can spend almost a day taking part in the dockside naval entertainments here before you even step aboard *The HMS Trincomalee*, Britain's oldest warship still afloat. The highlight for our children was the Marine Adventure Centre, where our daughter got to send messages with flags, talked through a voice pipe and tried navigating by Polaris, probably my wife's method of getting us to Hartlepool (we got lost three times in Port Clarence). Also on the recreated 19th-century dock are several terraced shops including Eustace Pinkback's Gunmates, where our son had the opportunity to pick up and then drop a heavy cannonball on his little finger. There are also two shows, Fighting Ships and Press Ganged, which we left early when our four year old was scared of an able seaman flogging a man for falling asleep on guard duty. The tour of the ship (elevator for buggy pushers)

Hartlepool Maritime Experience

Sailor Talk

Jack nasty face   A sailor who is disliked by his peers
Splice the main brace   It's rum time
Bristol fashion   To do something efficiently
Whistling psalms to the taffrail   Providing advice that is ignored
Nelson's blood   It's rum time again

focuses on what life was like for sailors in Nelson's time, and the attraction is further enhanced by a play ship, a restaurant with no children's menu and the intoxicating aroma of beer wind-blown from the nearby Lion Brewery, possibly contributing to my wife muttering incoherently to herself for almost five minutes in the passenger seat as she tried to direct us back out towards Port Clarence.

Open daily Mar-Oct 10am-5pm and daily Nov-Feb 10.30-4pm. **Adm** adults £7.75, children, seniors and conc £4.75, families (two adults, up to three children) £20. **Amenities** café with highchairs, parking. **Credit Cards** All except AX.

> **INSIDER TIP** ⟩⟩
>
> The free Museum of Hartlepool, based on the same complex as the Maritime Experience, is worth visiting to hear the legend of how a monkey washed ashore was hung in Hartlepool during the 19th-century Napoleonic Wars when it was suspected of being … wait for it … a French spy. Today Hartlepool United football team has as its mascot H'angus the monkey, while in 2002 Stuart Drummond campaigned for the office of mayor dressed as H'angus the monkey wearing the football mascot's costume and not only won (quite scary) but (even more scary) was

returned again three years later. The museum has dressing up and hidden treasure for children to find in sandpits.

Housesteads Roman Fort ALL AGES

Bardon Mill, Hexham, Northumberland, 📞 *01434 344363, www. nationaltrust.org.uk*

This, the most complete roman fort in Britain, forms part of Hadrian's Wall and is accessible through a hilly walk from the car park, which buggies can just about manage. The fort occupies a commanding position on a windswept escarpment with great views over the surrounding moors; hard to appreciate when your one year old is attempting to eat a disk of sheep poo. The best way to see the ruins – fairly unintelligible on their own – are through an English Heritage guide. Very family friendly – ours put the fort into context by talking about Belicanus, a soldier stationed here – they take you round the barracks, the quarters of the former commander and also the latrines, or as our daughter put it, 'Yes, let's go and see where the Romans did their poos'.

Open Apr–Sept Wed–Sun 10am–6pm (daily in the summer holidays). **Adm** adults £1.95, children £1.45. **Credit Cards** cash and cheques only.

INSIDER TIP ›

On your way back along the causeway why not look out for the colony of 100 grey seals that live here, instead of, say, having the awful family car quiz we endured about the making of a medieval manuscript my wife had devised. 'OK everyone. What do you do to the velum after you've soaked the calf skins?'

Seven Stories ★ ★ AGES 1–10

30 Lime Street, Newcastle-upon-Tyne, ☏ 0845 2710777, **www.seven stories.org.uk**

Named after its seven floors and the contention there are only really seven stories in the world (most of which are Harry Potter's we suspect), this attraction has daily live storytelling sessions at 11am and a host of children's activities ranging from dressing

up to glueing and painting. The museum is hard to find as the council won't allow it to put up signs (that wouldn't be fair on the rest of the quayside attractions) so it's best to ring ahead and get directions otherwise you might shout at your wife the second time you cross the Tyne bridge into Gateshead when she says, 'It said the Walker area and then it changed it. I don't know', while flapping her arms uselessly. Our children had fun charging about reading books, putting on a small stage show, and painting more rabbits while my wife, sulking after the car incident, reminisced about Pippi Longstocking, the red-haired freckle-faced mischievous female character created by Swedish writer Astrid Lindgren in the 1960s. Pippi was very smart and inspired a generation of feminists including my wife, who at Leicester University was voted feminist of the year. There is an

Saltburn-by-Sea

Saltburn-by-Sea became popular in the 19th century as an escape for rich industrialists from the grit and grime of factory production. The town is perched on a cliff edge, its beach accessed via a slightly rickety Victorian funicular (65p per adult per ride) ascending 120 feet in 5.5 seconds but which seems longer after you've learnt its power source is basically a few buckets of water. The Smugglers Heritage Centre (☏ 01287 62525) nearby tells the story of local legend, John Andrew King, who 200 years ago centred his smuggling operations on the inn next door. The museum is a few low-ceilinged rooms of wax figures in semi-darkness discussing the Kings Men and The Revenue in silly accents, although in one room children are asked to smell smuggled goods – rum, whisky, tea, coffee and the chocolate our son suddenly went berserk for.

Holy Island of Lindisfarne `ALL AGES`

The island can only be accessed via a narrow causeway subject to tidal conditions, which vary greatly. Before setting off check tides at the information board at the car park on the Beale side of the causeway or from the island info website (**www.holyisland.info/lindisfarnecastle**).

There are three main attractions on the island. Lindisfarne Castle, Lindisfarne Priory (📞 *01289 38900*, *www.english-heritage.org.uk*) and the Lindisfarne Heritage Centre. If you have limited time the priory is where you should head first. It was founded by Irish monk Aidan in 635, making it one of the earliest cradles of Anglo-Saxon Christianity. After Aidan came St Cuthbert in 651, who was so holy he used to pray in the North Sea and have otters dry his feet, although the fuss only really started 11 years after he died when he was dug up to elevate his bones into reliquaries for veneration and his body was found still miraculously intact. A cult soon grew up about him so that when Lindisfarne was eventually abandoned to Viking raiders his body was removed, and after an interlude of around 100 years when it was ferried hither-and-thither around Northumberland like a Chuckle Brothers routine, he wound up in Durham Cathedral, which was founded in his honour. To keep the children amused we found a jigsaw of the Lindisfarne Gospels and a leaflet our daughter could use to write her name in Anglo Saxon runes – fairly useless as she could not yet write her name in English. Although climbing the priory walls isn't strictly allowed, Bob in the kiosk turns a kindly blind eye to toddlers running about the lower

excellent child-friendly café, where the argument with my wife thawed thanks to the delicious ciabattas with cranberry sauce and brie that were far too tasty not to remark upon and it later ended entirely in the Book Den when, demonstrating my behaviour at the wheel was a by-product of driver fatigue, I fell blissfully asleep on the window seat propped up with cushions as my daughter read me/made up a tale from the pictures in *What planet are you from?* by Lauren Child.

Open Mon–Sat 10am–5pm (Sun 11am–5pm). *Adm* adults £5.50, children (under 17) £4.50, conc £4.50. *Amenities* baby-changing, café. *Credit Cards* all accepted.

YORKSHIRE

This county covers a vast area and its highlights include the beautiful city of York with its famous Jorvic Viking Centre as well as the largest railway museum in the country. The picturesque harbour town of walls with packets of chocolate gems shouting, 'This is so boring, I don't believe it'. The priory has no toilets and the nearest public loos are a few perilous (when potty training) minutes walk away.

Open *daily 21st Mar–30th Sept 9.30am–5pm; daily 1st Oct–31st Oct 9.30am–4pm; Mon, Sat, Sun 1st Nov–31st Jan 10am–2pm and daily again between 1st Feb–31st Mar from 10am–4pm.* *Adm* *adults £3.90, children £2, conc £3.10.*

The Lindisfarne Heritage Centre (📞 *01289 389004, www.lindisfarne. org.uk*) is around the corner from the priory on Marygate. Children can learn about local wildlife, folklore, hear examples of the island dialect and see a replica of the famous eighth- century Lindisfarne Gospels, the sight of which were said to have healing powers for pilgrims. At this friendly centre, with lots of interactive activities for children (brass rubbing of the gospels, jigsaws of the gospels, tracings of the gospels), our son Charlie, maybe a little fed up with the gospels, managed to crawl into and get stuck in a lobster pot.

Adm *adults £3, children (5–16) £1.*

The 16th-century Lindisfarne Castle (📞 *01289 389244, www.national trust.org*) is closed on Mondays and has great views of Bamburgh castle and the Farne Islands.

Adm *adults £5.70, children £3.10.*

Open *daily 10am–4pm.* *Adm* *adults £4.50, children £2.30.* *Amenities* *café, parking.* *Credit Cards* *all except AX and DC.*

Whitby is worth a visit. Here you can board a scaled-down replica of the ship James Cook sailed the world in, visit the abbey that inspired Bram Stoker to write *Dracula* and eat in one of the many award-winning restaurants. The town of Knaresborough is home to the quirky Mother Shipton's Cave where a famous prophetess lived, while in the World of James Herriot in Thirsk children can learn about the creator of the famous TV vet. The county also has a museum dedicated to the tragic Brontë sisters, a fantastic air museum and the stunning North York Moors.

Essentials

Whitby

By Bus There are two National Express (📞 *0870 5808080, www. nationalexpress.com*) buses a day travelling between London and Whitby. The trip takes approx seven hours and 50 minutes. From Manchester the same

Yorkshire Dales National Park

This national park consists of some 700sq miles of water-carved country. In the dales, or valleys, you'll find dramatic white-limestone crags, roads, and fields bordered by dry-stone walls, fast-running rivers, isolated sheep farms, and clusters of sandstone cottages. Two of the most interesting attractions are the 12th-century ruins of Bolton Priory and the 14th century Castle Bolton, to the north in Wensleydale. From strenuous hikes to easier circular walks the National Park Centre is a good starting point. (*www.yorkshiredales.org.uk*). The **North York Moors National Park** on the other side of the Vale of York, have a wild beauty all of their own, quite different form the dales. This is rather barren moorland and blossoms in summer with purple heather. The park is perfect for strolls or peaceful drives (*www.moors.uk.net*).

company have four services a day to Whitby, the journey taking between five and seven hours depending on what can be lengthy waits in Leeds.

By Train There are no direct services from London. The best way to get to Whitby is to travel on a National Express East Coast (☎ 08457 225225, *www.nationalexpresseastcoast.com*) train to Middlesborough and then catch a Northern Rail (☎ 0845 0000125, *www.northernrail.org*) service train on to Whitby. This final leg of your journey will take about an hour and a half and services are fairly irregular going every three or four hours or so but check ahead. To get to Whitby from Manchester the best option is to take a First Transpennine Express (☎ 0845 6001671, *www.tpexpress.co.uk*) train from Manchester Airport running every half an hour or so to Middlesborough. The journey is approximately three hours long. After

this follow the advice above to get on to Whitby.

By Car From Manchester it takes approx two hours and 45 minutes to Whitby. Take the M62 heading east, join the M1 then the A1 (M), the A64 past York, and finally the A169 and A171 into Whitby. From London to Whitby it will take between five and six hours. Take the M1 north then the M18, M62, A63, and the A614 to Bridlington, the B1249 and finally the A64 Scarborough road followed by the A171.

York

By Bus National Express (☎ 0870 5808080, *www.nationalexpress.com*) services travel hourly from London the journey taking between four and three-quarter hours to six hours depending on the wait at Leeds. They also travel hourly during the day between Manchester and York. The trip takes approximately two hours and 40 minutess.

By Train From London Kings Cross there are half-hourly services to York provided by National Express East Coast (℡ 08457 225225, *www.national expresseastcoast.com*). The journey takes around two hours. To get to York from Manchester on a First Transpennine Express (℡ 0845 6001671, *www.tpexpress. co.uk*) train will take approx 1 hour 30 minutes with services running half-hourly regularly throughout the day.

By Car It takes approx 1 hour 30 minutes from Manchester to York via the M62. You must then head east, join the M1 then the A1 (M) and take the A64 into York. From London the journey takes approx 4 hours. Take the M1 north then the M18, A1 (M) and finally the A64.

By Air Leeds Bradford Airport (℡ 0871 288288, *www.leeds bradfordairport.co.uk*) has extensive domestic connections (Aberdeen, Belfast, Bristol, Dublin, Exeter, Edinburgh, Glasgow, London Gatwick, Isle of Man, Newquay, Plymouth, Southampton) and also international flights to over 50 destinations covering some long haul and many European destinations. The main operators include bmi (℡ 0870 6070555, *www.flybmi. com*), flybe (℡ 0871 7000123, *www.flybe.com*), KLM (℡ 0870 5074074, *www.klm.com*) and Ryanair (℡ 0871 2460000, *www. ryanair.com*).

Visitor Information

The Harrogate Tourist Information Centre (℡ 01423 537300) is at Royal Baths Assembly Rooms, Crescent Road, Harrogate. The Hawes Tourist Information Centre (℡ 01969 666210) can be found at the Dales Countryside Museum, Station Yard, Hawes while the Haworth Tourist Information Centre (℡ 01535 642329 or 01535 645864) is based at 2/4 West Lane, Near Keighley, Haworth. The Knaresborough Tourist Information Centre (℡ 01423 866886 or 01423 537300) is at 9 Castle Courtyard, Market Place, Knaresborough and the Leeds Gateway Tourist Centre (℡ 0113 2425242) is at The Arcade, City Station, Leeds. The Thirsk Tourist Information Centre (℡ 01845 522755 or 01845 527759) is at 49 Market Place, Thirsk. The Whitby Tourist Information Centre (℡ 01723 383637) is at Langborne Road, Whitby while the York (De Grey Rooms) Tourist Information Centre (℡ 01904 550099) is based at The De Grey Rooms, Exhibition Square, York. The York (Railway Station) Visitor Information Centre (℡ 01904 550099) is at the Railway Station, Station Road, York. The Yorkshire Tourist Board (℡ 0870 6090000) has its base at 312 Tadcaster Road, York. For more local child-friendly events in Leeds check out *www.mylife inleeds.co.uk* by Travel Rants blogger Darren Cronian.

7 Northeast & Yorkshire

What to See & Do

Brontë Parsonage Museum ALL AGES

Church Street, Haworth, Keighley, West Yorkshire, ☎ 01535 642323, www.bronte.org.uk

This parsonage was where the Brontë sisters – Anne, Charlotte and Emily – lived with their brother Branwell and dreamt up classic 19th-century novels before their untimely deaths. Despite the children's quiz there isn't much for really young children to enjoy here and especially not for under twos averse to the hip seat given on entry (buggies are banned) and adept at crawling under roped-off barriers toset off sensor alarms. However, for older children and adults it gives a fascinating insight into the world's most famous literary family whose writing careers were developed in Haworth, amid the dramatic landscape of the surrounding moors. On a cold and windy day here it's easy to see how the myth making around the family has developed, as you imagine the sisters in this desolate setting conjuring their novels. For misunderstood and romantic

teens it is an essential stop. However, this life of unrelieved isolation was partly created unintentionally by the Brontës being published under the pseudonyms of Currer, Ellis and Acton Bell. Visitors can see costumes from TV dramatisations of *Wuthering heights* and also short term exhibitions focusing on the individual sisters and their family.

Open daily 10am–5.30pm Apr–Sept and 11am–5pm Oct–Mar. Adm adults £6, children (5–16) £3, under fives free, seniors £4, families (two adults and up to three children) £15. Amenities gift-shop. Credit Cards all cards accepted.

Dracula Experience AGES 11 AND UP

9 Marine Parade, Whitby, ☎ 01947 601923, www.draculaexperience.co.uk

Featuring beheadings, blood-curdling voices, special effects and live actors, the story of Dracula, dreamt up in Whitby by Bram Stoker (see box) is told here in a series of dark corridors that were a definite no-no for our daughter, who until the age of three was scared of the moon, steam, fluff and Henry the

Bram Stoker

Stoker was staying in Whitby in 1885 and reading up about the legend of vampires when the Russian Schooner, *The Demeter*, hit by a wild storm, drifted into the harbour on Tate Hill Sands. Mysteriously all the crew were dead, including the captain, who was lashed to the helm. The instant *The Demeter* ran aground Stoker is said to have witnessed a black dog leap ashore and run up the 199 steps to Whitby Abbey. A dog was thought to be one of the many forms into which a vampire could transform itself. Bram Stoker's story was born (evil laugh in here).

Castle Howard, York

Hoover. Fun for teenagers, they have a cape once worn by Christopher Lee on display here.

Open *Nov–Easter weekends only 9.45am–5pm, Easter–end of Oct (and also half-term holidays) daily 9.45am–5pm.* ***Adm*** *adults £2.50, children (under 13) £2.* ***Amenities*** *gift-shop.* ***Credit Cards*** *cash and cheques only.*

Captain Cook Experience
⭐ **ALL AGES**

Bark Endeavour, Pier Road, Whitby Harbour at Fish Quay, Whitby, 📞 *07813 781034, www.endeavourwhitby.com*

During a 45-minute ride on a pint-sized replica of the famous ship Cook sailed round the world in, you get views of North Yorkshire's Jurassic coastline in a voyage around Whitby harbour and along the coast to Sandsea. On this exhilarating ride into open seas through the harbour wall there is a chance of seeing seals and occasionally porpoises, dolphins and whales with some wonderful views looking back at

the abbey. The authentic replica of HMS Endeavour measures nearly 14 metres in length, 4 metres in width and is approximately 40% of the original ship's size. There are hardwood decks through with the three masts made from Douglas Fir and the whole ship was built by one of Whitby's oldest ship builders. As you sail the choppy waters you also get to hear sea shanties.

Runs *hourly (weather permitting) from Feb–Nov starting at 10am.* ***Adm*** *adults £3, children £2, seniors £2.* ***Credit Cards*** *cash and cheques only.*

Castle Howard ⭐ **ALL AGES**
York, North Yorkshire, 📞 *01653 648444, www.castlehoward.co.uk*

Castle Howard is one of country's finest stately homes, a gorgeous house with 1,000 acres of fabulous grounds. Visitors can discover hidden temples, statues, lakes and fountains, explore the winding paths of Ray Wood and enjoy the Walled Gardens, with its scented rose gardens. Still owned by the Howard family, whose ancestors have included two of Henry VIII's wives – Anne Boleyn and Catherine Howard – children are given a quiz, and along the tour route, staff will try and interest them in artefacts while also attempting to prevent toddlers from sitting on a priceless 18th-century gilt-wood settee by John Linnen. The house, full of pictures of the current Howard family including their two children Octavia and Merlin, was partially burnt down in the 1940s and since its renovation has been used in the filming of several period costume dramas including the *Brideshead Revisited* version that starred Emma Thompson. If you come in the holidays there are special tours aimed at two to 10 year olds lasting 30–40 minutes with themes such as Myths and Mysteries.

Open 16th Mar–1st Nov and 28th Nov–20th Dec. The gardens are also open on their own from 22nd Dec–15th Mar and 2nd –27th Nov at slightly reduced rates. *Adm* adults £11, children (4–16) £7 conc £10, families £9. Gardens only: adults £8.50, children £6, conc £8, families £23. *Amenities* café, parking, baby-changing. *Credit Cards* all except AX and DC.

Jorvik Viking Centre

⭐ ALL AGES

Coppergate, York, 📞 *01904 543400,* **www.jorvik-viking-centre.co.uk**

A vibrating time machine takes visitors back to the year 975 when York was the Viking town of Jorvik. After exiting the time machine, visitors journey in a small pod through scenes of Viking life including a fibre-glass man behind a stick stockade in a squatting position ('Having a pooh like daddy in the morning'). Other highlights include viewing a mineralized human stool uncovered in 1972 and measuring (if you're interested) 195mm × 55mm × 28mm and weighing 8.2 ounces, which contained whipworm eggs. There are also less scatological displays showing Norse words we have adopted (uggligr became our ugly), and a fun test to see how much Viking blood you possess through responding to a series of questions about your hair

FUN FACT ▸ **Vikings** ◂

- **Viking boys started drinking alcohol aged four.**
- Viking women could divorce simply by wearing their hair down.
- Many Icelanders descended from Viking stock have a condition called Dupuytren's Contracture, which means their hand grows into a claw. The reason this genetic flaw has survived is that a side-effect of the condition is a thick skull able to withstand an axe blow. An important attribute in the unruly Viking times and possibly in the future now the bankrupt country is heading back to the Stone Age.

FUN FACT » Toilet Humour «

In old days a bee used to be painted on men's stand-up urinals at such a height that if men urinated against it, it would prevent their shoes being splashed, the scholarly joke (oh, how we laughed) being that the Latin word for bee is 'apis'.

colour, and also, somewhat baffling, your sandwich filling of choice. Staff are on hand to explain about the Viking way of life (see box) and at the end there's a chance to see real bones with spear and sword injuries, something that, we assume, inspired our daughter's skeleton drawing before bed that night of what looked like a grisly compression fracture to the fifth lumbar vertebrae.

Open daily summer 10am–5pm and winter 10am–4pm. **Adm** adults £8, children £6, conc £7. **Amenities** baby-changing, outside café. **Credit Cards** all except AX.

Mother Shipton's Cave ALL AGES

High Bridge, Knaresborough, North Yorkshire, 📞 01423 864600, www. mothershiptonscave.com

The dank cave here, believed to be one of the oldest tourist attractions in the world, was where Mother Shipton (see box), a legendary prophetess with a nose and chin so hooked she looked like a nutcracker, is said to have lived and predicted among other things the Great Fire of London, the Internet, the plague, and the demise of Ant and Dec (OK, we made that up). The cave itself isn't much to look at, although the spring

Mother Shipton's Cave

Mother Shipton

Mother Shipton was born during a storm in 1488 to 15-year-old Agatha Sontheil, who was banished from Knaresborough for refusing to reveal who the father was. She sought refuge in the cave and lived there until the Abbot of Beverly sent her to a convent in Nottinghamshire. Ursula, her child, was taken in by a local family and grew up being taunted for her deformities. But she had a gift for predicting the future and when Sir Thomas Wolsley heard of it, had the Duke of Suffolk, Lord D'arcy and the Earl of Northumberland dispatched to check her out. Ursula, or Mother Shipton as she became known, knew they were coming, of course, and voiced the damning prophecy that they would all die on the pavements of York. The noblemen returned to court with her predictions for the Great Fire of London, the plague, the discovery of the potato and tobacco and the names Raleigh and Drake. Although Wolsley threatened to have her burned as a witch, he was too scared to carry out the threat and sure enough the three aristocrats were indeed all later executed as traitors by Queen Elizabeth I, their heads mounted on spikes in York. Mother Shipton died in 1561 – having lived twice as long as a normal life span then. She predicted the day naturally. Mentioned in Pepys' diaries and by Henry VIII's chronicler, many pubs were named after her in the 1500s and 1600s and she was the first-ever pantomime dame. Her other predictions included that thought would travel around the world in the winking of an eye, that man shall be seen in the air, and that iron will one day float. She also claimed that the end of the world would occur when the High Bridge of Knaresborough collapsed for the third time. Earlier wooden bridges have already fallen twice.

opposite is fun. Said to have healing powers, you can make a wish here, while the water is so dense with minerals it petrifies anything that it comes into contact with. You can see a petrified lady's bonnet and a man's Victorian hat left by a couple on their way to York races in 1853. In the cave museum there are other articles turned to stone – a glove of David Dimbleby's, a woolly hat left by Seth from TV soap opera *Emmerdale* and a pair of actress Sarah Lancashire's stilettos. Our children's highlight was making loud witchy noises in the dark cave then skipping back to the car along Beech Avenue.

Open Feb–Mar 10am–5.30pm weekends, 1st Apr–31st Oct 10am–5.30pm daily, Nov 10am–4.30pm weekends, closed Dec–Jan. Adm adults £6, children £4, under fours free, families (two adults and two children) £17. Amenities parking, baby-changing, café. Credit Cards all except AX.

National Railway Museum ALL AGES

Leeman Road, York, 📞 *08448 153139, www.nrm.org.uk*

The largest railway museum in the world contains more than 100 locos including *The Flying Scotsman*, the record-breaking *Mallard* and a replica of Stephenson's *Rocket*. Or as our one-year-old homas-the-Tank-Engine-mad son described it eloquently upon entering the hall, his eyes aglow with wonder, 'Oh….wow. Engines'. Other highlights include a futuristic Japanese bullet train and a lock of George Stephenson's hair. There are film shows about trains in the Platform 4 theatre, an outdoor children's playpark and a number of royal carriages for your wife to look inside and comment upon the seat trim. A word of warning – be wary of entering the Warehouse Room, where we got hopelessly lost amongst the aisles of railway memorabilia in the company of some very strange-looking train buffs in brightly coloured raincoats a little too excitedly handling muffled pop safety valves and signal lever frames.

Open *daily 10am–6pm.* **Adm** *free.* **Amenities** *café, buggy access.*

Wensleydale Cheese Visitor Centre AGES 11 AND UP

Gayle La, Hawes, 📞 *01969 667664, www.wensleydale.co.uk*

On the long drive here, after we ran out of Teddy Bear Starbursts, we began in desperation, when our daughter started acting up, to sell this attraction to her on the basis of its association with Wallace and Gromit ('Do you want to see Wallace and Gromit – well behave yourself'). As it turns out, however, there is not as much association between The Wensleydale Cheese Visitor Centre and Wallace and Gromit as we had been led to believe. We got this impression from the fact Wallace's favourite cheese is Wensleydale and the pictures of them both on a poster we had seen advertising the centre. We arrived too late for the cheese-making experience (10am–3pm), and ended up standing in front of a few empty steel milling tubs learning from a man in a white coat how Wensleydale was supreme champion at the 2002 Nantwich International Cheese Show while batting off desperate questioning from our daughter about where Wallace and Gromit were. While we learnt a bit about a process called blocking and saw a video about how Franciscan monks brought cheese making back from France in the 12th century, it was hard to concentrate on these cheese facts against the chorus of 'You said we'd see Wallace and Gromit, dad'. On the upside, the scenery around here is stunning:

patchwork limestone, walled hillsides, spectacular waterfalls with bare moorland to verdant green slopes making for great walking. *www.wensleydale.org*

Open *Mon–Sat 9.30am–5pm, winter times may vary so check ahead.* **Adm** *adults £2.50, children £1.50.* **Amenities** *café with highchairs, baby-changing, parking.* **Credit Cards** *All except AX and DC.*

The 1853 Gallery ALL AGES

Salts Mill, Shipley, Saltaire, West Yorkshire, ☎ 01274 531163, www. saltsmill.org.uk

Containing the world's largest collection of David Hockney's artwork, in an upstairs bookshop above the gallery there are also lots of tables that children are encouraged to sit and read at. A meeting point for local mums and toddlers because of the friendly café that heats up baby food, our daughter drew, fittingly, her first mixed-media work featuring a rabbit and involving crayons and a sachet of ketchup from her fish-finger sandwich.

Open *Mon–Fri 10am–5.30pm (Sat–Sun 10am–6pm).* **Adm** *free.* **Amenities** *parking.* **Credit Cards** *all accepted.*

The World of James Herriot
★★ ALL AGES

23 Kirkgate, Thirsk, North Yorkshire, ☎ 01845 524234, www.worldof jamesherriot.org

The vets' series *All Creatures Great and Small*, based on the books by James Herriot, dealt with flat-capped, no-nonsense Yorkshire farmers, prone to using the phrase 'Nowt you can do for her', who'd thrust raw onions up their animals' behinds as cures and then, when this failed, ring the vet at 4am. The series starring Christopher Timothy as Herriot, Robert Hardy as Siegfried and Peter Davison as Tristan ran from 1978 to 1983 and attracted mass audiences. The stories were based on the real events at this former vet's practice, where Alf Wight, the James Herriot of the books, lived and worked. The audio guide, narrated by his son Jim, takes you round the recreated 1940s'-style house, while elsewhere there's a children's interactive room where our daughter did a brass rubbing of a cow, coloured in a goat, tested her sheepdog skills using a magnet to round-up sheep and looked askance at a model of an early test for inflammation of the

The World of James Herriot

FUN FACT ❯❯ **James Herriot** ❮❮

- **Unable to identify the real characters who came to his vets' surgery** Alf Wight created a *nom de plume* for himself. He chose James Herriot because it was the name of the then-popular Birmingham City goalkeeper.
- Alf Wight had so many rejections for his manuscript that the thud of its return on the front doorstep he described 'as more distinctive than that of a cow with a prolapsed uterus'.
- Alf Wight wrote his books in half-hour bursts at the typewriter in front of the TV in the evenings. He didn't start writing until he was 50.

---

bladder in a horse. There are regular storytelling sessions, an education room for crafts open in the holidays and in the gift-shop on the way out children can buy a key-ring cow whose bottom they can put their hand up by ripping away some stitching.

Open *Mar–Oct 10am–5pm and Nov–Mar 11am–4pm.* ***Adm*** *adults £5.75, children (5–15) £4, conc £4.50, families (two adults and two children) £15.50.* ***Amenities*** *disabled ramps and buggy access, baby–changing.* ***Credit Cards*** *all except AX.*

Whitby Abbey ALL AGES

Whitby, 📞 *01947 603568, www. english-heritage.org.uk*

Fittingly at the imposing remains of Whitby Abbey, inspiration for Bram Stoker's *Dracula* (see box), my baby son bit me on the forearm, not to 'welcome me to immortality' but because we'd run out of rusks and he was teething. Founded in 657 by St Hilda, the ruined abbey, perched high above Whitby, is a great place for children to run about, find out what a seventh-century

Benedictine monk ate, colour in yet another illuminated manuscipt and then have a tantrum because the tea room serves no ice cream. There is good buggy access and activity sheets for children but wrap up warm on all but very sunny days, as the abbey is windswept and freezing.

Open *daily 21st Mar–30th Sept 10am–6pm and Thurs–Mon 1st Oct–31Mar 10am–4pm.* ***Adm*** *adults £4.90, children £2.40, conc £3.90, families £12.20.* ***Amenities*** *car park, tea-room.* ***Credit Cards*** *all accepted.*

York Castle Museum ALL AGES

Museum Street, York, 📞 *01904 687687, www.yorkcastlemuseum. org.uk*

This is a child-friendly museum with feel-inside boxes and an eclectic range of exhibits such as a pig-killing hammer, a cobbled Victorian street scene and an ash midden privy. We would also like to tell you more about the wedding dress displays and other highlights but cannot as we were too traumatized here by the café staff, who ruthlessly enforced their 'bring no picnics' rule,

Cobbled Victorian street scene in the York Castle Museum

and so publicly shamed us halfway through our round of cheese-and-pickle rolls that we half-suspected we might be forced to wear bright gold homemade sandwich badges on our clothes and pointed hats for the remainder of our visit. Outside the museum, in the shadow of the Clifford Tower, there is a carousel (£2 a go); good diversionary material when your children get unfathomably stuck in the Rural Yorkshire area of the museum asking indelicate questions about the 'ram preventer'. You must leave your buggy in the entrance.

Open daily 9.30am–5pm (10am in term time). **Adm** adults £7.50, children £4, under fives free, families (two adults, two children) £20. **Amenities** backpacks given to those handing in buggies, baby-changing. **Credit Cards** All except AX.

Yorkshire Air Museum and the Allied Forces Memorial ALL AGES

Halifax Way, Elvington, York, 📞 *01904 608595, www.yorkshireairmuseum. co.uk*

As I watched my daughter firing rounds from a Lewis gun simulator mounted at highchair height at several German Me110 twin-engine fighters each performing a 'curve of pursuit', I had the odd qualm about the appropriateness of this museum for children. And that was before she leant up against a defunct thermo nuclear device 30 times more powerful than the A-bomb dropped on Hiroshima and asked, 'what's this, dad?' My fears were exacerbated after my son hurt his leg when a boxed glass set of Yorkshire squadron badges fell on his leg in another aerodrome building. The man at the gate had told me when we'd entered, 'It's not Alton Towers, you know. There's no Harry the Hurricane. It's a memorial'. I didn't appreciate the importance of this place until we reached a large hangar containing a brick wall on which were written hundreds of moving personal messages from loved ones to those stationed here who died in World War II. After another room devoted to the heroics of Squadron 609, I began to feel churlish for my earlier fault finding. Under the wide roofs of these aerodromes and watching old men peering into cockpits they'd sat in 60 years ago, I felt an avenue of understanding open up. The firing of guns wasn't always the wrong thing to do. Once upon a time it was the right and bravest thing that could be done. And the men based here had done this and wanted to come back and remember their friends. Walking round the Fighter Command Exhibition, an old man, after watching us for a while, shuffled across to say about our children quietly munching chocolate buttons during a film about the Blitz, 'If they were my grandchildren I'd be very proud'. I felt instantly proud of them and moved at the same time to be recognized in a favourable light by a man who had fought in the war. 'And if you were their grand-dad', I now wish I had replied, 'they would be very proud of you too'.

Open daily 26th Oct–28th Mar 10am–3.30pm and 29th Mar–24th Oct 10am–5pm. **Adm** adults £6, children (5–15) £4, seniors £5, families (two adults and up to three children) £18. **Amenities** café, parking. **Credit Cards** All except AX.

FAMILY-FRIENDLY ACCOMMODATION

EXPENSIVE

Chambers Serviced Apartments ★

30 Park Place, Leeds, 📞 *0113 3863300, www.morethanjustabed.com*

I had the worst night of my life in this apartment, when I woke up at 5am in the morning suffering from, as it later transpired in Leeds Royal Infirmary, a kidney stone. From what I remember of this serviced two bed apartment, it was very clean and also full of every mod con you could lean on while waiting to go to hospital. Reception staff are incredibly

Chambers Apartments, Leeds

helpful and you've up to three times the size of a normal hotel bedroom, so the whole family can spread out. It's a stylish and sleek place to stay with a choice of one to two-bedrooms with or without balconies to penthouse rooftops available, a dining table and chairs, so you can entertain, and lots of services at the touch of a button. There's underground parking, laundry and dry cleaning services, free WiFi available throughout and a DVD library. Serviced Apartments may not be an obvious choice for all but they can be a good bet, especially if you're staying for a longer period of time in a city when they become more affordable and less claustrophobic than some hotels.

Rates two-bed apartments from £230 per night. *Amenities* travel cots, highchairs, washer-dryer, dishwasher, fridge freezer, microwave, phone, tea and coffee making, breakfast pack. *Credit Cards* all accepted.

Craster Towers Apartments
★★

Craster, Northumberland, ☎ 01665 576674, *www.crastertower.co.uk*

This enormous four-bed penthouse apartment over two floors and with sea views is based on the top floor of one of the country's oldest occupied aristocratic homes. The Craster family, who the famous kipper-producing village is named after, has lived in magnificent turreted Craster Towers for more than 850 years. The landings are as wide as some flats, there is a

superb kitchen diner, a wood-burning stove in the cosy living room and the chance Fiona and Michael Craster might pop upstairs to tell you about the friendly poltergeists that live on the floors below. Dunstanburgh Castle is within walking distance and there are seven wonderful beaches nearby, including Howick's Seahorses beach, where we spent a morning collecting limpet shells, catching tiny fish in a pink net, completely on our own like characters from a Famous Five story.

Rates £950–£1800 per week. *Amenities* parking, table football, iPod docking station, wifi, microwave, fridge freezer, oven, honesty-box phone, children's games, coffee maker, washing machine, dryer. *Credit Cards* all except AX and DC.

Gisborough Hall Hotel ★

Gisborough, North Yorkshire, ☎ 0844 8799149, *www.macdonaldhotels. co.uk*

We celebrated our daughter's fourth birthday in interconnecting room 109 at this country-house hotel, the juxtaposition of the occasion and location making us feel like a cross between Bono and Alan Partridge. For her presents our daughter received a Winnie the Pooh pencil suitcase, a dolly that cried when you pressed its tummy, and, at Jesper's pet shop on Gisborough High Street, Part One of the Ancol rabbit grooming system. Part of her birthday treat was meant to be looking at the llamas in the fields next to the hall, but they were too far away so instead this treat became not having to witness the beheading of Dracula with a kukri sword in the Dracula Experience in Whitby (instead Daddy went in alone). The hall is a great family spot. There are grounds to run about in and staff are especially friendly. As well as singing 'happy birthday' to our daughter at breakfast despite the fact she had dirtied three table clothes with chocolate cocoa pops, they also gave her a cuddly Gisborough Hall teddy.

Rates executive family rooms are around £174 per night; interconnecting rooms range from £175–£350. Amenities children's board games in the lounge and drawing room, parking, Internet access. In Room phone, TV, tea and coffee making. Credit Cards All except DC.

Hazlewood Castle

Paradise Lane, Hazlewood, Near Leeds, North Yorkshire, 📞 *01937 535353, www.hazlewood-castle.co.uk*

This beautifully restored castle mentioned in the Doomsday Book had four other cars in the car park when we arrived in our Vauxhall Astra estate – a Mercedes, a Porsche, a Bentley and a Rolls-Royce. Yet despite the incongruity of our automobile status relative to that of other guests, staff managed to ungrudgingly transport our black bin liner of dirty clothes to reception with the same respect accorded to the most expensive of suitcases. The hotel, which was once owned by the Vavasours (or va-va-vooms as my wife called them), has large grounds for children to explore, a secret door in a bookcase to

the restaurant our son became obsessed with and some family suites including ours (Tanvey) that are supposedly haunted (ours by the ghost of a monk, who hung himself here during the Reformation, who my wife sensed 'moving through me' while cleaning (in the bathroom) her ear with a cotton bud. There is no lift so leave buggies at the foot of the grand staircase. Our baby alarm didn't work here because of the thickness of the walls.

Rates family suite in the castle £285 per night B&B and £255 for the same in the courtyard. Amenities wifi, parking. In Room DVD player, widescreen TV, phone, restless dead 16th-century souls not yet at peace. Credit Cards all cards accepted.

MODERATE

Best Western Cedar Court Hotel

Park Parade, Harrogate, North Yorkshire, 📞 *01423 858585, www.cedarcourthotels.co.uk*

It was in the restaurant of this hotel we apportioned the blame for our fraught day out to the Wensleydale Cheese Visitor Centre ('Ben, if Wallace had suggested visiting an attraction like the Wensleydale Cheese Visitor Centre that far away that late in the day, Gromit would have raised an eyebrow at him. You know it was daft'). The hotel, with efficient staff, is popular with businessmen and handy for town centre attractions while our children enjoyed two things – hiding under tables in the restaurant during

Best Western Cedar Court Hotel, Harrogate

check-in, and emptying almost an entire bath's worth of water onto the floor of the bathroom during a game of 'Let's play log flume'.

Rates £84–£150 B&B per night (double for interconnecting rooms). **Amenities** wifi £5 per hour (£9 for 24 hours), parking. **In Room** TV, phone, hairdryer, tea and coffee making. **Credit Cards** all accepted.

Griffon Forest Lodges ★★

Scotchman La, Flaxton, York, ☎ 01904 468787, www.griffonfirest.co.uk

We adored our beautiful wooden lodge with two bedrooms and a raised decked hot-tub where we lay at the end of a lazy Sunday here, the sun glinting through the trees, spotting squirrels and rabbits with our daughter while our baby son, scared of bubbles, shouted 'No', every now and again about getting in. The lodges, set in a wonderful forest, are equipped with toys including the jenga blocks our children fought over as if they were rare jewels. There is a handy shop, which doubles as an off-licence, good nearby walks and oven. The mainly flat 1,000 acre site has good walks on tracks exclusively for walkers and cyclists, fishing at the nearby trout lake and its sister operation Sandburn Hall with golf, badminton and tennis.

Rates Keeper's Lodge per week (two beds – a double and a twin) £446–£898. Woodman Lodge (double, twin and single) £489–£1038. **Amenities** indoor tennis and badminton (for hire), walks, DVD player, CD player, widescreen TV, all lodges have hot-tubs, cycle hire, travel cots and highchairs (£10 per week), Internet access, wet room. **Credit Cards** all except AX.

The Parkhead Country Hotel

New Coundon, Bishop Auckland, Durham, ☎ 01388 661727, www. parkheadcountryhotel.co.uk

This friendly no-frills hotel was epitomized by the exchange I had at breakfast when the waitress (wonderful about our children throwing their sausages at each other).
Me: 'Have you any fruit to go in my cereal?'
Waitress: 'No'.
'No strawberries'.
'Sorry'.
'An apple?'
'We have no apples'.
'No bananas in the hotel?'
'No'.
'Have you got any nuts?'
'I'll go and check', and she came back with – wait for it – a packet of dry-roasted peanuts from

behind the bar. Very nice too they tasted in my Kellogg's All Bran. Best for families are the interconnecting chalet-style rooms close enough to the hotel for baby monitors to work enabling you to eat in the bar restaurant where there is an overhead TV screen that (after winning the pub quiz here) we tiredly watched for a full five minutes believing it to be a police stake out on *The Bill*, but which we only realized was a CCTV camera fixed on the hotel car park when we saw our own Vauxhall Astra.

Rates *family room £85 per night, interconnecting rooms.* **Amenities** *parking, wifi in the bar, travel cots.* **In Room** *TV, tea and coffee making.* **Credit Cards** *All cards accepted.*

INEXPENSIVE

Boggle Hole Youth Hostel

Boggle Hole, Mill Beck, Fylingthorpe, Whitby, 📞 *0845 3719504,* **www.yha. org.uk**

Sounding a bit like something out of *The Lord of the Rings*, the beach in front of the Boggle Hole youth hostel is a great spot for beachcombing. An ex-mill, Boggle Hole (which we like to keep saying) was full of families and has a car park 600m away so it's best to drop your bags and family off first. Boggle Hole. Boggle Hole. Boggle Hole. OK, we're done now.

Rates *family rooms with four beds £31.95–£67.95 and six-bedders £47.95–£102.95.* **Amenities** *lounge, quiet room, travel cots, kitchen, high-chairs, breakfast and dinner can be provided.* **Credit Cards** *MC, V.*

Kielder Leaplish Waterside Park ★★

Kielder Water, Leaplish, Northumberland, 📞 *0844 8471100,* **www.ho seasons.co.uk**

The staff were fantastic when our daughter fell over on a gravel path doing her 'cheese dance' in the birds-of-prey centre, bit through her bottom lip and was taken to Hexham Hospital. Shocked by the amount of blood, our daughter was given three lollies, a plastic doll and

Holiday Lodge in Kielder Leaplish Waterside Park

patted kindly by Geordies in the reception room cooing 'dint worry pet – such a brave bairn', so affectionately my wife burst into tears and also had to be told 'dint worry pet'. Kielder, based on the banks of the largest man-made reservoir in Europe, has regularly been voted the most tranquil spot in England. However, it wasn't that tranquil for us; our other emergencies included finding a bat in our living room and chasing our daughter through a field of potentially live ordnance after she demanded a wee in the Military Zone (friendly welcoming roadside sign – 'Do not touch any military debris. It might explode and kill you') in nearby Otterburn. Having said all that, we did enjoy ourselves here. The birds-of-prey centre is fantastic, there are boat rides across the reservoir, and a crazy golf course and play area for the children. Our wooden Hareshaw Premier Lodge included a double (with en suite) room, a twin room overlooking the reservoir, a huge dining room-kitchen and a balcony to sit out on in the evening to look out for bats.

Rates two-bedroom lodges from £323–£884 per week. *Amenities* oven, fridge freezer, washing machine, parking, TV, DVD player, indoor pool, sauna, outdoor synthetic ice rink, travel cots for hire. *Credit Cards* all accepted.

FAMILY-FRIENDLY DINING

EXPENSIVE

Greens of Whitby ★

Bridge Street, Whitby, 📞 *01947 600284, www.greensofwhitby.com*

There are times when, with two small children under five, however good the food, however friendly the restaurant, eating out as a family is not worth the hassle. This was almost one of them. On our way here we were cheered by a crowd queuing outside Trenchers fish and chip shop when we pulled away after the 15th circumnavigation of the roundabout outside. We couldn't find anywhere near Greens to park and when we did, the restaurant was full of that sight you dread as a parent – smart-looking diners eating in a hushed respectful atmosphere. Our daughter drew on the napkin and fell off her chair while our son refused to sleep in the buggy despite being pushed around the town between courses. The good bits – the food was some of the best we ate in the Northeast, and the staff were unfazed by all of the above. We returned home after getting lost feeling so frazzled that when I found a Gideon Bible in my bedside table and read: 'At your wit's end, turn to psalm 56', I did.

Open summer Mon–Fri 12pm–2pm and 6pm–10pm (weekends 12pm–10pm); winter 12pm–3pm and 6pm–10pm (weekends 12pm–10pm). *Main Course* £9.50–£23.50. *Amenities* highchairs, smaller portions for

children at half price, baby-changing.
Credit Cards All except DC.

The Treehouse ★

Alnwick Garden, Denwick Lane, Alnwick, Northumberland, 📞 01665
511852, www.alnwickgarden.com

A family-orientated treetop restaurant with branches growing
through the floor, which is set in
spectacular Alnwick Gardens,
where my wife turned into her
mother for an hour ('Oh, those
roses. Can you smell them?
Divine'). There is a good children's menu, no danger of children toppling to the ground (my
wife's major reservation beforehand) and if you're lucky some
inquisitive squirrels to keep them
amused while your wife breezily
informs you as you tuck into
your Northumberland cheese
platter that 'just one tiny speck of
Angel's Trumpet', a plant she saw
in the famous Poison Garden
'and you'd drift off to sleep and

would never wake up again. It's
the assassin's favourite'. The restaurant serves great Woodland
Platters and was full of children
soaked from head to toe after a
walk round the water features of
Alnwick Gardens that seek to
demonstrate among other things,
the scientific properties of menis-
cus, the coanda water effect and
the exact pitch of anger a mother's voice can rise to after a new
pair of shoes is soaked in the
Grand Cascade.

Open lunch 11.30am–2.45pm and
dinner on Thurs, Fri and Sat from
6.30pm. **Main Course** £13–£19.
Amenities children's menu, highchairs. **Credit Cards** all except AX.

MODERATE
Betty's Café Tea Rooms ★★

1 Parliament Street, Harrogate,
📞 01423 814070, www.bettys.co.uk

A retro-style café serving more
than 300 different varieties of

Cycle the moors the Brontes made famous

Penistione Hill, West of Haworth (at the back of the Bradford city
council car park), (📞 01274 432666. http://recreation.yorkshirewater.
com/?OBH=3743).

You can pretend to be that black-eyed "imp of Satan," Heathcliffe,
chasing after his beloved Cathy on the desolate Wuthering Heights
moors on a circular 13 and half mile cycle route here. The Haworth and
Denholme ride, as well presenting ample opportunities to shout: "You
had a temper, like my jealousy. Too hot, too greedy. How could you
leave me? When I wanted to Possess you" at the top of your voice, also
offers spectacular views over valleys taking in the Thornton Moor and
Leeshaw reservoirs. There's a good map showing the various staging
points along the way available to print out if you follow the link at the
above website. The path is a mixture of moorland and tarmac and
some areas are remote so go in pairs.

cake, chocolate and bread, where our children were served speedily and handed toys when they kicked up. Children are given bibs and wipes are available, along with baby food and colouring-in kits. The café has views over the Stray, there's no booking ahead (you queue to get in) and a live pianist takes the edge off the squawks for 'I want more cake'. The waitresses are in old-fashioned black and white and my wife liked the cake stands although not my continual Mother Shipton-style predictions (see box) that included 'If the condiment tray falls for the third time, the meal shall end'.

Open *daily 9am–9.30pm.* **Main Course** *£7–£11.* **Amenities** *baby-changing, a buggy park at the door.* **Credit Cards** *all except AX.*

Nandos

12 High Street, Ousegate, North Yorkshire, ☎ 01904 679103, www. nandos.co.uk

At this relaxed centrally located Portuguese chain restaurant specializing in peri peri chicken, children are given an activity pack including stickers, crayons, puzzles and colouring-in sheets. They have highchairs and there is African art for toddlers to observe on the wall while you bore your wife about the emotional impact of seeing a thermonuclear weapon at the Yorkshire Air Museum (see p 198). 'That something so small could contain a destructive force capable of wiping out a city! Where there are nettles, there are dock-leafs. In nature there's always an antidote. These weapons have none – they have created an

imbalance'. The restaurant is a short walk to the city's attractions, which can be done marginally quicker if your wife is hurrying ahead with the children 'because you're bringing them down about the apocalypse, Ben'.

Open *Sun–Thurs 11am–10.30pm and Fri–Sat 11am–11.30pm.* **Main Course** *£6.10–£10.* **Amenities** *baby-changing.* **Credit Cards** *all cards accepted.*

Old West Quay

Maritime Avenue, Hartlepool, ☎ 08701 977127, www.brewersfayre.co.uk

Although unexciting, this chain restaurant is handily placed next to the Hartlepool Maritime Experience with a soft-play area. Children are given activity packs that include crayons and colouring-in books. There are also regular special offers including, when we dined there, two main meals for £9.

Open *daily 10am–12am (Sundays 10am–11pm).* **Main Course** *£6–£12.* **Amenities** *highchairs, children's menus, baby-changing.* **Credit Cards** *all cards accepted.*

Portofino

12a Mosley Streer, Newcastle upon-Tyne, ☎ 0191 2615512, www. portofino-newcastle.com

We had lunch under the beautiful vaulted ceiling of this 19th-century former insurance company building and now a pizzeria. Close to the quayside, this place has a children's menu as well as super-friendly Geordie staff.

Open *Mon–Fri 12pm–2.30pm and 5pm–10.30pm (Sat 12pm–10.30pm.*

Mountain biking in the Dalby Forest

Low Dalby, Near Thornton Dale, North Yorkshire YO18 7LT (01751 460295, *www.foresty.gsi.gov.uk*).

There are more than 30 miles of scenic trails here through North Yorkshire's Dalby forest. Trails are graded according to their level of difficulty. The toughest red-graded routes include hazards such as jumps, steps, and steep inclines. Blue trails are for intermediates, while the green one we opted for here was a gentle two and half-mile family pootle that started and ended at the Dalby courtyard. Open: 7am-dusk. Amenities: café, parking (pay and display – £7 summer, £4 winter), gift-shop, cycle hire.

Main Course from £7. *Amenities* highchairs, baby-changing. *Credit Cards* all except AX.

The Magpie Café ★★

14 Pier Road, Whitby, North Yorkshire, 01947 602058, www. magpiecafe.co.uk

This award-winning restaurant in a former 18th-century merchant's home overlooking Whitby harbour was where we took our daughter for her fourth birthday. Come in the rain (the staff hand out brollies) as the rest of the time the queues are daunting. Mentioned in *The Good Food Guide 2009*, the restaurant is unpretentious with seafaring pictures on the walls and no-nonsense waitresses you half expect to tell you 'to pull yourself together' when you can't decide between haddock and chips or sausages. Our daughter was given crayons and paper to draw Disney characters on and there was a pit of demerara sugar for our son to snatch sachets from and drop to the floor. The waitresses kept bringing new paper when our daughter ran out and the only bugbear was the pressure that the queue visible through the window gives to the speed you attack your food. The food was delicious, my haddock and chips so fresh the fish would probably have swam in my brown sauce if I'd made the puddle any deeper. Buggies must be folded up.

Open daily 11.30am–9pm. *Main Course* £12. *Amenities* gluten-free meals, highchairs, baby-changing. *Credit Cards* all except AX and Electron.

INEXPENSIVE

Earl Grey Tea Rooms ★

Howick Hall and Gardens, Alnwick, Northumberland, 01665 572232, www.howickhallgardens.org

A good stop for a light lunch after a wander around Howick Gardens, this café is full of children's toys, including a doll's house that our daughter played with/slammed our son's fingers in. The tearooms are part of the old hall, once home to the famous reforming 19th-century Grey family and was where Earl Grey tea was devised. To eat here you must pay to visit the gardens (£5 for adults, children free), which include a tree-house, herons, red squirrels and according to my rapidly ageing wife 'some of the better rhodo-dendron hybrids'. As your children bang salt cellars down on the glass-topped wicker tables and threaten at any moment to shatter them as you wait for your tea of choice, you can reassure yourselves with the fact detailed on the menus that at least you haven't got 15 children like the second Earl Grey.

Open 1st Feb–1st Apr Sat, Sun and Wed 12pm–4pm, 1st Apr–31st Oct daily 12pm–5.30pm and 31st Oct– 10th Nov daily 12pm–4pm. **Main Course** sandwiches £4.65. **Amenities** highchairs. **Credit Cards** all except AX.

Marigolds Café

Waterside, Knaresborough, North Yorkshire, 📞 *01423 869773*

A beautifully located café in the shadow of Knaresborough via-duct close to Mother Shipton's Cave with children's toys, and both an under and over fives menu. After lunch you can hire a rowing boat (adults £4, children £3) and cruise down the River Nidd shouting to the riverbanks more Mother Shipton style predictions ('When children stand in the boat then shall the shouting begin').

Open daily 10am–4.30pm (closed Nov–Jan). **Main Course** steak sandwich £6.75. **Amenities** highchairs, baby-changing. **Credit Cards** cash and cheques only.

Undercroft Restaurant at Durham Cathedral

The College, Durham, 📞 *0191 3863721, www.durhamcathedral. co.uk*

This is a good place for a cheap lunch after a free tour of what Bill Bryson has described as the 'finest cathedral on the planet'. The restaurant has children's toys, half portions at half price and highchairs. The food ranges from soups and jacket potatoes to sandwiches and shepherd's pie. The cathedral, which took 40 years to build and is the last resting place of St Cuthbert (or Cuddy as he is known locally), has a children's quiz, a church room where children can try on surplices to the accompaniment of monastic chanting, and a benign attitude to the shouting of the opening credit to the *Tweenies* in its cloisters.

Open 10am–4.30pm. **Main Course** £2.95 for a basis soup, to £5.95 for a shepherd's pie. **Amenities** highchairs, half portions for children at half price, toys. **Credit Cards** all except AX.

8 The Lakes & North West

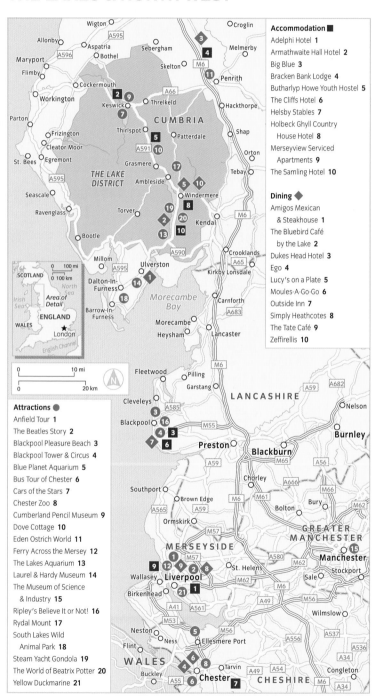

Accommodation ■
Adelphi Hotel **1**
Armathwaite Hall Hotel **2**
Big Blue **3**
Bracken Bank Lodge **4**
Butharlyp Howe Youth Hostel **5**
The Cliffs Hotel **6**
Helsby Stables **7**
Holbeck Ghyll Country
  House Hotel **8**
Merseyview Serviced
  Apartments **9**
The Samling Hotel **10**

Dining ◆
Amigos Mexican
  & Steakhouse **1**
The Bluebird Café
  by the Lake **2**
Dukes Head Hotel **3**
Ego **4**
Lucy's on a Plate **5**
Moules-A-Go-Go **6**
Outside Inn **7**
Simply Heathcotes **8**
The Tate Café **9**
Zeffirellis **10**

Attractions ●
Anfield Tour **1**
The Beatles Story **2**
Blackpool Pleasure Beach **3**
Blackpool Tower & Circus **4**
Blue Planet Aquarium **5**
Bus Tour of Chester **6**
Cars of the Stars **7**
Chester Zoo **8**
Cumberland Pencil Museum **9**
Dove Cottage **10**
Eden Ostrich World **11**
Ferry Across the Mersey **12**
The Lakes Aquarium **13**
Laurel & Hardy Museum **14**
The Museum of Science
  & Industry **15**
Ripley's Believe It or Not! **16**
Rydal Mount **17**
South Lakes Wild
  Animal Park **18**
Steam Yacht Gondola **19**
The World of Beatrix Potter **20**
Yellow Duckmarine **21**

The Lake District is widely considered to be the most romantic spot in England. Its rugged beauty and crystal clear lakes have made it the most common location for couples to pop the question. Bill Clinton proposed here (to Hilary in 1973) as did (oh dear) Sir Paul McCartney to Heather Mills in 2001. The poet William Wordsworth wrote many of his greatest works here and had clearly never been to Postman Pat Village at Longleat Safari Park when he declared that it was 'the loveliest spot that man has ever known', while the painter John Constable thought the Lakes had 'the finest scenery that ever was'. Besides the moody views and gentle boat cruises there's plenty for children including a zoo, walks, cycling, a steam train, aquariums and a Laurel and Hardy Museum. Even so, nowadays the Lakes are rife with boutique hotels and classy restaurants, and, perhaps because of this, spoiled swans who'll snootily turn their beaks up at Sunblest bread, expecting at the very least *focaccia*.

Liverpool, the former capital of European culture, is well known for its sense of humour, with many top comedians and Les Dennis hailing from there. The city has produced the Beatles and the famous large-haired footballing teams of the 70s and 80s, while its residents are nicknamed after a former lamb-based stew – Lobscouse. Perhaps as a legacy of its Irish blood – many millions of migrants from the Emerald Isle have settled in Liverpool over the centuries – it is a place apart from the rest of England. This is evidenced by its incredible strength of community and also by its general weirdness, which we witnessed first-hand when it 'rained cooking oil' according to the *Liverpool Echo*, the day we arrived. Despite still suffering from a perception that it's a crime hotspot Liverpool's regeneration and particularly the Albert Docks are great for families with attractions including: Tate Liverpool, BugWorld Experience, Beatles Story, Shiverpool Ghost Tour, International Slavery Museum and the Maritime Museum. Meanwhile, World Museum Liverpool has high-tech gizmos to bring history to life for all. To the south, Chester has its famous Roman walls; and Manchester, home of *Coronation Street* and the hands-on Museum of Science and Industry is a short drive away down the M62. Blackpool on the other hand exists in its own bubble – pleased to consider itself the tawdry Las Vegas of England, the party capital of the country attracts more stags and hens per head than anywhere else in the UK and for this reason, as colourful as the spectacle can be, it's best avoided at night. Blackpool is not for the faint-hearted. It is Las Vegas with a beach, Las Vegas with a temper, Las Vegas where the only gamble is whether you'll make it back to your hotel without someone being sick on your shoes. During the day families rule the sands, however, and there's the Pleasure Beach to visit and the famous Blackpool Tower circus. Then to top it all off, a donkey ride on the sands.

CHILDREN'S TOP 10 ATTRACTIONS

❶ **See lions**, elephants and larger-than-average youngsters from the Liverpool suburbs getting wedged in the Marmot Mania tunnel at Chester Zoo. See p 214.

❷ **Touch the** 'This Is Anfield' sign in the player's tunnel at Liverpool's famous football stadium. See p 217.

❸ **Lift a mini** with your little finger at Manchester's Museum of Science and Industry. See p 220.

❹ **Hand-feed** giraffes at the South Lakes Wild Animal Park. See p 228.

❺ **Stand next to** the world's largest pencil at the Cumberland Pencil Museum. See p 226.

❻ **Eat food served** by pirates at the Disneyesque Outside Inn restaurant in Blackpool. See p 239.

❼ **Tour Liverpool** on land and water on the renovated World War II amphibious landing craft, the *Yellow Duckmarine*. See p 220.

❽ **Wake to the sound** of Lar gibbons dueting at Armathwaite Hall Hotel. See p 231.

❾ **Stay at the** Liverpool Adelphi, where it is believed Hitler once worked as a waiter See p 233.

❿ **Visit the** country's most impressive circus, set in the foot of Blackpool Tower. See p 222.

CHESTER & AROUND

The people of Chester like three things: shopping, dressing up like Romans and murdering the Welsh. Chester people have been murdering the Welsh for centuries and are so keen on it they have ensured, despite advances in human rights, that it's still (technically) legal to murder Welshmen with a crossbow within the city walls after 9pm. Chester also has the best-preserved Roman city walls in Britain, the second-most photographed clock in Britain (the Eastgate Clock), and, more importantly, is also where the teen Channel 4 soap *Hollyoaks* is based. Besides (if you are my wife) looking out for actor Jeronimo Best (the annoying Spanish dance teacher, Fernando) from the top deck of a city sightseeing bus, families can boat along the River Dee or have their picture taken with one of the many costumed Roman centurions sweating like greasy pasties near the Eastgate Clock. Chester Zoo and the aquarium in Ellesmere Port are both within striking distance.

Essentials

By Rail From London Euston there are half-hourly services from Virgin Trains (☎ *0845 0008000, www.virgintrains.co.uk*) for Chester with a journey time of about two hours. From Glasgow you also take a Virgin

Train but change at Warrington Bank Quay (they run every hour) and then use an Arriva Trains Wales (☎ 0845 6061660, *www.arrivatrains.co.uk*) service on to Chester. From Manchester to Chester take a Virgin train direct. They run every 20 minutes and the journey will take about an hour.

By Bus There are National Express (☎ 0870 5808080, *www.nationalexpress.co.uk*) services every two and half hours or so from London Victoria coach station to Chester. The journey takes between five and six and a half hours. From Manchester the same company provides five coaches a day to Chester. The journey takes just over an hour. From Glasgow to Chester it's at least a seven-hour journey and buses leave only twice a day.

By Car From London to Chester will take around three and half hours using the M1, M6, A500 and then the A51. From Manchester take the A57M, the A5103, the M56, M53 and the A56, the journey taking just under an hour. From Glasgow it's the M8, M73, M74, A74A, M6, M56, M53 and then the A56 for a journey of under four hours.

Visitor Information

Chester Tourist Information Centre (☎ 01244 402111, *www.visitchester.com*) is at the Town Hall, Northgate Street, Chester. The Ellesmere Port Tourist Information Centre (☎ 0151 3567879) is based at Unit 22b, McArthur Glen Outlet Village, Kinsey Road, Ellesmere Port.

What to See & Do

Blue Planet Aquarium
⭐ **ALL AGES**

Kinsey Road, Ellesmere Port, ☎ 0151 3578804, www.blueplanetaquarium.co.uk

Boasting the largest shark tunnel in Europe, this aquarium was full of strange, excited and, we guessed, fairly posh Scouse schoolchildren discussing the injurious effects of standing on a stonefish they'd learnt from the Deadly and Dangerous Fish Exhibition. ('Convulsions, hypertension, paralysis, respiratory weakness and collapse. You'd be marmelised, mate'). Our daughter's low point was almost choking on some polished cobalt I bought her for a treat from a coin-operated machine (I thought it was a gobstopper) and her high point was stroking rays in the touch-pool ('they feel like toast, daddy'). Charlie, our one-year-old son, meanwhile, ran excitedly up and down the shallow ramps between tanks, largely uninterested in the fish, putting his newfound ability to walk through its paces like a motoring correspondent checking out the handling on a new Mercedes. There's a recreation of the Amazon rainforest, a mocked-up Lake Malawi, the adventure playground has bouncy whales

The Blue Planet Aquarium

and marine talks take place in the aquatheatre.

Open *daily 10am–5pm (6pm weekends).* **Adm** *adults £14.50, children (under 15) £10.50, conc £1.50, families (two adults, two children) £48.* **Amenities** *café, parking, baby-changing, wheelchair hire (£10 returnable deposit).* **Credit Cards** *all except AE and DC.*

Bus Tour of Chester ALL AGES

City Sight-Seeing Bus, ☎ *01244 347452, www.city-sightseeing.com*

One of the best ways to get an overview of Chester is from the top of a bus. The hop-on/hop-off tours are family friendly with youngsters given pens, sweets and a colouring-in book they can, if they are our son, shred and attempt to feed later to the wide-boy squirrels in Grosvenor Park. Buses leave every 15–20 minutes (4th May–31st Aug) and daily (4th Apr–4th Oct) from Chester Railway Station and Bus Exchange taking in the cathedral, amphitheatre and the

city walls. The on-board commentator will pass on interesting local history and also increasingly less interesting local history if you get caught in a traffic jam near the Eastgate Clock (largely about House of Fraser maybe coming to Chester to increase its retail pull). You can combine your ticket with a boat cruise down the River Dee, the trips leaves handily from The Groves bus stop.

Adm *adults £8.50, children (5–15) £3, seniors £7 and family tickets (two adults, two children) £19. With the boat trip adults £12, children £4.50, seniors £9.50, families (two adults, two children) £27.50.* **Credit Cards** *all except AE.*

> **INSIDER TIP** »
>
> On a boat trip down the River Dee in Chester, please be aware, if you aren't concentrating because the children are running about trying to jump in the water, that the words 'before finally emerging into the Irish Sea' apply to the river NOT the boat ride itself, as my panicky wife thought ('My God, Ben! The Irish Sea! How long is this trip? It's £2 an hour in the NCP car park.')

Chester Zoo ✩ ALL AGES

Cedar House, Caughall Road, Upton-by-Chester, Chester, ☎ *01244 380280, www.chesterzoo.org*

They have 7,000 animals here including every substantial beast you'd expect of a superior zoo along with 'stand-up monkeys' (meerkats), a minute spectacled bear plus a monorail (£2 extra). Children can get their faces painted, or have a tattoo of a tasteful anchor airbrushed onto their upper arm and there is an impressive wooden play park to sit in to have a picnic. There are also some gardens such as the Andes Garden showing the terrrain and range of plants from the mountains of the Andes. My son enjoyed the lions while our daughter's highlight was watching a schoolgirl from Rainhill getting wedged in the Marmot Mania tunnel because of her overlarge sandwich bag, prompting mournful shouts from the darkness to her concerned/highly amused friends, 'Get Mrs Harris'. My own favourite moment was overhearing a man with a heavy German accent at an ice-cream stand near the elephants asking for, 'Von Nobbily-bobbily'. There's an excellent sea-lion show so don't miss feeding time, animal talks by presenters, Fun Ark and Ape Around play areas and a pinbadge trading craze that has taken off, so you can swap badges with staff or by stopping at displays.

Open *daily 10am–4pm.* ***Adm*** *Off peak adults £10.86, children (3–15) £8.13, under 3s £0.90, family (two adults, two children) £34.54. Peak time £14.95, children (3–15) £11.30, under 3s £0.90, conc £13.55, family £50.* ***Amenities*** *café (child lunchbox £3.95), parking, coffee shop.* ***Credit Cards*** *all accepted.*

LIVERPOOL, MANCHESTER & AROUND

The best place to start in Liverpool is the Albert Docks where you can ride on the *Yellow Duckmarine*, visit the Beatles Museum and the Liverpool Tate and take the ferry across the Mersey. Further out for any football fan, the Anfield Tour is a must-see, while Manchester is a short hop down the M62. While Manchester hasn't the character of Liverpool, it does have many Victorian red-brick buildings of the sort you see cats sitting outside of during the depressing title sequence of *Coronation Street*. We sound dismissive but it's hard not to compare these two great cities. If Liverpool and Manchester were two brothers, Manchester would be the younger more sensible one with a proper job keen to start the Industrial Revolution while Liverpool would be the talented, incorrigible older one preferring to lounge about the Mersey and play headers and volleys with a tin can. For families the highlight of Manchester is the hands-on MOSI (Museum of Science and Industry).

Essentials

By Rail Direct services from Virgin Trains (☎ 0845 0008000, **www.virgintrains,co.uk**) go from London Euston to Liverpool Lime Street every hour or so. The journey takes two hours and 10 minutes. From Glasgow Virgin Trains leave for Preston every half-hour. Change here and take the Northern Rail (☎ 0845 0000125, **www.northern rail.org**) service for Liverpool. The journey takes three and half hours. From Birmingham New

Street London Midland (📞 *0121 63422040, www.londonmidland. com*) services leave every half-hour to Liverpool Lime Street. The Merseytravel network provides direct train connections from the city centre to principal local destinations, including Southport, Aintree, Wirral Peninsula and St Helens (*www. merseytravel.gov.uk*).

By Bus National Express (📞 *0870 5808080, www.nationalexpress.co. uk*) services from London Victoria coach station to Liverpool leave every couple of hours. The journey takes about five and a half hours. There is one direct service from Glasgow to Liverpool per day taking five hours and 20 minutes. Indirect services take many hours longer and there are three extra services of these per day. From Birmingham services to Liverpool go throughout the day and journey is three hours.

By Car To get to Liverpool from London take the M1, M6, M62 and then the A5080. The journey will take about four hours. From Glasgow take the M8, M73, M74, A74M, M6, M58, A5036 and the A59 and from Manchester the best route is the M60, M62 and the A5080. It will take about 45 minutes.

By Sea Mersey Ferries offer connections to the Wirral Peninsula and links from Dublin, Belfast and the Isle of Man. Dublin and Belfast services are operated by Norfolkline Irish Sea Ferries from the Twelve Quays terminal at

Birkenhead (*www.norfolkline ferries.co.uk*). The Isle of Man service is operated by the Steam Packet Company from the Pier Head (*www.steam-packet.com*).

By Air Liverpool John Lennon (📞 *0871 5218484, www.liverpool airport.com*) has domestic flights to the Isle of Man and Belfast and international flights to the United States, France, Germany, Canada, Italy and Spain. Its major operators are: KLM (📞 *0871 2227474, www.klm.com*), easyJet (📞 *0905 8210905, www.easyjet. com*), Flybe (📞 *0871 700000, www. flybe.com*) Wizzair (📞 *0904 4759500, www.wizzair.com*) and Ryanair (📞 *0871 2460000, www. ryanair.com*).

Visitor Information

The Liverpool Visitor Centre (📞 *0151 2332459, www.visit liverpool.com*) is based at 36–38 Whitechapel, Liverpool. There are further tourist information centres: at Liverpool (John Lennon Airport) in the Arrivals Hall, South Terminal (📞 *0151 2332008*) and at the Liverpool Maritime Museum, Albert Dock, (📞 *0151 2332008*).

INSIDER TIP

The cheapest way to get around Liverpool and visit the sights is on a Livesmart card. The card (adults £25, children £15) entitles the holder to free entry into The Beatles Story and the Liverpool Football Museum, ride the Mersey Ferry and go on the City Explorer sightseeing bus. The tickets are valid for three days, starting on the day you first use the ticket. For more information and to buy a ticket contact *www. yourticketforliverpool.com* or Visit Liverpool (📞 *0151 2332008*, *www.visitliverpool.com*).

Anfield Tour ALL AGES

Liverpool Football Club, Anfield Road, Liverpool, 📞 *0151 2606677, www.liverpoolfc.tv/club/tour.htm*

'Even on the slippy floor of the away team changing room Man Utd's Cristiano Ronaldo has never fallen over – even when we drew a penalty spot'. You can expect pithy football banter along these lines on a tour of England's most famous football ground. Highlights include posing in the team changing room underneath the shirt of Steven Gerrard and sitting in manager Rafa Benitez's seat in the stands although my favourite moment was standing in the tunnel

Young fans can take the Anfield Tour

listening to a tape of the roaring crowd at the height of Liverpool's 1970s' dominance – just what away teams were subjected to for up to 10 minutes before emerging onto the pitch – while touching the 'This is Anfield' sign (pithy comment number two: 'Which tiny Michael Owen was too small to reach'). My family fared less well. Our son required an emergency nappy change in the ref's room, my daughter almost got us barred for attempting to run onto the just-watered pitch, and my wife's sole interest in this, the stadium I dreamt of playing in as a right-footed winger in school, was the following comment: 'It's cleaner than I expected'. The Anfield Museum meanwhile is full of trophies and a film showing the miracle of Istanbul that saw the Liverpool football team (which I must admit I support) triumph against the odds over AC Milan to win the coveted European Cup. The tours run on the hour (half-hourly during peak times) seven days a week between 10am and 3pm except on match days and the day before a televised game at the stadium.

Adm *tour and museum – adults £10, children (under 16) or seniors £6, families (two adults, two children) £25. Museum only–adults £5, children (under 16) £3, families £13.* **Amenities** *parking, buggy-friendly elevator to the museum.* **Credit Cards** *all except AE.*

Ferry Across the Mersey ALL AGES

Mersey ferries, 📞 *0151 3301444, www.merseyferries.co.uk*

Ferry across the Mersey

We expected squawking seagulls, tooting ferries and women in miniskirts. To begin with, I must admit the ferry my wife had eulogized about from her childhood days was a bit of a disappointment. It was raining so hard on the *Royal Iris* we could hardly see the Liverbird building, there were no 1960s' factory workers eating chips out of the *Liverpool Echo* – just tourists in raincoats – while onboard commentary was fairly uninspiring ('the ventilation shaft was opened in 1934 by King George V'). However, during our return leg we were won over by Liverpudlian spirit when we were let off part of the fare and another mum, seeing our son with no socks – his were drenched – gave us a pair she'd just bought. Plus, at Birkenhead, the ticket collector gave our children a helium balloon each that he had been saving for his own children. The ferry runs between

Albert Dock and Seacombe and Birkenhead on other side. Between 9am and 10am, and again after 3pm, it operates as a commuter service, but outside those hours it becomes Explorer Cruises for tourists. As part of the Big Mersey Adventure you can combine the cruise with a visit to space-themed Spaceport (*www.spaceport.org.uk*).

Fares in commuter times an adult return is £2.30, children (5–15) £1.70. In cruise times, an adult return is £5.30 and children £2.95. Fares are cheaper with a Livesmart card.

The Beatles Story ALL AGES

*Britannia Pavilion, Albert Dock, Liverpool, ☎ 0151 7091963, **www.beatlesstory.com***

On an informative tour of recreated scenes from the lives of the Fab Four, children are given their own audio guides and get to dance/jump up and down spilling their carton of juice to

Beatle Facts

- The Beatles were rejected by every record label until George Martin heard the demo. He hated it, calling their sound 'unusual' (diplomatic for rubbish), but then he saw them and was blown away by their charisma. If they had this affect on a silly old man, 'what would everyone else think?'
- Stuart Sutcliffe, a former band member, was so bad on the guitar that Paul unplugged him during gigs without him knowing.
- The song *Strawberry Fields* is about a Salvation Army home in Liverpool, which evoked childhood memories for John Lennon during an hallucinogenic intoxication.
- *Hey Jude* was written by Paul in his car while on his way to visit Julian, John Lennon's son, who was disturbed by his parents' divorce. Paul wrote this song to cheer him up.
- John Lennon's eyesight was so bad that he was officially registered blind.
- Ringo took his own baked beans to India because he couldn't stomach the thought of local food.
- A toilet roll from The Beatles' *Abbey Road* session was auctioned for £40,000.

Twist and Shout in the Cavern Room. Halfway round a TV screen shows Beatlemania in full emotionally wrought flow with hundreds of women screaming, fainting and crying at an airport as the Beatles disembark their plane or as our daughter, dredging her memory for comparable frantic outbursts, interpreted it: 'I think someone took their gingerbread mens, Dad'). The museum, busy with schoolchildren pinging headphones off each other's sore, red ears, ends in mini shrines to each of the mop-topped gang, the final room being a stunning white piano with no-one sat in front of it. Everything is white except the evocative pair of round glasses and the word 'Imagine'. Underneath this there is the baffling legend 'this is not here', giving us something to debate in Starbucks afterwards – was the display not there as it was all in our imagination? Or was John Lennon not there as he had been shot dead? Or was it something far deeper and impossible to decipher when you are spooning Hipp Organic carbonara into the reluctant mouth of an under two while his sister is running around shouting, 'I want that biscuit what I saw with chocolate on it and icing on it that that lady has in a packet'.

Open daily 9am–7pm (last adm 5pm).
Adm adults £12.25, children (5–16) £6.35, under 5s free, conc £8.30, families (two adults, two children) £31.50. **Amenities** café, elevator for

buggies and the disabled. **Credit Cards** *All except DC.*

The Museum of Science and Industry ★ ★ ALL AGES

Liverpool Road, Castlefield, Manchester, ☏ 0161 8322244, www. mosi.org

Here children get the chance to lift a mini with their little finger and walk through a Victorian sewer complete with foul smells while adults can compare their palm pilots to the world's first enormous computer, and experience the deafening noise of working in a cotton mill. Other high spots include listening to famous Manchester scientist James Dalton, who discovered atomic theory, talking about his achievements and in the child-centric Xperiment Gallery trying on goggles that fool your eyes into seeing everything back to front. In People's History our daughter enjoyed dressing up and there is a good café with highchairs where we overheard a competitive father informing his daughter if she could spell 'beef bourguignon' then she could have a child's £3.95 portion.

Open *daily 10am–5pm.* **Adm** *free.* **Amenities** *café, baby-changing, parking.*

Yellow Duckmarine ★ ALL AGES

Anchor Courtyard, Britannia Pavilion, Albert Dock, Liverpool, ☏ 0151 7087799, www.theyellowduck marine.co.uk

This is not a submarine. It is a World War II landing craft – an amphibious vehicle that drives on land and also floats on water,

Yellow Duckmarine

not underneath the water. It tours around Liverpool city centre like any normal sightseeing bus and then splashes down into Salthouse Dock for a short boat ride. I say this because my wife, for reasons possibly connected to the Beatles song *We All Live in a Yellow Submarine*, thought we were actually going underwater in it, even though the vehicle had canvass flaps for windows held together with velcro. I say this because I do not want you to have to sit at traffic lights near the World Museum with an inflatable orange life jacket strapped to your chest like we did. The 30-minute tour starts at the Gower Street bus stop outside Albert Dock, where, while you wait for your ride, you get to hear young scallies making bogus calls to the emergency services from the payphone. The land-based tour features commentary, laced hilariously with duck-based gags, strengthening Liverpool's claim to have the finest sense of humour in the country. ('What is a duck's favourite food? Cheese and quackers'. See what we mean?) Our daughter Phoebe was allowed a go on the microphone, our son tottered around safely, and my wife, originally from Widnes, pointed out which shoe shops in St John's shopping centre she used to work in on a Saturday morning. If you have children under two, ring up in advance to let staff know. Buggies can be folded up and stored. The tours run seven days a week and start at 10.30am. You needn't bring an oxygen tank.

Open *tours start at 10.30am and run hourly every day.* **Adm** *off peak: adults £9.95, children (under 16) £7.95, seniors £8.95, families (two adults, two children) £29; peak (public holiday weekends, school holidays Mar– Sept): adults £11.95, children £9.95, seniors £10.95, families £34.* **Credit Cards** *all except AE.*

BLACKPOOL & AROUND

The first time I visited Blackpool was on a friend's stag. It was during the last World Cup and the town had been invaded by groups of lads from rival cities in the Northwest. Schooled in softy Buckinghamshire, our idea of aggro was being told to 'pipe down' for singing too loudly to a Kajagoogoo song in assembly. That weekend we were shocked by the fighting and glass throwing but mostly by the number of men with significant parts of their ears bitten off. That said, in the day-time, while the tattooed revellers sleep off hangovers, or dab antiseptic on their frayed ear whorls, families are at liberty to discover the country's finest circus in the footings of the Blackpool Tower, donkey rides and the roller-coasters of the Pleasure Beach, as well as a freaky museum and a dazzlingly child-friendly restaurant.

Essentials

By Rail From London (Euston) Virgin trains (☏ *0845 0008000*, *www.virgintrains.co.uk*) travel to Preston hourly and then you must change to a Northern Rail (☏ *0845 0000125*, *www.northernrail.org*) service on to Blackpool North. The journey takes three hours. From Glasgow to Blackpool take the Transpennine Express (☏ *0845 6001671*, *www.tpexpress.co.uk*) service to Preston and then change again to a Northern Rail service onto Blackpool North. The journey will take around three hours.

By Bus From London to Blackpool there are six National Express (☏ *0870 5808080*, *www.nationalexpress.co.uk*) coaches a day. The journey takes six and a half hours. From Glasgow to Blackpool there are two services a day and the journey is between six and seven hours. There are five coaches from Liverpool per day and the journey is one hour and 30 minutes.

By Air Blackpool International Airport (☏ *08700 273777*, *www.blackpoolinternational.com*) has domestic flights to the Isle of

Man and Belfast and international flights to, among other destinations, Venice and Rome.

By Car From London it's the M1, M6, M55 and the A583. The journey will take about four and a half hours.

Visitor Information

The Blackpool Tourist Information Centre (📞 01253 478222) is based at 1 Clifton Street, Blackpool.

For more information try *www.visitlancashire.com*.

What to See & Do

Blackpool Pleasure Beach ALL AGES

Ocean Boulevard, Blackpool, 📞 *01253 3411033, www.theblackpool pleasurebeach.com*

Founded 1896, Blackpool Pleasure Beach remains Britain's number one tourism attraction and you can stay for as long as your nerves hold out... There are all sorts of rides to splash and wind you here, although in the Beavers Creek area for toddlers be warned – the park is so stringent on height and age restrictions we practically had to fill out forms to get our son on Ellie's Caterpillar. Singled out in the queue during a spot-check we were asked our son's age, and when we gave it, we were asked if he could walk and when we said he could, we were asked – I am not making this up – to prove it, which our son gamely did by running full pelt into the knee of a man from Fleetwood and then bursting into tears. Other attractions include the Revolving Helicopters and Morgan's Circus, although more fun for our son was when my wife accidentally took her hands off our overweighted buggy handles and he shot backwards. For adrenalin seekers it's paradise: *Infusion* has five loops plus a double line twist on a suspended looping coaster; *Avalanche,* the UK's only bobsled coaster, races 50mph down a 1160ft long course; *Bling* lifts a whopping 100 feet then spins at speeds of 60mph; while Pepsi Max Big One is one of Europe's tallest rollercoasters (235 ft). There's also go-carts, carousels, dodgems, mini scooters, pirate rides, tea cup rides, a puzzle maze and indoors bowling, ice skating and Ripley's Believe it or not! Included in the admission price is a Dance and Water Show in the fountain area and the family-friendly South Beach Show, featuring puppet shows, magicians and that sort of thing.

Open weekends only Feb, Mar and Nov 10.30am–6pm, Apr–June 10.30am–5pm (weekends 6pm), July–Aug 10.30am–6pm (weekends and school holidays 8pm, Sept 10.30am–5pm (weekends 8pm). 1st Oct–23rd Oct 11.30am–5pm (weekends 8pm). 24th Oct–1st Nov 10.30am–8pm (weekends 9pm). Adm peak: adults £30, children £25; off peak: adults £25, children £19. Amenities baby-changing. Credit Cards all accepted.

Blackpool Tower and Circus ★ ★ ALL AGES

Promenade, Blackpool, 📞 *01253 622242, www.theblackpooltower. co.uk*

Donkey Rides

There used to be 28 groups of donkeys on Blackpool beach. Now, thanks to a fall in popularity in donkey riding and building work on the seafront, there are just 15. The donkeys are dwindling, soon we suspect to be gone forever. If your children fancy a 200-metre trot between the two piers, rides cost around £2. Our daughter, not the most politically correct young girl in the world, rode Bruno and although she couldn't quite grasp the essential difference between a donkey and a horsey (as she kept calling him) she loved every minute of geeing him along to go 'faster, come on faster. You are so slow Bruno. Daddy, can I gee him up by kicking him?'

With views to Wales and the Lake District, admission includes entry to an aquarium, the famous ballroom, and, more importantly for children, to the country's finest circus beautifully nestled in between the ornate feet of the tower. An elevator, scary even before the chirpy-come-sinister attendant's joke ('that squeaky noise is the brake pads. They're wearing out'), takes visitors to the 380-feet summit, where our daughter, along with several men from Huddersfield, demonstrated her sense of immortality completing the Walk of Faith – standing on a two-inch plate glass viewing platform with clear views to street level far, far below. The aquarium is small and uneventful, the ballroom is busy with pensioners reminiscing about the Gay Gordons, although the circus, where my wife finally stopped telling me about how Rita from *Coronation Street* was run over by a tram in Blackpool when Mooky the clown entered the ring, is superb with tumblers and high-wire acts from all over the world.

Open *mid Mar–mid July daily 10am–5pm, mid July–7th Nov daily 10am–11pm, 8th Nov–mid Mar 10am–5pm (weekends only).* ***Adm*** *off peak: adults £13.95, children (under 18) and conc £10.95; peak: adults £16.95, children and conc £13.95.* ***Amenities*** *four restaurants, baby-changing.* ***Credit Cards*** *all except AE.*

Blackpool Tower

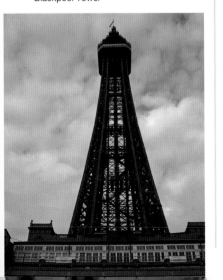

Ripley's Believe it or Not!

Ripley's Believe It or Not! **ALL AGES**

Units 5 and 6 Ocean Boulevard, Pleasure Beach, Blackpool, ☎ 01253 341033, www.ripleysblackpool.com

Here, in this one setting, you can learn about a man who designs shoes for cows and you can see a guy writing with his hands and feet in different languages, not to mention a six-legged lamb. Also I challenge you not to be impressed by a replica of George Washington made entirely from one-dollar bills and a flute made from actual human bone. There are stairs and no elevator so buggy pushers should leave them at the cashier's desk.

Open daily 10am–4.30pm (later if the Pleasure Beach is still open). **Adm** *adults £8, children £5, seniors £7.* **Amenities** *no toilets.* **Credit Cards** *all except AE.*

INSIDER TIP ≫
You can get reductions of up to 50 per cent at Ripley's Believe It or Not! by visiting the website and printing money-off vouchers.

THE LAKE DISTRICT

England's largest national park contains Scafell Pike, its highest mountain, Wastwater, its deepest lake, and also the pretty town of Bowness-on-Windermere. With its stunning scenery and picturesque lakes, this was a popular tourist destination even before the romantic writings of William Wordsworth in the 19th century catapulted it to fame. Your children will, of course, know it better as the setting for John Cunliffe's classic children series, *Postman Pat*. The good news is there are now many more attractions for youngsters bored of sitting on crystal-clear waters staring at mountainsides. There are zoos, interactive museums and even an attraction devoted to children's novelist Beatrix Potter. The bad news is that some rather stuffy, pretentious hotels and restaurants often focus on their older, more well-heeled residents. The atmosphere can thus be formal, so it's a good idea to check ahead rather than assume children are welcome.

Essentials

By Rail The main rail station in the Lakes is Oxenholme. From

London Euston there are direct Virgin train (☎ 0845 0008000, *www.virgintrains.co.uk*) services that take two hours and 38 minutes. From Glasgow to Oxenholme the same company has regular services that take one hour and 47 minutes. From Manchester Piccadilly direct Transpennine Express (☎ 0845 6001671, *www.tpexpress.co.uk*) services take one hour and 10 minutes and leave throughout the day.

By Bus National Express (☎ 0870 5808080, *www.nationalexpress.co. uk*) has a once-a-day service from London to Windermere, taking eight hours. From Glasgow the same company has a once-a-day service to Kendal. The journey takes seven and a half hours.

By Car From London to Windermere take the M1, M6, A590 and the A591. The journey will take about five hours.

Visitor Information

The Ambleside Tourist Information Centre (☎ 01539 4322582) can be found at Central Buildings, Market Cross, Ambleside. The Barrow in Furness Tourist Information Centre (☎ 01229 8766505) is at Forum 28, Duke Street, Barrow in Furness. The Bowness Tourist Information Centre (☎ 01539 442895) is at Glebe Road, Bowness-on-Windermere. The Coniston Tourist Information Centre (☎ 01539 441535) is at Ruskin Avenue, Coniston. The Kendal Tourist Information Centre (☎ 01539

797516) is at the Town Hall, Highgate, Kendal. The Keswick Tourist Information Centre (☎ 01768 772645) is at Moot Hall, Market Square, Keswick. The Kirby Lonsdale Tourist Information Centre (☎ 01524 271437) is at 24 Main Street, Kirby Lonsdale. The Penrith Tourist Information Centre (☎ 01768 867466) is at Robinson's School, Middlegate, Penrith. The Ullswater Tourist Information Centre (☎ 01768 482414) is at the Main Car Park, Glenridding, Penrith. The Ulverston Tourist Information Centre (☎ 01229 687120) is at Coronation Hall, County Square, Ulverston. The Windermere Tourist Information Centre (☎ 01539 446499) is at Victoria Street, Windermere.

Cars of the Stars ALL AGES

Motor Museum, Standish Street, Keswick, ☎ 01768 773757, www. carsofthestars.com

Highlights include Del Boy's three-wheeler from *Only Fools and Horses*, and Mr Bean's pea-green mini. The cars, without much information on them or context, are disappointingly roped off and when our toddler tried to touch Michael Keaton's Batmobile a harsh Dalek-like voice barked out over the tannoy, 'Stay away from the cars'. In the gift shop you can buy an autograph of Mr T from TV's *The A-Team* and be told by the curator, 'It was for his own safety', as if the Batmobile front-mounted machine guns were maybe actually loaded and could

have been triggered by a chocolatey hand.

Open daily 10am–5pm, except Dec
when it is weekends only. *Adm*
adults £5, children (3–15) £3. *Amenities* giftshop *Credit Cards* cash and
cheques only.

Cumberland Pencil Museum ALL AGES

Southey Works, Main Street, Keswick,
📞 01768 773626, *www.pencil
museum.co.uk*

We knew this museum was
going to be superb when we read
the giant sign outside – SEE
THE WORLD'S LARGEST
PENCIL. The boast conjured
up such wonderful images. We
sat in the car waiting for our son
to finish off his nap and pictured
pencil manufacturers in rival
towns across the world shaking
their heads with wonderment

and disappointment at the
incredible news – 'They've broken the record in Keswick. Add
a length of graphite, Hans, we're
taking this 2B up to 65 feet'.
Not only does the museum contain the world's largest pencil, it
also has A SECRET WARTIME
PENCIL, a pencil clandestinely
manufactured by the British
government with a hidden compass and map inside to help
Allied pilots during World War
II. You enter the museum via a
mine, learn about Barrowdale
graphite, the drawing material of
choice of Michelangelo 400
years ago, and there's a drawing
zone for children to retire to
after they've had their picture
taken with the world's largest
pencil.

Open daily 9.30am–5pm. *Adm* adults
£3, children (under 16) and seniors

On the Water

As you'd expect in the Lake District there are many different cruise
options, although probably the best for families is the Steam Yacht
Gondola (📞 01539 441533, *www.nationaltrust.org.uk*) which leaves
from Coniston pier between Apr–Nov more or less every hour starting
from 10.30am until 4.15pm (May–Sept) and until 3.15pm (Apr and Oct).
A sort of Venetian gondola with a wood-burning engine, the round trip
aboard includes commentary about the Campbell family of land and
water-speed record-breaking fame, as well as facts about children's
author Arthur Ransome. You'll pass the spot where Donald Campbell
met his end in *Bluebird* when seeking to travel 300mph on water for the
first time, and learn that it was on this lake that Ransome drew inspiration for his famous story *Swallows and Amazons*. The cruise lasts about
45 minutes – quite long enough when you're following children about
the boat holding on to the back of their shirts so they don't topple over
the edge into the water after Campbell.

Price £7, children (5–15) £3.50, families (two adults and up to three children
£17.50). *Credit Cards* all except AE and DC.

Meet all sorts of animals at Eden Ostrich World

£1.50, families (two adults and up to three children) £7.50. **Amenities** coffee shop, free parking, disabled access. **Credit Cards** all except AE.

Eden Ostrich World ALL AGES

Langwathby Farm, Langwathby, Penrith, Cumbria, 📞 *01768 881771,* **www.ostrich-world.com**

Calling this place Ostrich World is a bit like calling our house Loaf of Bread World – after all, in it we have, among many other items, two loaves of bread. The centre has two ostriches we saw in a back field. It is not a world of ostriches at least not that we could see on this occasion. There were more emus than ostriches, more goats and more sheep and more chipmunks and rabbits so why wasn't it called Goat World or even Guinea Pig World? OK, we admit we are annoyed with this attraction. There were too many signs around the place warning us about things. We were warned that pregnant woman shouldn't touch the sheep and lambs. That the emus might peck. That the rheas could too, and that the goats might bite. We were warned that you can't eat your own food here when the café is open and that you must 'Supervise your children at all times'. We did, however, like the chipmunks doing their loop the loops and there was a chidren's quiz.

Open daily 10am–3.30pm (Nov–Feb not Tues except in Feb half-term). Adm adults £5.95, children £4.95, conc £5.45, families (two adults, two children) £20. **Amenities** baby-changing. **Credit Cards** Delta, MC, V.

Laurel and Hardy Museum ALL AGES

4c Upper Brook Street, Ulverston, ℡ *01229 5822922, www.laurel-and-hardy.co.uk*

Containing probably the largest collection of Laurel and Hardy memorabilia in the world, the small request cinema here is a great place to witness your children laughing at slapstick from the bowler-hatted duo. ('Daddy, he just bit that man's tie – that is so funny I don't believe it').

A pilgrimage for generations of comics from Ken Dodd to Eric Morecombe, the artefacts here – old letters, newspaper articles etc. – are arranged in such a higgledy-piggledy fashion they look like they have been pasted on the walls by a mad stalker unable to contain his lust for the pair. One minute you might be reading a story about Clint Eastwood being Stan Laurel's real father (from the always truth-seeking *Daily Mail*) and the next staring at something as incongruous as Stan's old treacle toffee box lid. The museum isn't ostensibly child-friendly – it has no real facilities and a rather scarily dirty toilet – although the approachable curator sat answering our questions about how many Laurel and Hardy sayings he could think off the top of his head and didn't blink an eye when our son accidentally broke the head off an Ollie statue.

Open daily 10am–4.30pm. **Adm** adults £3, children £2, families (two adults and up to three children) £6. **Amenities** toilet. **Credit Cards** cash and cheques only.

South Lakes Wild Animal Park ☆ ALL AGES

Broughton Road, Dalton-in-Furness, ℡ *01229 466086, www.wildanimalpark.co.uk*

I stared at the crocodiles browned in a muddy pool in the kangaroo enclosure here for 10 minutes, amazed at the possibility they could so easily escape and devour visitors through a flimsy wooden fence. It was thrilling to watch them static in the stagnant water, their mouths slightly ajar, until an ibis stood on the back of one of them and it rolled over. The crocodile had turned out to be a log. Feeling foolish I had assumed it was a real crocodile, I started to spread word through the park. Did you see the crocodiles? I asked a clutch of children nearby. They had, and nodded. 'Well they're not real,' I said, before the teacher guided them adroitly away towards the emus. Our children, it has to be said, had a great time hand-feeding the giraffes with foliage from the raised balcony area, watching lions attack their food up a 6m tree, and observing the penguins have their dinner, although by now I was questioning everything. Those emus. That noise they made in their throats – it sounded like water disappearing down a plughole – wasn't that a bit suspicious? Wasn't it all very *mechanical?* Then there was the

There are two former homes of the Lakes poet to visit here.

Dove Cottage ALL AGES

☏ *01539 435544, www.wordsworth.org*

Based at Grasmere, this is where Wordsworth spent his time of 'plain living and high thinking.' It was to Dove Cottage that he returned after long walks round the lakes to write some of his most famous works including his 'I wandered lonely as a cloud' line. There is an education room, where they have chidren's activities during school holidays between 9.30am and 5.30pm, such as painting, colouring and making up poems using fridge magnets. There was also a poet in residence, Adam O'Riordan, when we visited, who does readings at 2.30pm on Wednesdays, and can be talked about by your smitten wife at 8am the next morning and also again at 9am and 10am and then half-hourly following lunch after she has goggled him and discovered according to reviews that he 'engages us with rangy narratives which zoom in from cosmos to coffee cup, yet can also turn his careful hand to woozy landscapes which capture the fractured apparitions of cities and love affairs'.

Open *daily 9.30am–5.30pm daily.* **Adm** *adults £7.50, children £4.50, families £17.50.* **Credit Cards** *all except AE and DC.*

Rydal Mount in Rydal near Ambleside ALL AGES

☏ *01539 433002, www.rydalmount.co.uk*

This is where we wandered stressfully as parents in the grounds of Wordsworth's other home when our daughter, bored of romantic poetry, and of my wife and I arguing about Adam O'Riordan, demanded something nice to eat that 'is not a treat and not a sandwich but something nice.' Children get a quiz sheet which, when they answer all the questions from it, leads to a key-ring reward. The rooms are restored to how they looked in Wordsworth's time and there is an interesting cutlass chair (designed so you could sit down without taking your sword off) that I sat down on to finally have my say about Adam O'Riordan, 'He's a loose-buttoned fop and, no, we will not be visiting the Ledbury Poetry Festival as part of this book's research so you can steal up to him and ask for his autograph and show him your own work about that cornfield in Worcester'.

Open *summer Mar–Oct 9.30am–5pm daily; winter Wed–Sun 11am–4pm.* **Adm** *adults £6, children (5–15) £4, conc £5.* **Credit Cards** *all accepted.*

bear snoring next to the fence – the drone was uncannily battery-like. You can also cure snake phobias through handling them here, while other highlights include tiger and penguin

Open 3rd Nov–Easter daily 10am–4.30pm. 4th Apr–1st Nov 10am–5pm. **Adm** from Nov–Mar adults £7, seniors and children (3–15) £4. From Apr–Nov adults £10.50, seniors and children £7. **Amenities** café with children's menu, highchairs and baby-changing. **Credit Cards** All except AE.

The Lakes Aquarium ALL AGES

Newby Bridge, Cumbria, 📞 01539 530153, www.lakesaquarium.co.uk

It was here our daughter won an Oscar the Otter badge, our son walked into a concave glass tank of bream and my wife turned ashen-faced after catching a glimpse of some red-eared terrapins. After you have steered your turtle-phobic wife away from the hazard, now shuffling like a vulnerable pensioner with a shattered hip ('They were right near the surface. They could have jumped out. There were loads of them'), you come face to face, in a virtual diving bell, with hippos, crocodiles and bull sharks. There are also interesting talks about otters (Did you know they eat pebbles to help grind up the food in their stomachs?) and children are given an Oscar the Otter quiz sheet. Otter talks take place at 10.30am, 1.30pm and 3pm, and talks about the wildlife of Morecombe Bay are at 11.30am, 1.30pm and 4pm. Next door is the steam train to Haverthwaite

(40 minutes round trip, adults £5.70, children £2.85); we suggest you get on board and eat some Quiggins Kendal Mint Cake whilst sipping from a bottle of Lonesome Pine Laurel and Hardy beer to try and calm down. ('Ben, I know you think I'm ridiculous but you're scared of heights. Imagine if every day we visited an attraction that meant you climbing a three-section ladder'.)

Open daily 9am–5pm. **Adm** adults £8.75, children (3–15) £5.75, seniors £7.50. families (two adults and two children) £20. **Amenities** café, parking. **Credit Cards** all except AE.

The World of Beatrix Potter ALL AGES

The Old Laundry, Crag Brow, Bowness-on-Windermere, 📞 01539 488444, www.hop-skip-jump.com

The whimsical tales of the famous children's author are brought to life here in an indoor recreation of her beloved lakeside countryside complete with sights, smells, sounds, and my wife saying earnestly to me, 'The music's so relaxing – it actually makes me want to be a woodland creature, doesn't it you?' There is a short film about the author, and also a Peter Rabbit garden.

Open summer 10am–5.30pm, winter 10am–4.30pm. **Adm** adults £6, children £3. **Amenities** disabled access, café with children's books to read (though no Beatrix Potter, oddly). **Credit Cards** all except AE.

The World of Beatrix Potter

FAMILY-FRIENDLY ACCOMMODATION

EXPENSIVE

Armathwaite Hall Hotel

Brassenthwaite Lake, Keswick, Cumbria, 📞 *01768 776551, www. armathwaite-hall.com*

Set in 400 acres, this country-house hotel offers free entry to next door's Trotters Wild Animal Park (get your voucher from reception) from where early in the morning if you open your bedroom window you can hear dueting Lar gibbons. There are weekend and school holiday programmes for children including falconry demos on Sunday mornings, and even a course called – we kid you not – Young Etiquette, involving lessons for children on how to use a knife and fork, which glasses to use for what drinks and how it is bad form to 'shovel peas'. The hotel has stylish rooms (ask for one with a bunk-bed room next door) and also wins the prize for having the quirkiest waitresses – one of whom served us a giant saucer of Marmite that my wife mistook for Daddy's Sauce and spread on a sausage, and another, showing a healthy contempt for the beauty and very nature of the Lake District, who replied when we asked what the name of the nearby lake was, 'I don't know. There are loads of lakes around here'.

Rates family room (two bedrooms, one with bunk-beds) £170 per adult (£25 per extra child). Amenities spa complex with infinity pool, hot tub, sauna, steam room, hydrotherapy pool, gym, snooker table (under 16s not allowed), parking. In Room TVs, hairdryer, tea and coffee making. Credit Cards all accepted.

Holbeck Ghyll Country House, Windermere

Holbeck Ghyll Country House Hotel ☆

Windermere, Cumbria, 📞 *01539 432375, www.holbeckghyll.com*

The highlight of our stay here wasn't the spectacular views of Lake Windermere or even the three-bedroom Gatehouse Cottage we stayed in with an open fire. It was our sprightly 82-year-old baby-sitter Joan, who, within minutes of meeting us, had dropped her keys to the carpet to demonstrate how she could bend down like a gymnast, had referred our son's baby milk as a 'titty bottle' and had then revealed the secret of her still-active life – cleaning the hotel brass at 8am and gossiping about the hardiness of carpets vis-à-vis stains. Our one gripe was in the restaurant, where the slightly cold maitre d' was sharp with us about skipping between the gourmet and the normal menus and sniffy about buggies in his restaurant. That said, they probably have the best cheese board outside France. Overcome with lust for this cheese board, I managed to have a completely new form of argument with my wife after I, apparently, ordered the cheeses *suggestively*. 'You said, that one's really running. Then you said, can I see inside the rind? Then there was "mmm cabbagey, my favourite". That's what you said. You're lucky – if you didn't like cheese so much, I'd have had a real go'.

Rates *at the Gatehouse £225 self-catering per night. For dinner, B&B in the main hotel £145 per person.* **Amenities** *health spa, tennis courts, putting green, croquet lawn, walks.* **Credit Cards** *all except DC.*

The Samling Hotel ☆

Ambleside Road, Windermere, Cumbria, 📞 *01539 431922, www. thesamlinghotel.co.uk*

A beautiful family-friendly hotel with great views of Lake Windermere, where staff were so accommodating the waiter volunteered to nip out and buy Marmite when they had none at breakfast. There is a croquet lawn enabling your son to crack his sister over the head ('fworry, Daddy') with a mallet and a superb restaurant, where we overheard possibly the poshest conversation of our entire trip round England, concerning a world-weary 16-year-old boy who had nothing to do all summer 'apart from teach Theo Greek'. He was dining with his mother, whom he called 'impertinent' for asking … whether he liked his dessert. One word of warning – unless you want to wind up at the bottom of Lake Windermere be careful exiting the hotel. There is a very sharp and dangerous bend in the road at the bottom of hill to negotiate. If you need to go right, go left first and double back. The food is fantastic and the luxurious room with space for a single bed for our daughter and a cot for our son had views across the lake.

Rates £310 per night B&B. *Amenities* hot-tub, croquet, library, restaurant. *In Room* phone, TV, robes and slippers, hairdryer, DVDs. *Credit Cards* all except AE and DC.

MODERATE

Adelphi Hotel

Ranelagh Place, Liverpool, ☎ *0871 2220029, www.britanniahotels.com*

The largest hotel in the north of England provides disappointingly little for families but is worth a short stay for its central location, 19th-century Edwardian grandeur and its dubious boast that Adolf Hitler once worked there as a waiter. Other famous guests whose stays did not, we feel sure, coincide with any of Hitler's shifts in the dining room (although they would have been very interesting) include Winston Churchill, Harold Wilson, Roy Rogers and Charles Dickens. There is a swimming pool (open 7am–8pm weekdays and 10am–4pm at weekends) where our children played pirates for two hours and staff are tolerant of young ones pegging around the corridors with chocolate-gem stains round their mouths shouting 'ha ha, me hardies'. Jenny's Carvery is a good place to try the roast beef, while Crompton's is more for fine dining. The Albert Dock nearby is stacked with great attractions including: Tate Liverpool, BugWorld Experience, Beatles Story, Shiverpool Ghost Tour, International Slavery Museum and the Maritime Museum. World Museum Liverpool has high-tech gizmos to bring history to life for youngsters while the Empire, Playhouse and Everyman have a theatre, musical and classical programme.

Rates on average £130 per room per night B&B. Interconnecting rooms (there are only 10) £260. *Amenities* swimming pool, sauna, steam room, gym. *In Room* TV, phone, hairdryer, tea and coffee making. *Credit Cards* all accepted.

Big Blue

Ocean Boulevard, Pleasure Beach, Blackpool, ☎ *0845 3673333, www. thebigbluehotel.com*

This is a sleek, 157-room hotel and we had a room that overlooked the Pleasure Beach, which our children loved almost as much as their bunk-beds with their own TVs to watch *Grandpa In Your Pocket* on. The room's entertainment centre has DVD and CD players and playstations, plus there's a café bar and brasserie where children can create their own fresh pizzas. A stay includes discounted wristbands for the Pleasure Beach and the whole place scores high on mod cons although there were gripes. We were asked to pay a £5 tray charge to have a bottle of warm milk sent up for our son in the morning and at breakfast we were told this by a waitress with a glassy-eyed look of boredom: 'boiled egg's a pound extra'.

Rates family room with bunk-beds £99–£129 B&B. *Amenities* parking, free wifi, gym. *In Room* phone, TV, tea and coffee making, PlayStations to hire. *Credit Cards* all except Solo.

Bracken Bank Lodge

Lazonby, Penrith, Cumbria, 📞 *01768 898241, www.brackenbank.co.uk*

At this eccentric 16th-century grouse-shooting lodge set in 700 acres and often frequented by royalty, there are toys and silky chickens for children to stroke. Owner Stuart Burton's grandfather was responsible for shooting many of the animals whose pelts line the walls while his father brought back so many live crocodiles from Africa almost every croc you see in a British zoo today is a descendant of one he bagged. Falconry shows can be arranged and there is a full-size snooker table, over which you can reprise the story of how your grandfather was mauled to death by a leopard in Gujarat India between the wars – a lie you told your wife when you first met her that she ACTUALLY believed and you have had to stick to for almost 17 years. The owners trace their ancestry back to King Edward I's reign and are friendly if slightly obsessed with a village called Plumpton. We kept a tally of their utterances of it (14). There is one family room with a double and a single bed and a lovely en suite bathroom with a roll-top bath. They don't serve food but have a folder full of recommendations nearby.

Rates £35 per night per room B&B. *Amenities* parking, clay pigeon shooting (over 12s only). *In Room* four-poster bed, en suite bathroom with roll top bath. *Credit Cards* all except AE.

Helsby Stables ☆

The Courtyard, Helsby, Near Chester, 📞 *01928 723222, www.thecourtyard helsby.com*

I used to joke with a friend about how life would be more enjoyable by a 'pub bus'. The pub bus we dreamed of was equipped with a bar and would pick you up from your house, serve you drinks along the way and drop you at various pubs before taking you home. Mixing in elements of the ice-cream van, it would have a jingle to entice you from *The Bill*. Perhaps Sham 69's, 'We're going down the pub'. In the Helsby Stables I discovered this theory had become a reality. The Helsby Arms runs a bus service picking up drinkers and then dropping them back home at the end of the night. Unfortunately for us it has come too late. This character-rich two-bed self-catering cottage with contemporary furnishings has a parking space and a small garden large enough for two children to attack each other with breadsticks in. The only small problem we had apart from not being able to get drunk together in the pub was the lack of a stairgate, although we got round that by making our own with hefty luggage piled precariously up on the top step.

Rates £600 per week (out of season £450). *Amenities* dishwasher, oven, washer-dryer, fridge-freezer, wifi and a wide-screen TV, tea and coffee, children's DVDs, microwave, iron and ironing board, hairdryer. *Credit Cards* all except DC.

Merseyview Serviced Apartments

East Float Dock, Dock Road, Wallasey, Near Birkenhead, ☎ *0844 7365899, 07941 562879, www. merseyview.com*

Based at an old warehouse where Ricky Tomlinson was crushed to death by a container in the Hollywood blockbuster *The 51st State* and also from where the world's first submarine *Resurgam II* was launched, this three-bed family-friendly apartment has a very efficient owner-manager, Gail, who will scold you in a motherly fashion if you don't read your folder of info thoroughly enough before asking a question. The apartment

comes with its own parking space, a washer-dryer, fridge freezer, oven, TV, and most importantly a cupboard full of children's toys. A short drive to Seacombe ferry (which will take you to Liverpool), it has three very large bedrooms and it is also close to a Tesco's where I brought a packet of blackberries each as long as a human finger. I couldn't decide whether to eat them or post them immediately to the botany division of the Natural History Museum (see p 28).

Rates £100–£200 a night (from £500 for a week). *Amenities* vacuum, hairdryer, DVD player, iPod docking station, hifi, free wifi. *Credit Cards* all except AE and DC.

INEXPENSIVE

Butharlyp Howe Youth Hostel

Easedale Road, Grasmere, Cumbria, ☎ *0870 7705836, www.yha.org.uk*

A Victorian house with extensive grounds, there is a play area for children and outdoor games equipment, board games and bikes available for hire. The hostel has functional rooms and is only open between Feb and Oct.

Rates family room £58–£84. *Amenities* laundry, TV, lounge with Internet access. *Credit Cards* MC, V.

The Cliffs Hotel ⋆

Queen's Promenade, Blackpool, ☎ *01253 595559, www.choicehotels.co.uk*

There are children's clubs at this Edwardian hotel for parents who feel they need a break after a whole day spent at the Pleasure Beach losing substantial sums of small change (almost £8) on grab-a-bear booths. The clubs, stacked with toys from table tennis, Wii and a dance machine to crafts, basketball and rally driving, are open from 10am to 10pm. One is for youngsters aged 4–12 and the other for teenagers. There's also soft-play for under fours although children must be accompanied. The restaurant has a children's menu, which changes daily and features a colouring and activity sheet. The hotel, an early century building on the renowned Queen's Promenade, has a tram stop right outside, a disco in the evening and an indoor heated pool. There are 50 family rooms, including several larger than average ones with bunk-beds (or bumper beds, as our daughter calls them). There's also a pool, spa and sauna. Nearby attractions include Blackpool Zoo, Karting 2000, the Water Park, Blackpool Tower and Circus, Louis Tussaud's and Sea-Life.

Rates £75–£140. **Amenities** spa, sauna, gym. **In Room** phone, TV, tea and coffee making. **Credit Cards** AE, MC, V.

FAMILY-FRIENDLY DINING

EXPENSIVE

Lucy's on a Plate ★★

Church Street, Ambleside, 📞 01539 431191, www.lucysofambleside.co.uk

Some of the best food in the Lakes is served here in a family-friendly atmosphere that includes a personalized welcome from Lucy, the owner, written on that day's menu to all pre-booked diners. Families, often greeted by Lucy in person, are usually seated in the conservatory where there are toys for children to play with, allowing husbands the peace necessary to politely tell off their wife over some excellent grilled halumi wrapped in ham for (a) wasting money that day buying too much Coniston Fudge, (b) having their house number engraved on slate and (c) continually going on about the poet in residence at Dove Cottage, Adam O'Riordan, and what he might think of her secret poem about the cornfield she saw through the passenger window in Worcestershire and hid between the pages of the road atlas, and which contains the rhyme 'evanescent barley the colour of a Salvador Dalí'.

Open daily 10am–5pm and 6pm–9pm. **Main Course** £10–£25. **Amenities** highchairs, baby-changing. **Credit Cards** all except DC.

Simply Heathcotes

Beetham Plaza, 25 the Strand, Liverpool, 📞 0151 2363536, www.heathcotes.co.uk

Staff entertain children with balloon animals, they get to shake and make their own fruit cocktails while all the ingredients are fresh and the children's menus come with pens to colour it in. There are healthy options like pasta as well as more meaty-based dishes you can pretend you are busy chewing when your wife starts to tell you yet again about her days working as a Busty Wench in the nearby Camelot theme park.

Open Mon–Sat lunch 12pm–2.30pm, Mon–Fri dinner 6pm–10pm, Sat dinner 6pm–11pm, Sunday all day. *Main Course* £12–£20. *Amenities* highchairs, baby-changing, parking. *Credit Cards* all except DC.

Amigos Mexican and Steakhouse

30 Cavendish Street, Ulverston, ☎ 01229 587616, www.amigos mexican.com

This efficient, friendly restaurant, serving great nachos, is close to the newly erected statue to Laurel and Hardy and has been going over 11 years. This may be because of a great mix of steaks, ribs and tortilla dishes, king prawns in crispy batter plus sizzling fajitas (the house speciality) and delicious hot 'n' spicy dishes in a fun atmosphere. To go with the interesting selection of cocktails and jugs of Sangria there's the great and awful but always enjoyable Mexican-type music. Amigos has a children's menu for under 12s and children are encouraged to crayon pictures on their napkins, enabling adults to overhear revolutionary sounding Cumbrians discussing what 'pseudo Lakelanders have against Furness' and also some knocked off Viagra rife in the town that apparently 'makes your eyes sweat'.

Open Tues–Sat 6pm. *Main Course* £10.95. *Amenities* highchairs, baby-changing. *Credit Cards* all except DC.

Dukes Head Hotel

Front Street, Armathwaite, ☎ 01697 472226, www.dukeshead-hotel. co.uk

We'd had a hard day. Firstly our daughter had broken three of her new Lakeland pencils drawing a rabbit on the way to the Neolithic Castlerigg stone circle. Secondly, the stone circle wasn't very relaxing, having been taken over by drum-beating pagans arguing with National Trust members about wax from their candles dripping on the ancient rocks. Thirdly, the ice-cream van parked in a lay-by had gone when we returned to the car, prompting tantrums. Fourthly, the Fox and Pheasant pub we were booked to eat dinner at let us down. Thus we arrived at Dukes Head on the edge of a catastrophic meltdown. Our meals of venison casserole and pheasant (smaller portions for the children and a reduced price) were brought speedily and the relaxed staff calmed our children down by pulling faces at my son and asking questions of my daughter thus allowing my wife and I to resume our debate about the buzzing light spheres witnessed at Castlerigg by T. Singleton in 1919 (My theory – nonsense. My wife's – 'But you never know,' meaning, of course, she believes in aliens and is a nutter).

Open daily 12pm–1.45pm and 6.30pm–9pm. *Main Course* £8.95–£15.70. *Amenities* highchairs. *Credit Cards* all except DC.

Lake District Floods

In November 2009, Cumbria experienced the most severe flooding in its history. The Lake District was engulfed with raging floods following the heaviest rainfall ever recorded in Britain. Thousands were affected by the devastation, with roads and bridges closed and flood-hit communities in Cumbria cut off as the county's infrastructure was severely damaged. As well as communities, homes and businesses, important historical points of interest such as Wordsworth House in Cockermouth were also affected. Visitors to the Lake District should be aware that communities and organisations such as the National Trust have pulled together to work hard in helping each other, putting walls up, repairing paths, rebuilding their environment and connecting this beautiful landscape back to the rest of the world. This is a close-knit community and we urge you to help this wonderful region as you travel through it and be sympathetic to its people who are slowly rebuilding their lives.

Ego

14–16 Grosvenor Street, Chester,
℡ 0144 346512, www.ego
restaurants.co.uk

Children are exceptionally well looked after in this contemporary Mediterranean-style restaurant where food is all freshly prepared and they have fun sheets, a children's menu, toys, and, on Sunday, a special table for face painting.

Open *daily 12am–10.30pm.* **Main Course** *£9.95–£19.95 (although evening set menus two courses for £11.95).* **Amenities** *highchairs, baby-changing.* **Credit Cards** *all except DC.*

Moules-A-Go-Go

39–41 Watergate Row South, Chester, ℡ 0144 348818, www.moules agogo.co.uk

There are colouring-in books and crayons as well as a children's menu serving the mini moules our four year old enjoyed so much she had two quarter kilos of them. They also serve excellent Belgian beers. Nearby is the Dewa Roman Experience where you can see Roman, Saxon and Medieval remains buried beneath Chester. There's a chance to try on Roman armour, fire a catapult or create a mosaic as well as lots of 'horrible history' type activities such as the 'Roman Smells' challenge.

www.dewaromanexperience.co.uk

Open *Mon–Fri 12pm–3pm and 6pm–10pm, Sat all day and Sun 12pm–9pm.* **Main Course** *from £9–£17.* **Amenities** *highchairs, baby-changing.* **Credit Cards** *all except AE and DC.*

The Tate Café

Albert Dock, Liverpool, ℡ 0151 702 7581, www.tate.org.uk

This is a good place to sit down to a fresh, locally sourced lunch after a confusing wander (if you are four) through a Gustav

Klimt painting, design and modern life exhibition, where our daughter lay on the gallery floor and drew rabbits on a ripped-out page from my notepad while intermittently shouting, 'I want children's things'. There's a healthy-choice children's menu and Cheshire farm chocolate ice-cream to calm the situation down when your wife loses her temper after you have shouted 'up periscope' for the fifth time in acknowledgment of her foolish misunderstanding of the underwater capabilities of the *Yellow Duckmarine* (see p 220) The gallery is free to enter.

Open *Oct–May Tues–Sun 10am–5.50pm and June–Sept Mon–Sun 10am–5.50pm.* **Main Course** *£7.55.* **Amenities** *highchairs.* **Credit Cards** *All except AE.*

Zeffirellis ★

Compston Road, Ambleside, 📞 *01539 430465, www.zeffirellis. com*

A trendy yet unpricey restaurant with Van Morrison playing at low level and a glazed waterfall that would have been a soothing backdrop if our baby son had not kept standing up in his high-chair like a pearl diver about to leap off a cliff face. We created such a disturbance that staff waived their buggy ban enabling us to finish our Vesuvian Real Bean Chili, albeit to the accompanied of an incensed, wailing one year old gritting his teeth like a wild beast and flinging his head about while strapped into his buggy. The restaurant, which serves very good food, was full of families with slightly older children politely ignoring our

The Grizedale Forest Park & Visitor Centre

Grizedale, Hawkshead, Cumbria, LA22 0QJ (📞 *01229 860010. www. forestry.gov/grizdaleforestpark*)

On a nine and a half mile ramble through this oak and conifer woodland you'll see dozens of outdoor sculptures, witness views on a clear day to Morecambe Bay and Coniston Fells, and if you're lucky you might see a red deer and possibly a buzzard. Although the red squirrels here have more or less vanished you'll probably see also roe deer. Covering 12,000 acres there are a host of cycle routes and walks ranging from the red-graded 15km North Face mountain bike course, right down to the untaxing buggy friendly one-mile long Ridding Wood trail we chose that saw us take in around 15 art works. If you want to see more art, including Andy Goldsworthy's famous wriggling stone wall (it weaves between the trees) try the Star Trek-sounding, Filurian Way.

Open *(visitor centre) summer 10am-5pm, winter 10am-4pm. The forest itself is open from first light.* **Amenities** *bike hire, café, gift-shop, parking (£2 for 2 hours, £4 all day).*

Pirate night at the Outside Inn, Blackpool

suffering while discussing anti-shock trekking poles.

Open *daily 5.30pm–10pm.* **Main Course** *£7.50–£9.50.* **Amenities** *highchairs, baby-changing.* **Credit Cards** *all except AE and DC.*

INEXPENSIVE

Outside Inn ★★★

Hallam Way, Whitehills Business Park, Blackpool, 📞 *01253 798477,* *www.outsideinnblackpool.co.uk*

Part of an unassuming Premier Inn on the outside, inside this restaurant dazzles. More than £3 million has been spent on recreating an incredible wonderland of lanterned trees, ruined castles, waterfalls and Tudor houses. We came on Pirate Night (they have these once a month). Staff members were dressed as buccaneers, there was a treasure chest of sweets children could help themselves to and everyone was great. If it all gets too much for the younger ones, there is an under fives whacky warehouse with a

netted ball pit to retreat to. Excellent for young families.

Open *daily 11am–11pm.* **Main Course** *from £5.* **Amenities** *soft-play room, highchairs, children's menus, baby-changing.* **Credit Cards** *all accepted.*

The Bluebird Café by the Lake

Lake Road, Coniston, 📞 *01539 441649, www.bluebirdcafe.com*

This café, with great views across Coniston Water, doesn't have a child's menu although serves reasonably priced rolls. There is Donald Campbell memorabilia on the walls and for £35 you can buy a model of his famous world-breaking car that you can later knock into Coniston Water when you swing round too fast to look at Peel Island.

Open *mid Feb–late Nov 10am–5pm and Dec–mid Feb Sat and Sun only 10.30am–4.30pm.* **Main Course** *(e.g. cheese and onion sandwich) £5.10.* **Amenities** *car park, highchairs.* **Credit Cards** *all except AE and DC.*

Index

D

E

F

G